# WHO READS *ULYSSES*?

T0373541

MAJOR LITERARY AUTHORS
VOLUME # 19

STUDIES IN
# MAJOR LITERARY AUTHORS
OUTSTANDING DISSERTATIONS

*edited by*
William E. Cain
Wellesley College

*A ROUTLEDGE SERIES*

OTHER BOOKS IN THIS SERIES:

# WHO READS *ULYSSES?*
## The Rhetoric of the Joyce Wars and the Common Reader

Julie Sloan Brannon

ROUTLEDGE
New York & London

Published in 2003 by
Routledge
270 Madison Ave,
New York NY 10016
www.routledge-ny.com

Published in Great Britain by
Routledge
2 Park Square, Milton Park,
Abingdon, Oxon, OX14 4RN

Transferred to Digital Printing 2009

Library of Congress Cataloging-in-Publication Data

Brannon, Julie Sloan.
    Who Reads Ulysses? : the rhetoric of the Joyce wars and the
common reader / by Julie Sloan Brannon.
        p. cm. — (Studies in major literary authors ; v. 19)
Includes bibliographical references (p.) and index.

1. Joyce, James, 1882–1941. Ulysses—Criticism, Textual. 2. Joyce, James, 1882–1941—
Criticism and interpretation—History—20th century. 3. Authors and readers—History—
20th Century. 4. Criticism, Textual—History—20th century. 5. Books and reading—
History—20th century. I. Title. II. Series.
    PR6019.03 U6293 2003
823".912—dc21

2002007261

ISBN10: 0–415–94206–3 (hbk)
ISBN10: 0–415–80347–0 (pbk)

ISBN13: 978–0–415–94206–5 (hbk)
ISBN13: 978–0–415–80347–2 (pbk)

**Publisher's Note**
The publisher has gone to great lengths to ensure the quality of this reprint
but points out that some imperfections in the original may be apparent.

For Todd, Christopher, Jonathan, and Annalivia

# Contents

# Preface

There is always something slightly hypocritical about a scholarly book purporting to champion the common reader. In a work that is marketed mainly to university libraries and other scholars, with scant likelihood of finding its way to the bookshelves at Borders, discussing the common reader feels more than a little like gossiping about people when they're not in the room—and more particularly, people we barely know. But somehow, such a metaphor seems highly appropriate when discussing the Joyce Wars: at their heart, the controversies outlined in this study are, simply, gossip. During the Kidd-Gabler controversy, the anticipation over what Kidd would say or do next overshadowed any of the real issues being "discussed." The controversy over the Rose edition roughly ten years later was more of the same. In this book, I do not attempt to declare a winner in what was by many accounts the scholarly equivalent of a barroom brawl; rather, I look at how—and why—a battle over arcane editorial issues became (paradoxically) both more and less meaningful than a schoolboy slugfest. Supposedly, the common reader was the beneficiary of these battles in that readers would finally get Joyce's work the way it was meant to be or, in the case of the Rose edition, they would get a *Ulysses* that was strictly for them, unencumbered by the weight of the Ivory Tower. These "goals" were never reached, and it seems clear at this point that one of the reasons for this failure is that few have really considered who reads *Ulysses* in the first place, or why they read it. My own goal in this study was to provide a beginning for such scholarly consideration, through examining the peculiar moment in time dubbed "the Joyce Wars."

In the five or so years since I began to write this study, there has been a growing interest in the role and identity of the common reader. Prior to 1998, there were few attempts outside the field of library science or booksellers' marketing surveys to chart the tastes or agendas of the non-professional reader; certainly literary scholars found little reason to do so. The reader, it was implied, was there to be instructed in literary taste and discrimination. That these readers may have had other ideas was rarely considered, or if it was considered it was always in the context that the literary taste of the masses was primarily for boorish, formulaic, poorly written trash. This type of hand wringing over the choices of the low- and middlebrow audiences has a long, venerable tradition today carried on by William Bennett, Allan Bloom, and E. D. Hirsch. In many ways, they are correct: the vast majority of fiction produced and purchased in this country is that of genre fiction—romances, science fiction, and mystery thrillers—and, literarily speaking, the majority of these works are riddled with flat characters, simple plotting, predictable action, and sometimes turgid prose. They require little effort on the part of readers, and leave few lasting impressions—neither of which can be said about *Ulysses*. And yet, *Ulysses* itself enjoys a popular life that would seem to belie its inaccessibility, and this status would seem to point to a common reader that can, indeed, consume more gourmet fare than Grisham or Steel can provide.

In fact, after many fruitless forays over the last five or six years into the world of online booksellers, I was able to purchase a copy of a book that constructs just such a reader for *Ulysses*: William Powell Jones's *James Joyce and the Common Reader*. But even this work, first published in 1955, points to the gulf between the academy and the common reader. Jones states in his preface to the second edition (1970) that his "original purpose ... was to gain more readers for Joyce" and that he "sought to approach 'the intelligent reader without artifice but with respect'" (viii), indicating that he believed readers outside the academy can and do read Joyce's works but that the common reader (whom he identifies via Johnson's famous description) has neither been addressed by scholarship nor respected by the academy. Jones indicates that "the title of [his] book received some criticism"—he doesn't say why—but the implication that Joyce's works have been appropriated by the academy is strong: "the beginner needs to be shown that he can cut through the difficult symbolism and esoteric criticism ... to the works themselves. [He] tried to prove that most of Joyce not only was intelligible to the general reader but could be exciting too" (viii). Even though Jones assumes intelligence on the part of the reader, the subtext of his commentary—"the beginner needs to be shown"—constructs the reader as passive, awaiting instruction from scholars in how to enjoy Joyce properly. So even scholarly books that overtly attempt to reach the common reader still construct that reader as alienated by both Joyce's work and the criticism surrounding it, and such books apparently find criticism within the Ivory Tower.

The published documents of the Joyce Wars fit into this larger cultural discourse in which academia and the common reader are at odds, and neither side appears likely to give the other much credence. The relationship between the two, though, is more complex than the typical rhetoric of the "culture wars" tends to make it appear. In this study, I attempt to map out a way to understand that complex relationship and the institutions of its transmittal and replication. The traditional understanding of those institutions places the common reader in a passive role, waiting for critics, academics, and the book publishing elite to decide what constitutes the Literary. But this process is complicated by the fact that ultimately readers decide for themselves whether or not a book is worth reading; no amount of critical praise can keep a book on the Bestseller list if people don't like it. And no amount of time spent on the list can guarantee canonical status for a book if it doesn't appeal to academia on some level beyond entertainment value.

This traditional formulation of the passive common reader has been challenged by several scholars over the years,[2] but only recently has there been a sustained attempt to understand the role that audience has played in the formation of literary culture. Lawrence Rainey, Mark Morrison, Joyce Wexler, and Allison Pease, among many others, have studied how the publishing culture of the early twentieth century shaped Modernism.[3] Yet little attention has been paid to how present day audiences, for whom Modernism is already codified, reified, and ossified as canonical, receive texts like *Ulysses*. In this book, I examine the Joyce Wars as a window into this unexplored area because of their public nature: the debates raged in literary periodicals with a large non-academic readership, and spilled over into newspapers and general- interest, "middlebrow" periodicals like *Time* and *Newsweek*. It is curious that an essentially professional debate about textual theory and editorial decisions became so large a part of our public literary culture for a time. The Joyce Wars, as they appeared in the public eye, became part of a larger discourse in which scholars and common readers have little to do with each other. Scholarship is often seen as irrelevant to the practice of reading for most people outside the academy, and the Joyce Wars did nothing to erase this boundary. In fact, as the documents of the controversies show, the debates were easily assimilated into a discourse of personality, celebrity, and mudslinging. The issues of authorship, materiality of books, copyright, and the role of readers in literary culture were overshadowed by the Springer-esque quality of what the public press implied was simple, petty careerism.

The documents under consideration here fall into two categories: the primary, which are the articles and letters of the combatants themselves, and the secondary, which are the newspaper accounts, reviews, and interviews of the principle players. The tone of the debates was first set in the public's mind not by the primary documents but by the initial articles that preceded the Joyce Wars proper, most strikingly in the *Post* article that described John Kidd in terms of David to the Joyce establishment's Goliath. But let us not forget that the players stepped into their parts, some more willingly than others, and kept the disagreement on the level of spectacle. Prior to the appearance of that article, both Kidd and Gabler had been privately speaking their cases to the Joyce community. None of this back story reached the public, but the cast of characters was in place and ready to go by the time that *Post* article brought the plot to the public's attention. The end result of the debates, at least for those outside the academy, was that the spectacle became more important than the meaning behind it—it was entertaining, and because of that it was easily dismissed.

Such spectacle would hardly cause a blip in the public's radar if it weren't about James Joyce and his most famous work. The Joyce Wars were press-worthy only because of the iconographic importance that *Ulysses* plays in our literary culture. It is a curious worship; the book called the most important of the preceding hundred years is also notorious for its inability to be read without special help. In this contradiction *Ulysses* seems Biblical and the literary critics and scholars its priesthood. Such religious terms are not unwarranted, given the very nature of the word "canon" and the strange place literature has in our culture. I explore in Chapter One the quasi-religious terms with which we engage literature, and the resulting awe we have for the figure of the author; this is neither new nor surprising to most of us in the postmodern (post-postmodern?) era. Yet this demystification has done nothing to halt the process of author-worship, and even though we in the Joyce community *say* that we no longer believe in a definitive text, like Vladimir and Estragon we still keep waiting for one.[4]

And it appears that such deferral will continue for a good while; changes to the copyright law in both the United States and Britain in the last few years have made the publishing situation of *Ulysses* more contentious than ever. Robert Spoo's thorough scholarship on these issues reveals that the 1922 *Ulysses* appears to be a public domain work, yet the novel will remain under copyright protection in the United States for up to another half-century; in Britain, 1996 changes to the law (in order to conform to the European Union Term Directive) reinstated the copyright for *Ulysses*, which had entered the public domain there in 1991 but now enjoys copyright protection until 2011.[5] The Joyce estate, whose role in the Joyce Wars can hardly be overlooked, seems determined to maintain control over Joyce's work and reputation for as long as possible and by any means necessary. On the surface, such a stance is reasonable; any property owner would fight to hold on to a lucrative property for as long as the law allows.

Yet the most recent public appearances of Joycean controversy center on adaptations or even small uses of *Ulysses*; in these cases it is the Joyce estate's rhetoric, in the person of the author's grandson Stephen Joyce, that reveals a reluctance to "allow" the general public even passing acquaintance with Joyce's works. For example, permission was denied to the producers of the recent film *Nora*, based on Brenda Maddox's biography of Joyce's wife Nora Barnacle, to use any part of Joyce's texts. But it doesn't stop there; Stephen Joyce refused the use of a few words from *Finnegans Wake* in a musical work commissioned for broadcast over European radio, and he "demanded" in 2000 that the organizers of a public festival in Edinburgh cancel a cabaret performance of "Penelope" because, in his words, it turned his grandfather's work into a "circus act."[6] Director Stephen Walsh in 1991 began production of a new film version of *Ulysses* aimed at the general cinema audience, and Stephen Joyce was reported as being "hostile to the project" which has cut sections of the book and rearranged others—notably putting Molly Bloom's monologue at the beginning of the film rather than the end, a move that speaks to the power of that section to represent *Ulysses* as a whole in popular culture (a singularity I discuss in Chapter Two). Walsh's own thoughts on the status of *Ulysses* are revealing: "It's funny, *Ulysses* is considered the most important book of the 20th century and yet nobody has read the damn thing. We're going to open it up to a wider audience" (quoted in Cullen). Presumably that wider audience might be moved to actually read the "damn thing," and thus not only see for themselves whether or not Walsh's film does it justice but also add to the Joyce estate's coffers through book sales. One can only surmise that Stephen Joyce's hostility to the film stems from Walsh's willingness to film *Ulysses* as though it were any other book, feeling free to reshape the narrative to suit mainstream cinematic techniques of story-telling. Clearly, Stephen Joyce—and those rascally academics he so despises—value a static *Ulysses* (and by implication a static Joyce), the equivalent of a literary museum piece or a dusty talisman of an absent god. Such a stance can hardly be welcoming to the general reader.

In addition to opposing performances of Joyce's works, Stephen Joyce has also successfully prevented Cork University Press from using excerpts of *Ulysses* in an anthology, *Irish Writing in the Twentieth Century—A Reader*, edited by David Pierce. Rather than pay the high permissions fees demanded by the Joyce estate, the publisher tried to sidestep the fee dispute by including an excerpt from the Rose *Reader's Edition* (which was then embroiled in a lawsuit brought by the Joyce estate—see below). This action resulted in an injunction and the publisher, rather than destroy an entire print run, removed the offending section and replaced it with a notice that Joyce's works could not be included because of copyright dispute. And so now, an anthology of twentieth century Irish literature does not include Ireland's most famous literary son.

Refusals, inordinately high permissions fees, and demands to halt production—it appears that Stephen Joyce feels that his custodianship of *Ulysses* and his grandfather's reputation relies on limiting access to the works. But literary works of art, in some sense, do not belong solely to the "owner"; if they are truly great or influential works (define that how you will), they enter into a public realm beyond that of the commercial transaction of buying a book and are therefore virtually impossible to control. Parodies, pop culture references, and visual or musical performances circulate these works and authors throughout culture with little respect for the rights of authors over their creations. Shakespearean phrases have become such a naturalized part of our lexicon that few people really know which plays they come from or which characters said them. I discuss in Chapter Two that *Ulysses*, too, has entered our public language in ways that may or may not reflect the image of Joyce dear to academia—or the Joyce estate.

Part of the estate's suit against the Rose edition contained reference to the "passing off" portion of copyright law; the estate maintained that the *Reader's Edition* has irreparably harmed the reputation of Joyce's work by passing off an inferior copy of *Ulysses,* a curious stand that yokes an edition aimed at the common reader to a notion of mediocrity, and a move that may further underscore the inaccessibility of the text. The courts wisely rejected this part of the suit. However, the court did rule that the Rose edition's use of the previously published Rosenbach manuscript infringed on the copyright of that material, and halted further production of the *Reader's Edition.*[7] The estate's refusals and litigation reify impressions that, as Andrew Reimer of the Sydney *Morning Herald* wrote, "*Ulysses* is far more than a mere work of literature. It is a cult object worshipped with arcane rituals" (6 Sept. 1997: 9). Perhaps, because *Ulysses* has become synonymous with Joyce in both the public and the academic consciousness, Stephen Joyce has a personal stake in protecting his grandfather's reputation by attempting to shape the public perceptions of *Ulysses* as a literary monument suitable only for worship. Such a stance is ironic, given the censure that greeted *Ulysses* upon its publication, and illustrates better than anything else how the cultural status of the book has changed over time.

I wish to take this opportunity to correct a flaw in the following study, and that is a neglect to contextualize more clearly the historical view of the common reader in the academy. By the early twentieth century, mass literacy had reached unprecedented levels. The rise of the publishing industry coincided with the rise of an industrialized economy, a rise in levels of leisure time never before seen, and the growth of an audience that increasingly turned to reading as a way to fill that leisure time. Margaret Dalziel's excellent study of popular literature in the nineteenth century was undertaken in an attempt to provide a basis for comparison to the popular literature of the present (which for her was 1957); her aim, in part, was to answer the question, "Is there . . . any good reason for the view so forcibly advanced by [Q. D.] Leavis in *Fiction and the Reading Public*, and so widely held since, that popular literature and popular taste have deteriorated greatly during the last hundred years?" (175). For Dalziel, the Leavisite view was tied up in moral judgments "in a way and to an extent that we avoid in criticizing more serious writing," an avoidance that apparently relies on the writer's motive: serious literature's forays into violence, horror, and depravity can be overlooked because of the writer's "attitudes [that] we can respect even if we do not share them," but for writers "whose motives and attitudes we do not trust" such depictions are acceptably judged by their morality (174). The age-old tension between art and commercialism remains a defining criteria for what constitutes the Literary. Dalziel shows that Leavis had a poor understanding of audience and reading matter of the nineteenth century, and credibly shows that Leavis incorrectly derides the deterioriation of taste based on the diaries of some unique working class readers and a "cursory examination" of cheap publications that were not, in fact, as widely read as Leavis supposes (175–176). But Dalziel does not question the Leavisite formulation that the common reader is an impressionable idiot savant—she herself uses terms like "half-educated," which easily slips into a subtext of "half-witted"—and continually reveals a willingness to believe that common readers cannot distinguish between bad literature and good. This is a mistake that continues today, and one that reifies the position of the literary critic/scholar as gatekeeper of culture. It is my contention that the common reader does indeed know when a book is badly written, but is more often willing to overlook bad writing in search of entertainment and surcease from the demands of life in a consumer economy. This conclusion is borne out in Janice Radway's *Reading the Romance* (1991), which is a striking look at readers of one of the most maligned literary forms. The readers in Radway's study, through extensive reading of their subject, have formed fairly sophisticated levels of analysis of the romance form. Radway also found that these women approached their reading with an agenda that belies the impressionable passivity attributed to them by much feminist scholarship: these readers were seeking ways to temporarily escape their roles as dutiful wives and mothers while not necessarily challenging the social pressures which kept them there. This complex agenda (of which a feminist discussion would be rich and provoking) interests me in relation to my own study for one simple reason: it reveals a glimpse into a truth long denied by the academy that its own agendas are not the only literary agendas, and that the common reader does not necessarily need scholars to tell them what to read—or how.

Further, my own definition of the common reader has been radically widened from when I began this study, partly thanks to a course I recently taught on Oprah's Book Club and Literary Establishments. My students continually challenged my own definition that the common reader was best delineated as a reader of serious fiction—because I, too, succumbed to the idea that genre fiction wasn't even worth examining in a literature course, except as an example of cultural documents of particular historical moments. My students viewed the reader as "anyone," which for the purposes of the class left me rather frustrated. But I began to see, through their persistence, that perhaps Dr. Johnson's famous dictum about the common reader was a far more democratic description than I gave it credit for being. As Carey Kaplan and Ellen Cronan Rose discuss in *The Canon and the Common Reader* (1990), Johnson's own background caused him to "almost invariably [qualify] and [undercut] his most fiercely conservative statements"; and though his writing "was devoted to legitimizing literature as a noble calling . . . his essential integrity required him to acknowledge that his writings were not purely irresistible effusions of Truth and Beauty[, they were] also a means to make a living" (18). Johnson apparently saw no conflict between art and commercialism. Rose and Kaplan show that Johnson defined the common reader in opposition to an "elitism of the pre-print era that saw literature as belonging essentially to a courtly minority enjoying pleasures too recherche for ordinary mortals," and that "after making some staggering and apparently irrefragable generalization, he backtracks and acknowledges change, human limitation, and the forces of history" (19). Johnson, while codifying the Literary, did not see that realm as fixed or removed from ordinary people. And his own definition of the role of the common reader is as useful today as it was two hundred years ago: "for by the common sense of readers, uncorrupted by literary prejudices, after all the refinements of subtility and the dogmatism of learning, must be generally decided all claim to poetical honours" ("Life of Gray").

It is tempting to stop with that pronouncement, but I would be remiss if I did not acknowledge that, while elegant, it hardly begins to address the problem of estrangement between the common reader and the academy. Perhaps such division is insurmountable, and we should just accept the current state of affairs. But given the political realities of shrinking budgets for the study of humanities, the disturbing trend of seeing universities as markets with the attendant view of students as customers, and the growing use of non-tenure track teachers in place of full-time faculty, I think that the general distrust of academia felt by the public needs to be addressed. I certainly don't have all of the answers to this dilemma, but I do have an unwavering conviction that literary study in a capitalist culture is both necessary and relevant. And I hope that, rather than simply causing us to salaciously rake over old coals, the following pages provoke discussion of the role of the common reader in forming literary culture. For at one time, all of us were "common readers," and as scholars we should acknowledge that shared tie with those readers outside of academia.

*N.B.*: I have attempted to update the copyright information as much as possible in the body of the text, but some information relating to changes in copyright law are placed in the chapter notes. In addition, John Kidd is no longer with Boston University and the James Joyce Research Center housed there has been closed as of 1999. I have placed the most recent information available on Kidd and his edition of *Ulysses* in the chapter notes as well.

*Julie Sloan Brannon*
*Jacksonville University*
*Jacksonville, Florida*
*2002*

## NOTES

[1] "'Reader's Edition' of *Ulysses*," Letter. *Irish Times*. 8 July 1997: 13.

[2] E.G., Janice Radway's *Reading the Romance: Women, Patriarchy, and Popular Literature* (1984, 1991), which looks at what real readers find in the much-maligned romance novel as opposed to the kind of feminist bashing these works usually receive from scholars (if they are discussed at all). Radway's book offers the refreshing perspective that the common reader is not stupid and she is quite capable of distinguishing good writing from bad, but that her agenda does not mirror the scholar's—nor should it.

[3] Lawrence Rainey, *Institutions of Modernism: Literary Elites and Public Culture* (1998); Mark Morrison, *The Public Face of Modernism: Little Magazines, Audiences, and Reception, 1905–1920* (2001); Joyce Wexler, *Who Paid For Modernism?: Art, Money, and the Fiction of Conrad, Joyce, and Lawrence* (1997); Allison Pease, *Modernism, Mass Culture, and The Aesthetics of Obscenity* (2000).

[4] I am indebted to Robert Spoo for conversing with me electronically on this issue, and for pointing out this contradiction in the Joyce world.

[5] "Copyright Protectionism and Its Discontents: The Case of James Joyce's *Ulysses* in America," *The Yale Law Journal* 108.3 (1998): 633–667; "Copyright and the Ends of Ownership: the Case for a Public-domain *Ulysses* in America," *Joyce Studies Annual*, (1999); forthcoming, "Injuries, Remedies, Moral Rights, and the Public Domain" Introduction to special issue "Joyce and the Law" of the *James Joyce Quarterly*, Volume 37, Numbers 3 and 4.

[6] Medh Ruane, "The war of words over Joyce's literary legacy," *The Irish Times*, 10 June 2000. *The Irish Times Archive* online. 25 Apr. 2002. http://www. ireland.com/newspaper/archive/; Kate Watson-Smyth, "Joyce's grandson tries to keep explicit Molly Bloom off the stage," *The Independent* (London) 31 July 2000. *The Independent.co.uk*. 27 Apr. 2002. http://www.independent.co.uk/story. jsp?story=49438. Referenced in Robert Spoo, "Injuries, Remedies, Moral Rights, and the Public Domain" *James Joyce Quarterly* 37 (2002) (forthcoming).

[7] Again, Robert Spoo continues his investigation into the strange copyright sagas of *Ulysses*. His article, "A Rose Is a Rose Is a Roth: New/Old Theories of Legal Liability in the Joyce World," (forthcoming in the *James Joyce Literary Supplement*) compares the current copyright issues assailing the Rose edition to those of the Samuel Roth pirated edition of 1927, and finds remarkable similarities. I would urge any reader who is interested in how such issues affect the current situation for both scholars and readers to consult Spoo's growing corpus of work in this area.

# Acknowledgments

Because no book is ever solely the work of the author, I would like to thank the following people:

Elizabeth Fuller of the Rosenbach Museum for her assistance during research of the Joyce holdings there;

The editorial offices of *Newsweek* and George Hunka at Hunger.org for generous permissions to reprint letters, articles, and illustrations;

*The South Carolina Review*, for permission to reprint portions of Chapter Two which appeared as the essay, "Joyce.com" in the Special Issue on Ireland in the Arts and Humanities 1899–1999, Volume 32, Number 1 (Fall 1999).

Fritz Senn, director of the Zurich James Joyce Foundation, for his assistance in locating press articles, and for his insightful reading and intelligent commentary on the manuscript;

The Florida State University for a Dissertation Research Grant during the Fall of 1997;

John Kidd for his willingness to converse with me during my research;

Hans Walter Gabler for graciously reading and correcting portions of this book;

Daniel Klyn, whose enthusiasm and interest for this project is greatly appreciated;

Michael Groden and Charles Rossman for promptly and generously answering questions via the J-Joyce Discussion list;

Robert Spoo, for his generous sharing of materials and time, and his careful and considerate reading of several chapters;

S. E. Gontarski, for guidance, for helping me sharpen my thought during the writing of this study, and for his unfailing support;

Ralph Berry, Bonnie Braendlin, and William Cloonan for asking excellent questions;

William Cain for choosing this study as part of the Studies in Major Literary Authors series, and for his advisory comments on revision;

Damian Treffs and the production staff at Routledge, for patiently answering my dumb questions and shepherding me through this process;

Karen DeMeester, for pointing the way to this topic, and also for her friendship which manifested, among so many other ways, in a willingness to listen to me talk about it long after her own interest must have waned;

Sheila Sloan and John and Helen Brannon, for their unwavering faith, love, and support;

Christopher, Jonathan, and Annalivia Brannon for reminding me that sometimes it's more important to dance to a Wiggles video than it is to write yet another book about James Joyce;

And last, but never least, Todd Brannon for patiently and supportively reading draft after draft even though, like Nora Joyce, he's never read *Ulysses*.

# INTRODUCTION

*O, rocks! . . . Tell us in plain words.*

—*Molly Bloom,* Ulysses, 4.343

Robert Spoo, reviewing the Danis Rose edition of *Ulysses* (*College English* 60 [March 1998]: 330–335), takes scholars to task for entertaining abstract notions of readership and, in Rose's case, for using "the abstract, elastic notion of the 'reader' as a stalking-horse for the broad exercise of editorial power" (332). Spoo calls for a theory of the relationship of Joyce and the academy to that larger culture and states that "it is high time that critics began to examine their relationship to the audiences they so blithely assume or invent. *Ulysses* will survive our disputations; it is the credibility of scholarship that is in question" (334–335). The literary critic/scholar[1] seems to be at odds with the common reader; one scholarly article appearing in the *Western Humanities Review* even contained the words "the Common Reader Versus the Literary Critic" (Marchant 221). This is a peculiar state of affairs considering that there is no real consensus in defining this reader. The common reader could be the consumer of mass paperbacks, those works historically derided by the academy as middlebrow and hopelessly banal; or, the common reader could be a member of that educated group of people who immerse themselves in works considered "literary" (a troublingly ill-defined term itself). The only solid statement that can be made about this reader is that she is, apparently, not a professional critic.

The traditional formulation of "the reader" (a term used interchangeably at times with "the common reader") has been that she is a passive recipient of literary culture, dependent upon the literary establishment—consisting of critics, scholars, publishers, and writers—for definition of what constitutes the "literary." With the exception of reader response theory, which places the authority of making meaning with the reader rather than the author, almost all literary interpretation and theorizing posits a

*1*

passive reader who receives the meaning(s) deposited in the literary work by the author or the dominant ideology (depending on the critic's theoretical orientation). Reader response, *in extremis*, removes the power of the literary critic to determine meaning. But even if, as Stanley Fish proposes, interpretive communities share "interpretive strategies not for reading but for writing texts, for constituting their properties . . . [and that] these strategies exist prior to the act of reading and therefore determine the shape of what is read rather than the other way around" (14), the division between the literary critic and the common reader continues. The literary establishment's interpretive strategies remain the dominant discourse in determining what gets defined as "literature," and often these strategies depend upon accepting that the literary critic, rather than the common reader, is best equipped to take on this task.

But this passive reader is a construct, a convenient rhetorical device for the literary critic who is, in essence, speaking for him- or herself. After all, offering a literary interpretation is itself an act of reading, predicated upon the interpretive community of the scholar. Yet the role of the common reader is more important than this rhetorical use would imply; there is an economics of literary production that depends upon the reader as consumer. The publishing industry, itself an important part of the formation of literary culture, depends upon the common reader to buy those books being marketed as worth reading by critics and scholars. Of course, the role of the common reader is more complex than a simple economic view would imply; the dynamic between the publishers, critics, and the common reader is intricate and not solely economic in nature. It is also less simplistic than the traditional view that critics and publishers define the "literary" and that the reading public accepts this definition, lining up dutifully to buy literary masterpieces. Economics, under a traditional understanding of the critic/scholar's role in this mechanism, supposedly plays no part in the academic study of the literary. The strange case of James Joyce's *Ulysses*, however, illustrates that this traditional understanding is naïve at best, disingenuous at worst, and may serve to widen the dichotomy between the academic literary critic and the common reader. The Joyce Wars, as the controversies over editions of *Ulysses* came to be known, encompassed not only the editorial issues of authorship and poststructuralist issues of textual instability, but also highlighted the differing agendas of the academic and the common reader. In what follows, I will consider the Joyce Wars with an eye toward understanding Joyce's function as a cultural icon, both inside and outside of the academy, as well as examine the role the Joyce Wars played in maintaining (or, in some ways, perhaps widening) the gulf between the common reader and the academy. Two of the unexplored aspects of these very public debates are the role of the common reader in sustaining Joyce as a cultural icon, and the assumption that Joyce's works require an uncommon reader to enjoy them. *Ulysses* in particular exists as a peculiarly academic and yet popular work that continues to garner interest

in the public press. The Joyce Wars, academically speaking, asked us to re-
consider who writes *Ulysses*; the editorial issues are complex and require
careful elucidation. The fact that the academic debates over Hans Walter
Gabler's 1984 edition found their way into the popular press seems to be at
odds with the esoteric nature of the editorial and scholarly questions involved; the fact that Danis Rose deliberately invoked the dichotomy between academic and common reader in 1997 by positing a need for a
"reader's edition" of *Ulysses* seems to reinforce the special status of that
book as intellectual property, with access to its meaning owned by the
academy. But such a simple dichotomizing view ignores the struggles which
underlie the Joyce Wars: Joycean iconography ensures that *Ulysses* will remain a book sought out by readers both in and out of academia, but the
agendas of those two constituencies differ in key ways. This study outlines
the major points of struggle in the Joyce Wars as they appeared in the popular press, examines how the rhetoric of those documents fits into the
larger discourse about *Ulysses* and scholars that exists already, and explores how the controversy over editions of *Ulysses* might illustrate the dynamic between the academy and the common reader.

   Understanding the common reader as a real, historical *participant* in the
formation of literary culture needs a more prominent place in literary
scholarship, a need which has only recently begun to be addressed. Scholars in the field of library science frequently conduct readership surveys,
and of course the publishing industry regularly assesses book purchase patterns, but infrequently do the results of such surveys find their way into literary theorizing. Richard Altick, Jonathan Rose, Janice Radway and
Richard Todd (among others) have all, to varying degrees, attempted to define just who reads what, and how these readers participate in forming literary culture. Altick's *The English Common Reader* was one of the first
scholarly looks at historical audiences as active participants in the rise of
the novel genre, examining the mechanisms of the rise in literacy rates—the
lending libraries, the printing presses, and the efforts of social reformers to
teach the lower classes to read (not always out of altruism). As an indicator
of who the common reader is now, however, Altick's fascinating study is inadequate. More recently, Janice Radway has examined the role of the common reader—specifically defined in her work as the subscribers to the
Book of the Month Club—in understanding the hierarchichal nature of literary culture in America.[2] These literary cultural studies aside, few scholars have attempted to bring the kind of statistical data on readers, such as
that published in 1983 by Nicholas Zill and Marianne Winglee,[3] to bear
on studies of the role of the reader in forming literary canons.

   One study which does just that, however, is Richard Todd's *Consuming
Fictions: The Booker Prize and Fiction in Britain Today* (1996). In Todd's
study, he defines the general reader of serious literary works as "a reasonably sophisticated, largely but not exclusively professional readership with
an interest in, but not unlimited time for, the leisured consumption of full-

length fiction," based on surveys taken by British booksellers (3). This definition seems adequate, given Zill and Winglee's statistics on American consumers of serious literary fiction (see *n.* 3). Further, this reader looks to publications like the *Times Literary Supplement* and the *New York Review of Books*, among others, to remain apprised of the appearance of new literary works and to read opinions about those works. In short, the "common reader" is a fairly well-educated and informed reader of serious literature (as opposed to genre fiction) who, while not a specialist, nevertheless exhibits a certain familiarity with matters of style, technique, theme, and genre conventions. For the purposes of this study, the terms "common reader" and "general reading public" are synonymous, and defined as the group of people outside academic circles who buy and read significant literary works for enjoyment and educational purposes.

Within critical discourse, however, this reader has no identity and, when she is not dismissed altogether as middlebrow, becomes subsumed within the academy as a particular kind of reader: an academic one with a professional stake in literary interpretation. The common reader thus loses her power in the formation of literary culture. One of the implications of overlooking the reader as participant is that any claims for the subversive nature of literature (or, conversely, its reinforcement of dominant ideology) remain in the realm of unproven—and unprovable—theory. Spoo addresses this implication when he discusses Christine Froula's recent *Modernism's Body*:

> At times she suggests that mere exposure to Joyce's writings will work the miracle of consciousness-raising that her book celebrates. . . . At other times it is clear that Froula wrote her book in the belief that Joyce's subversiveness must be taught, yet it is hard to imagine any common reader deriving much from her heady instruction. . . . Froula does not indicate how her challenging discourse might be . . . made to cross over to a public which, fed by the talk shows and the image-merchants, may actually be ready for subversive messages about gender. Indeed, it is not at all clear that . . . anyone unacquainted with the assumptions and jargon of the academy can experience the particular subversion-effect that Joyce allegedly encourages. Without a theory of the relationship of Joyce and the academy to the larger culture, the most that can be hoped for is a rash of subversions within the Ivory Tower. The uncomfortable suspicion arises that Froula is preaching to the subverted. (334)

While Spoo criticizes Froula for not addressing the practical effects of her analysis for the common reader, his own definition of that reader is clearly dismissive. His assertion that the common reader is "fed by the talk shows and image-merchants" reveals that Spoo himself defines the common reader as part of a vast wasteland of the middlebrow; and contrary to his implication, it is *not* clear that "anyone unacquainted with the assumptions and jargon of the academy" cannot experience the subversion of the Joycean text. Spoo defines the common reader in opposition to the academy here, and while his concerns about the "credibility of scholarship" are valid, he, too, perpetuates without examination the dichotomy between reader and critic. The uncomfortable truth behind this impulse in literary criticism is that the common reader is, in fact, the Other: the marginalized spectre against which literary critics define their own position in literary culture.

That position has always been a dubious one, particularly in America. Anti-intellectualism has long been a part of U.S. culture, with academia often being aligned with Communism, Socialism, and other left-wing ideologies (not always without reason). Furthermore, the much-discussed proliferation of poststructuralist theory, with its concomitant growth in the use of jargon unfamiliar to the non-specialist—not to mention its politics— has done little to bridge the gulf between academia and the non-academic world. The stereotype of the absent-minded professor, too focused on his work to notice his surroundings, has also enjoyed a long history in western culture. These two elements played a part in the first Joyce War as manifested in the popular press.

Much of the 1984 debate grew from the academy's own struggles with the advent of continental literary theories. The documents of the debate— most notably the infamous exchanges in the *Times Literary Supplement* and the *New York Review of Books*, but also articles in newspapers, popular magazines, and scholarly periodicals—indicate that the "combatants" fall loosely into two camps: traditionally-oriented scholars and (for lack of a better term) poststructuralist scholars. The Joycean scholarly community, like most others in the early 1980's, was struggling with the encroachment of continental theories upon its humanist territory. These postmodern theories of literature had been steadily making inroads into academia for over twenty years by the time the "Joyce Wars" began; by 1984, younger scholars trained in the new, more overtly political theories had become established (or were trying to establish themselves) in the academy. Of course, this shift was not localized to Joyce studies; throughout the university community, from the humanities to the sciences, the academy was (and still is) contending with the implications of postmodern theories. As Michel Foucault has argued, all power struggles are localized, and together they form a web of power struggles within a dominant discourse. The conflicts within Joyce studies are emblematic of those taking place in every field of the academy, which itself is involved in ongoing struggles within larger society regarding the university's function.

This tension between the university and the non-university worlds finds one expression in the common perception that most modernist literature is inaccessible to non-academic readers. The radical modernists—Joyce, Eliot, Woolf, and Pound, among others—alienated themselves (often purposefully, in the case of Eliot and Pound) from a wide audience with their experiments in subject and form. Yet, paradoxically, by the end of the twentieth century their innovations have entered the cultural epistemology in many ways: fractured subjectivity, meta-narrative, and other aspects of what is commonly called "stream-of-consciousness" technique have become staples in the arts, particularly the visual arts such as popular film, music video, and television. Given this state of affairs, one would imagine that Joyce would now be *more* accessible to the reading public; the fact that an aura of incomprehensibility continues to surround much of his work seems a peculiar development, and one which needs to be addressed. This aura, in fact, is highly unstable. Many Joyce readers come to his works from outside the academy, attracted solely by Joyce's reputation as master of modern literature. Others come to Joyce's works out of an attraction to his counter-culture status, garnered in the 1960's by *Finnegans Wake*. Understanding how Joycean iconography functions allows us to begin understanding how disparate ways of seeing Joyce can coexist in what I term "the public Joyce," the Joyce that exists outside of the academy.

The relationship of this audience of general readers to the academy is a complex one, and hard to specify without a host of disclaimers. One of the difficulties lies in the seeming lack of interest the two audiences show each other. As Gerald Graff has pointed out in discussing the rhetoric against literary theory:

> Academic commentary on Faulkner addresses a lay public about as much or as little as commentary on Derrida. It chiefly addresses "Faulkner studies," which predetermines independent of any lay audience what constitutes a problem worth taking up and what evaluations are orthodox and heretical. . . . Indeed, what makes literary theory seem so outrageously different from standard research and explication is that by flaunting its difficulty and esotericism it shows it has simply abandoned the sentimental pretense that it has an audience outside the field, that outsiders still care what academic literary commentators have to say. (64–65)

Graff describes the separation of professors from non-academics as a result of the institutional practices of universities: the conflicts between fields are never made part of the context within which students learn those fields, and the conflicts "end up as the business of those who specialize in them and quarrel over them in the professional journals devoted to those issues" (70). While Graff's aim of opening the conflicts within academia to scrutiny by what he terms "lay people" is admirable, he spends little time exploring why such conflicts would be interesting to those people in the first place. The audience for whom Graff would open up the conflicts is specifically that of students, rather than a general reading public; but the separation between the general public and academia is suspended for students and, as such, they function as a special case with a different agenda. Students are looking to earn a grade, and do not freely choose their reading material, and this distinction makes Graff's remedy for the separation between the public and the academy suspect. Why would the quarreling in professional journals be of interest to a reader outside of the academy?

Therein lies the peculiarity of the Joyce Wars: the conflicts between literary and editorial theories were not restricted to professional journals but took place in very public organs of literary thought. There was something about this moment in Joyce Studies which made it of enough interest that the *New York Review of Books* devoted almost a whole year to printing letters from the combatants. The question remains: why?

The answer partly lies in understanding the pedestal that Literature occupies in our culture. The religious impulse in literary studies illustrates the sacred nature of the literary text; even Graff uses priestly terms to describe critics by differentiating them from "lay people." The concept of the supranatural author, more sensitive and attuned to the hidden meanings of the universe than ordinary humans, is a still-popular Romantic ideal. This ideal in part explains the iconography surrounding the authors who constitute our received literary canon (even the word "canon" carries religious import, with its "canonization" of the Author-Saint). In fact, Foucault precisely summarizes this relationship between the university and a culture's literary ontology:

> . . . among all the narratives, why is it that a number of them are sacralized, made to function as "literature"? They are immediately taken up with an institution that was originally very different: the university institution. . . .
>
> . . . In the nineteenth century, the university was the element within which was constituted a so-called classical literature, and which was valued both as the sole basis of contemporary literature and as a criticism of that literature. Hence a very curious interplay occurs . . . between literature and the university, between the writer and the professor. . . . little by little, the two institutions . . . tended to merge completely. We know perfectly well that today so-called avant-garde literature is read only by university teachers and their students. We know very well that nowadays a writer over thirty is surrounded by students writing their theses on his work. We know that writers live mainly by teaching and lecturing.
>
> So here we have the truth of something: the fact that literature functions as literature through an interplay of selection, sacralization, and institutional validation, of which the university is both the operator and the receiver. (4–5)

To understand the academic construction of readership, it is necessary to understand how Joyce's status as canonized master is perpetuated through the instrument of the university. The single largest dispersal system of canonized literature is that of the lower division survey course. Morton P. Levitt reminisces that he first read *Ulysses* "in 1958, . . . sandwiched among *The Magic Mountain*, *Swann's Way*, *The Sound and the Fury*, and eleven other modern novels in a fifteen-week undergraduate course" (91). We can see that, at the very height of New Criticism's reign, Joyce's most famous work was considered important enough to offer in a survey course about the Modernist novel. Forty years later, the situation is much changed. *Ulysses* is infrequently taught at the undergraduate level, owing to time constraints; the survey course is unfriendly to any of Joyce's works except *Portrait* or "The Dead," his most anthologized work. Yet *Ulysses* is always mentioned when a list of the greatest writers of the twentieth century is put together, or when discussing influences on contemporary authors like Pynchon. At the very least, even if Joyce is not taught in an undergraduate survey course, one could hardly discuss the Modernist movement without him. His place in the canon, as displayed in the average undergraduate survey course, is assured. And the truth of the matter is that the vast majority of students at university end their literature classes after fulfilling the liberal studies requirement; it is in these courses that their ideas of what constitutes "great literature" will be reified. Indeed, Foucault states: "Our culture accords literature a place that in a sense is extraordinarily limited: how many people read literature? What place does it really have in the general expansion of discourses? But this same culture forces all its children, as they move toward culture, to pass through a whole ideology ... of literature during their studies. There is a kind of paradox here" ("Functions" 6).

This paradox is the scaffolding upon which the public nature of the Joyce Wars hung. Those who do read literature (and their number is greater than Foucault's statement suggests), having passed through the ideology of the sacredness of texts, read those texts under an idea which has been destabilized by postmodern thinkers like Foucault: that authorial intention can be determined, and that the texts being read are a result of that authorial intention. By the 1980's such textual stability had long been dismissed in the world of textual editing, but literary scholars had rarely found reason to scrutinize the theoretical implications of multiple editions of a work, all traceable to the revising authorial hand. Conversely, textual editors had rarely investigated the impact of literary theory on their own field and continued attempting to publish "definitive editions," even while literary theorists had begun to dismiss the idea of the writer as sole author of a work. The Gabler edition and the ensuing controversy helped to change all of that. The attacks on Gabler's edition, and the equally spirited defenses of it, may seem to those outside the academy as tempests in a teapot; yet they speak profoundly of the upheavals in literary criticism which reached their apex in the 1980's.

Debate over editorial theories on the placement of a period may seem slightly ridiculous even to those in the academy, but for those who study modern literature and its successors, it points to larger critical debates over the nature of text, the role of the Author, and the historically placed values of language and its meaning. Perhaps punctuation is incidental to scholars of earlier literatures, but for twentieth century works, where experimental writing often called into question the very ordering principles of consciousness itself (and the grammatical rules which kept that written consciousness in order), debate over the meaning of punctuation takes on a very different cast. Indeed, it is just those ideas of what Joyce's impact was on the literature that came after him which give an urgency to the *Ulysses* controversies of the 1980's. The appearance in 1997 of Rose's *Reader's Edition* raises larger questions of the social construction of just who James Joyce is and what he and his works stand for in the culture outside the academy. In a comment printed in the June 23, 1997 *Newsweek*, Rose makes an implicit challenge to traditional scholarship: "A person can read this in two weeks instead of a year . . . Let's say that I have removed from various rooms in Joyce's mansion cobwebs from the past" (8). Rose is apparently trying to wake Joyce's work from the nightmare of critical history; whether he succeeds or not remains to be seen. But Rose does not challenge the elitist idea of Joyce's work at all; by stating a need to translate *Ulysses,* he is in truth reinforcing this idea. Moreover, the preface to the edition seems aimed not at the common reader, but at the scholars who would take Rose to task for his editorial methods. It contains editorial jargon, esoteric arguments, and definitions better suited to a scholarly audience familiar with textual editing procedures. The preface appears to be written more for the participants and onlookers of the first Joyce War than a "general reader" coming to *Ulysses* for the first time. There is a strong feeling of appeasement about the structure of Rose's edition; in addition to the subtle apologia of the preface, he includes an alternate version of the "Penelope" episode without his added punctuation. With Molly's soliloquy serving as a kind of Sudetenland, the Rose edition's preface functions as a Munich Pact between the editorial concerns of the first Joyce War and the readership construction issues of the second. Rose is not Hitler, of course. Tanks will not roll down Eccles Street. But the media outcry against Rose's editorial changes warrants a closer look in considering the question of who "owns" *Ulysses*. The public Joyce and the academic Joyce are at odds in this debate over editions; it remains to be seen who will be the victor.

It is certain that whatever the results of the Joyce Wars were (or will be), as Charles Rossman states, "we have lost our bibliographical innocence forever" (45). The "we" of his statement, however, is the academy; it remains unclear whether or not the general reader has been cast out of textual Eden as a result of the scholarly quarreling over Joyce's most famous work. But moving the debates back into the academic closet will not revive the "credibility of scholarship." Nor will teaching the conflicts fill the gap that exists between the public and the academy, *pace* Graff. What the Joyce Wars can teach us—and by "us," I mean scholars—is that our scholarship depends in part on understanding just who reads the works under examination, and why they read them. Such an understanding will allow us to see how our own work functions in the discourse of Literature: in tandem with, not opposition to, readers outside of academia. We have an obligation in that dyad to continue the vital work of scholarship for the benefit of all who read literary works, to keep literature a vibrant part of our larger cultural discourse, and to ensure that what we do is indeed credible to readers both in and out of academia. The position of the Humanities is a tenuous one in our culture at present, evidenced by the growing trend of treating higher education as a market with students as consumers—what relevance, indeed, does *Ulysses* have to participation in a consumer economy? The Joyce Wars provide an excellent case study for examining Joycean iconography as it exists both inside and outside the academy, and for exploring some of the ways the gulf between the academy and the common reader continues to grow.

NOTES

[1]The terms "critic" and "scholar" are used interchangeably in this dissertation, although they used to mean quite different things. Even Spoo's quote shows them to have become cognates, with the need for *critics* to examine their assumptions being the basis for strengthening the credibility of *scholarship*.

[2]*A Feeling for Books: the Book-of-the-Month Club, Literary Taste, and Middle Class Desire*, Chapel Hill: University of North Carolina Press, 1997.

[3]"Literature Reading in the United States: Data from National Surveys and Their Policy Implications," in *Book Research Quarterly* (Spring 1989): 24–58. Zill and Winglee's analysis is thorough but disturbingly vague on differentiating between what they term "quality fiction" and "genre fiction," categories they blur by noting that some genre fiction is well crafted and highly imaginative, presumably qualities that "high literature" (a term they also use) exemplifies. But even this exhaustive study shies away from defining the common reader as either a consumer primarily of genre fiction or serious literature; they report that roughly "7 to 12 percent of the adult population" reads serious literature, but that " the size of the audience for literature could be two to three times larger, depending on where one draws the line between 'entertainment' and 'art'" (34).

# CHAPTER ONE

# JOYCE'S CANONIZATION,
## in which
# THE PROFESSORS ARE KEPT BUSY

*After all, to comprehend* Ulysses *is not among the recognised learned professions, and nobody should give his entire existence to the job.*
—Arnold Bennett

"The Joyce Industry": this is the self-applied name for the post-1960 boom in Joyce criticism. The first issue of *The James Joyce Quarterly* in 1963 inaugurated the arrival of Joyce studies as a full-scale critical field in its own right, and forty years later this journal is still at the center of that field. Simultaneous with this recognition of Joyce studies as a legitimate field of inquiry, the biannual International James Joyce Symposia grew from a fairly small gathering of seventy-five scholars in 1967 to a gathering of well over 250 participants from countries spanning the globe at the present time.[1] From the introduction of *Ulysses* to the wider American literary scene through the famous Woolsey decision of 1933, Joyce went from being a peculiar and obscure Irish writer (often alluded to as obscene but, as in the case of most censored writers, rarely actually read) to a major literary giant in a span of less than ten years, and the center of that activity has been in the United States—a country in which Joyce never set foot.

*Ulysses* continues to sell upwards of 100,000 copies a year worldwide.[2] Some of these copies, undoubtedly, are sold to students in the university system; but the book is also stocked on the shelves of commercial bookstores like Barnes & Noble, B. Dalton, and Waldenbooks. The university, then, plays a role in Joyce's reputation, but there are other forces at work, many of which have to do with the publicity machine which thrust *Ulysses* into the public's eye over eighty years ago. Joyce's reputation rests in part on the academic machinery which created the Joyce Industry as we know it, and the process which canonized his works produced a particular kind of Joyce, one which serves the needs of the academic institution which created him. This academic Joyce diverges from the general public's Joyce, a dichotomy I will examine more closely in Chapter Two; but the image of an iconoclastic author whose works are impossible to comprehend without critical intervention finds its roots in the academic Joyce and the critical machinery which supports him. The oft-repeated quote about keeping the professors busy has become a Joycean cliché, and functions in part to imply that Joyce wrote specifically for the professors rather than a broader reading public. The context of the quote, however, is a humorous one which undercuts the surface meaning; Jacques Benoîst-Méchin, the young man who translated "Penelope" into French for Valery Larbaud's reading in 1921, had begged Joyce for the scheme of the book. Joyce only gave him parts of it and said: "If I gave it all up immediately, I'd lose my immortality. I've put in so many enigmas and puzzles that it will keep the professors busy for centuries arguing over what I meant, and that's the only way of in-suring one's immortality" (Ellmann 521). Joyce's view of "the professors" was a wry (although ironically prescient) one. But the effect of this quote, offered *ad nauseam* and out of context in both scholarly and popular arti-cles as a serious comment on Joyce's intentions, reinforces the academic Joyce who wrote for the professors. And for the last fifty years the profes-sors have, indeed, been busy.

## INTRODUCING JAMES JOYCE

Through literary reviews and book salons in Europe, then through the ef-forts of Pound, Eliot, Beach and others, Joyce's reputation spread to the United States and the rest of the world. It should also be noted that these efforts to spread Joyce's work were spurred in no small way by Joyce him-self. From the beginning, the censorship of *Ulysses* allowed it to find an au-dience only through smuggled copies and reviews by fellow writers. It was through Valery Larbaud, Stuart Gilbert, and Frank Budgen that Joyce made sure people understood what *Ulysses* was about, helping Larbaud coin the term "interior monologue" and providing unlimited assistance for Gilbert's 1931 *James Joyce's* Ulysses and Budgen's 1934 *The Making of James Joyce's* Ulysses.[3] But even at the beginning of his writing career he was concerned about reaching a reading public, as shown in his correspon-dence with publishers about *Dubliners*.[4] Peculiarly, though, many critics tend to focus on these letters only as illustrations of Joyce's fight to keep his work intact and free of censorship, a reading given credence by Ell-mann's treatment of these skirmishes. And yet this reading ignores the fact that, like any writer, Joyce *wanted* to be published and read, and his corre-spondence with publishers shows a willingness to make concessions (see *Letters I*, 56; 59–63). Joseph Kelly, in *Our Joyce: From Outcast to Icon* (1998), describes Joyce's target audience for *Dubliners* as specifically Irish, and Joyce's letters support Kelly's argument. In a letter dated June 23, 1906 to Grant Richards on his reluctance to publish *Dubliners*, Joyce wrote: "I seriously believe that you will retard the course of civilization in Ireland by preventing the Irish people from having one good look at themselves in my nicely polished looking-glass" (*Letters I* 64). Kelly cites Joyce's oft-quoted "paralysis" statement to Constantine Curran which has guided critics in their analysis of these stories, and takes critics to task for applying this paralysis as "a moral or spiritual failing general to humankind and the world" (16). Kelly specifies the paralysis Joyce wished to portray in *Dubliners* as being unique to Ireland, and even more narrowly to a specific class of people living in Dublin at the turn of the century; by "globalizing paralysis," critics deny "any real possibility of curing the disease" (16). By reinserting Joyce's political life into discussion of *Dubliners*, Kelly offers us a view of Joyce at odds with the main body of criticism which surrounds Joyce's works. Kelly places the shift from the political to the aesthetic squarely on the shoulders of Ezra Pound:

> Not only did Pound get Joyce published and into the hands of readers, but he also readdressed Joyce's early fiction to an audience vastly different from the Irish middle class. Pound de-Irished Joyce's reputation, and, in the process, stripped his early fiction of its political force. What originally had been intended to criticize middle-class, Dublin Catholic society became a general comment on the universal human condition in the modern age. (63–64)

Pound's influence on the fortunes of the modernist movement cannot be overestimated, and Kelly makes a strong case that, because of Pound's aesthetic aims, Joyce's work (along with others gathered by Pound who are now considered the core of modernism) became linked with the elitist modernism of Pound's program. The price of being published under this program was that the works would reach a limited *cognoscenti* rather than the wider, particularly Irish audience that Joyce originally intended for his stories. Indeed, H.G. Wells's review of *Portrait* specifically located Joyce's work in the tradition of Irish literature: "Like so many Irish writers from Sterne to Shaw Mr. Joyce is a bold experimentalist with paragraph and punctuation" ("James Joyce" 23). This review was extremely influential, coming as it did from a respected English writer, and it helped spread Joyce's reputation as a young Irish writer to watch. But, as Kelly points out, Pound's reviews pulled both *Dubliners* and *Portrait* away from Ireland and Irish politics into a more universalized mode (76–77); of *Dubliners*, Pound wrote: "[Joyce] gives us things as they are, not only for Dublin, but for every city" and says that "It is surprising that Mr Joyce is Irish" (*Pound/Joyce* 28–29). Pound wrote of *Portrait* that Joyce belonged in the company of Flaubert and Dostoyevsky, and more pointedly the newer writers like T.S. Eliot and Wyndham Lewis; he placed *Portrait* on a world stage by saying that "it will remain a permanent part of English literature—written by an Irishman in Trieste and first published in New York City"(*Pound/Joyce* 88–90). Pound's other writings on Joyce further remove Joyce from a specifically Irish context. In "The Non-Existence of Ireland," appearing in *The New Age* on February 25, 1915, Pound wrote that

Joyce "fled to Trieste and into the modern world . . . He writes as a European, not as a provincial" (*Pound/Joyce* 32–33). The first readers of *Ulysses* were the subscribers to Pound's serial *The Egoist*, which had also published *Portrait* serially and then subsequently became a press and brought it out in book form. The Egoist Press also acquired the rights to *Dubliners* from its publisher Grant Richards in 1921, and so Pound became the sole outlet for Joyce's works prior to Sylvia Beach.

Pound helped ensconce Joyce firmly in the Continental literary scene, and Pound's connection with the American editors Margaret Anderson and Jane Heap enabled the first five chapters of *Ulysses* to appear in serial form in a decidedly avant-garde outlet, *The Little Review*. Ellmann describes Pound's relationship with *The Little Review* as primarily part of his program of 'making it new': "Pound was then in the course of shifting his . . . American allegiance from Harriet Monroe's *Poetry* to the *Little Review* . . . which was more avant-garde in its interests and which intended to print chiefly prose" (421). And so Joyce became an international modernist rather than a specifically Irish writer intent on social change in his home country; instead of creating the conscience of the Irish, Pound moved Joyce into creating the conscience of the modernist *literati*.

### ULYSSES' EARLY RECEPTION

Joyce's growing reputation notwithstanding, getting *Ulysses* published proved to be as arduous a task as Odysseus's voyage itself (a detailed publishing history of *Ulysses* is found in Chapter Three). As *Ulysses* was serialized in the *Little Review* it was subject to the censorship laws in the United States; Heap and Anderson went to trial in 1920 over the "Nausicaa" episode and lost. Its reputation grew based on reviews of the serialized episodes; its reputation also grew as a notoriously obscene work. The reviews from Continental writers and critics like Valery Larbaud helped boost subscriptions for the first printing. The suppression of *Ulysses* in the English-speaking countries gave the work (like all censorship does) a tantalizing aura which, in addition to its revolutionary method of narration, made *Ulysses* a *cause celèbre*. Morris Ernst, the lawyer who successfully defended *Ulysses* in the famous censorship trial of 1933, wrote, "the more our postal and customs officials burned copies, the greater the inducement for smuggling and bootlegging. It became a vogue to own one of those blue-paper-jacketed copies of *Ulysses* from Paris—a vogue that soon led to prices in the hundreds of dollars for one such copy" ("Four-Letter Words and the Unconscious" 33). When the ban was lifted by Judge Woolsey in 1933, *Ulysses* had a ready and waiting audience eager to see what the fuss was about.[5] This phenomenon played a large part in Joyce's public reputation (see Chapter Two), but to see how his works became entrenched in the academy requires us to look at the classification of *Ulysses* as a "difficult and literary" work during the trial, in conjunction with the growth of the academy after World War II and the turn of literary criticism into an academic enterprise.

## THE TRIAL

The story of *Ulysses* cannot be told without understanding the dynamics of the trial which allowed it to be published in the United States. The decision of Judge John Woolsey was groundbreaking, and relied heavily on the kind of evaluations already in place for the work. As Kelly states,

> Joyce gained and lost with Woolsey's decision. He gained the right to be published and distributed. But that right was predicated on his failure to move people. Woolsey's decision marked a capitulation to the "literary world," which produced guides to help readers interpret *Ulysses* in the detached method Eliot and Pound approved. (83–84)

The defense's strategy was simple: to claim that *Ulysses* was a serious and classic piece of literature and therefore by definition could not be obscene. Ernst offered carefully chosen excerpts from reviews by Rebecca West, Arnold Bennett, and T.S. Eliot which portrayed Joyce as a literary genius and, under a sort of literary *noblesse oblige*, they claimed that a genius could not write anything obscene at all: the work was honest and artistic rather than disgusting or prurient. Even if some portions of the book are pornographic, they argued, the total effect was artistic and therefore the book's literary value outweighed any particular instances of obscenity. Under the auspices of Bennett Cerf of Random House, the defense team surveyed librarians around the country as to the book's merit, and received mostly favorable responses; but as Kenneth Stevens writes, "the replies from librarians demonstrated that acceptance of *Ulysses* was significantly more subdued outside literary circles . . . Generally, however, the library responses were what the lawyers wanted. [The responses] revealed that patrons who most often asked about the book were college students and faculty, a social group which a judge might be less likely to consider smut-seekers" ("*Ulysses* on Trial" 62).

Judge Woolsey agreed with Ernst's characterization of *Ulysses* as a literary classic too difficult for the uneducated or young to understand, and declared the book a "tour de force" and a "sincere and serious attempt to devise a new literary method for the observation and description of mankind" (Moscato and Le Blanc 38). Bennett Cerf decided to include Woolsey's decision and a foreword from Ernst at the front of the edition; this decision had been made prior to the trial, as indicated in a letter dated March 22, 1932, outlining changes to his publishing contract with Joyce:

> It may prove advisable . . . to put in a brief note by a prominent attorney embodying the decision of the judge who legalizes the book. The inclusion of this decision in our volume will protect us in any future court action that may arise in connection with the publication. If the decision is not included, it is possible that on any succeeding action the court would not

allow us to introduce previous decisions as evidence. Such a decision obviously would mean that we would have to begin the fight all over again.
(Moscato and Le Blanc 103)

The end result of including the decision in the prefatory matter is to reinforce the opinion that *Ulysses* "is not an easy book to read or to understand" (Woolsey 36).

The strategy of positioning *Ulysses* as a "modern classic" during the
trial relied on the fact that *Ulysses* had only been read by a relatively small
number of people, thereby making it part of an elitist literature, and on the
book's radically new and difficult prose style. Certainly Ernst depended on
the evaluations of literary critics for his argument, and one of the earliest
reviews hailing Joyce's genius was that of Edmund Wilson. In an essay
which first appeared in *The New Republic* (18 Dec. 1929) and was
reprinted in his famous collection *Axel's Castle* (1931), Wilson discusses
all of Joyce's works (including *Work in Progress*) and places *Ulysses* firmly
in the tradition of both Symbolism and Naturalism. In spite of his reservations about Joyce's lack of "respect . . . for the capacities of the reader's attention" (215–16), he finds that even the tedious episodes of *Ulysses* (his
examples are "Cyclops" and "Oxen of the Sun") "contribute something"
to the book by showing how man has "written about himself in the past"
and how "naïve or pretentious it seems"; he contrasts these parodies to the
way Joyce's shows consciousness: Joyce has shown "how [man] must recognize himself today" (217). Wilson addressed the morality of the book in
answer to its reputation as "dirty":

> [T]he first readers of *Ulysses* were shocked, not merely by Joyce's use of
> certain words ordinarily excluded today from English literature, but by
> his way of representing those aspects of human nature which we tend to
> consider incongruous as . . . inextricably mingled. But the more we read
> *Ulysses*, the more we are convinced of its psychological truth, and the
> more we are amazed at Joyce's genius in mastering and presenting, not
> through analysis or generalization, but by the complete recreation of life
> in the process of being lived, the relations of human beings to their envi-
> ronment and to each other, the nature of their perception of what goes on
> about them and of what goes on within themselves . . . to have exhibited
> ordinary humanity without either satirizing or sentimentalizing it—this
> would already have been sufficiently remarkable; but to have subdued all
> this material to the uses of a supremely finished and disciplined work of
> art is a feat which has hardly been equalled in the literature of our time.
> (219–20)

Wilson's assessment of Joyce astutely transforms the difficulty of the book
for readers and the censorship issue: he makes the "dirty" parts of the
book evidence of its genius, and its difficulty (even when Joyce appears to
ignore readers altogether) a mark of its poetry. Wilson's review is remarkable in itself, a cogent assessment that never idolizes Joyce to the extreme
of accepting or valorizing his excesses, while at the same time it clearly sees

Joyce's literary innovation for what it is: an example of the new direction fiction was taking in the early twentieth century. It proved to be a landmark in Joyce criticism and one which played a role in Ernst's trial strategy.[6] Kelly posits that *Axel's Castle* "helped make modernism a legitimate field of study, and it helped canonize Joyce in the process" (142); yet Wilson's essay on Joyce was not aimed at an academic audience but rather one of general readers, since it was originally published in a general interest periodical. That his work was appropriated by the academy to legitimize modernism clearly illustrates a shift in literary criticism from a journalistic forum to a scholarly one.

Another influential review which helped cement the book's reputation as an erudite masterpiece was T.S. Eliot's "*Ulysses*, Order, and Myth," which appeared in the November 1923 issue of *The Dial*. This essay has proved over time to be one of the most prominent interpretations of *Ulysses*, and Eliot did much to shape critical reaction to the book. In his essay, Eliot positioned *Ulysses* firmly in the elitist tradition which he and Pound felt was so necessary to modern literature; in discussing the possible influence Joyce's book might have Eliot wrote: "The next generation is responsible for its own soul; a man of genius is responsible to his peers, not to a studio full of uneducated and undisciplined coxcombs" (in Benstock 25). Eliot's essay was one of the first to point out the importance of the Homeric parallel to *Ulysses*, and it proved so influential that, taken together with Stuart Gilbert's study seven years later, the mythological framework which Joyce used to shape *Ulysses* was for a time practically the only lens through which it was seen. This view of the book necessitated a classical education for interpretation, and affirmed that *Ulysses* was indeed only for the educated elite. Eliot's essay also gave an organic unity and a self-containment to the work[7] which would influence countless studies during the 1940's and 1950's, what Geert Lernout in *The French Joyce* dubs the "symbol-hunting" period of Joyce studies (23).

Nearly twenty years after "*Ulysses*, Order, and Myth" appeared, Eliot would edit the first anthology of Joyce's works, a slim volume entitled *Introducing James Joyce: A Selection of Joyce's Prose* (1942). This book also stressed a unity in Joyce's work, but posited such a unity over the course of his career.[8] Ira Nadel points out that "Eliot's choices reflect a principle . . . to provide not the best of Joyce but to establish continuity from one book to another by focusing on passages 'in which the author was present as child or as young man, either as observer or as protagonist'" ("Anthologizing Joyce" 509). Indeed, Eliot himself states in his introductory note to this popular anthology that the passages he selected from *Ulysses* were chosen not only to continue this "autobiographical thread," but also because the "later episodes . . . are less comprehensible in isolation"; he states that there were passages he wanted to include "which would have lessened the abruptness of the transition from *Ulysses* to *Finnegans Wake*" but "style rather than content would have justified them" and would have "altered the purpose" of the anthology (6). Clearly, Eliot privileges the teleological aspect of Joyce's *oeuvre*.

Nadel contrasts Eliot's focus with Harry Levin's in his classic anthology *The Portable Joyce* (1947; published in England as *The Essential James Joyce* in 1948): "Levin deals with Joyce's reputation, his artistry, politics, influence, and reception. By contrast, Eliot avoids these matters" and makes autobiography and continuity between works the central concern (511). Nadel further underscores the power Eliot's own interpretations had over subsequent scholarship, quoting a talk Eliot gave in 1943 on the subject:

> Don't try to read *Finnegans Wake* until you have read *Ulysses*; don't read *Ulysses* until you find you enjoy the *Portrait of the Artist* . . . ; and read *Dubliners* first of all. That is the only possible way of coming to understand the work of one of the great writers, not of our own time only, but of all European literature. (*The Listener* 14 Oct. 1943; in Nadel, 514)

The impulse to read Joyce's *oeuvre* as a progressive and teleological entity perhaps begins with Eliot, but does not end with him. Certainly, Eliot's views shaped the kinds of critical responses Joyce's works have received. *Ulysses* is usually seen as the quintessential modernist work, and *Finnegans Wake* as the prototypical postmodernist work. The urge to see *Finnegans Wake* as a progression from *Ulysses*, as postmodernism is sometimes seen as a progression from modernism, seems understandable on the surface. But it is open to speculation whether, had Joyce lived, he might have written something else and what shape that something else might have assumed. Joyce himself said that he wanted to write something "very simple and very short" (Ellmann 731); this remark may have been a joke, but nevertheless Joyce's works might not have ended with *Finnegans Wake* had he survived. Reading his works as a closed system is a perspective only allowed in hindsight, and one which Eliot's anthology helped perpetuate.

*Introducing James Joyce* enjoyed a fairly wide audience; Nadel points out that, by the time Levin's anthology appeared in England in 1948, Eliot's volume had sold over 16,000 copies and gone through several printings (514). Eliot's book was conceived as "an 'introduction' for new readers" of Joyce (6). But Levin's book, because it was fuller than Eliot's, soon displaced the earlier work, and it was Levin's first book on Joyce, *James Joyce: A Critical Introduction*, that almost single-handedly ushered Joyce into the academy by making him "academically respectable"; it was "independent of Joyce's personal involvement" and situated Joyce's work "in a general modernist European framework" (Lernout 22). Wilson's *Axel's Castle* also demonstrated these qualities, but Levin was a scholar rather than a literary critic. It was in the years after the war and during the extraordinary growth of the universities in the United States that Joyce became firmly established as academic property at the same time that literary criticism merged with scholarship to form the profession as we know it today.

ENTERING THE UNIVERSITY

In 1941, at Joyce's request, Levin wrote *James Joyce: A Critical Introduction*. Joyce had read a review that Levin wrote of *Finnegans Wake*, and was so impressed by the young scholar that he contacted James Laughlin, the publisher of New Directions who was putting together a series on "The Makers of Modern Literature." Levin's work did not depend on Joyce's involvement, but Joyce shows a firm hand in shaping his own reputation in recommending Levin for the job. The book was revised in 1960, and in the new introduction Levin looks back on a phenomenon his own work helped launch:[9] "Has there ever been so short a transition between ostracism and canonization" (xiii)? Besides Kelly's recent book, two other works have attempted to map this territory in Joyce's critical fortunes: Jeffrey Segall's study, *Joyce in America*, discusses the early reception of *Ulysses* in the United States of the 1920's through the 1950's, and Geert Lernout's *The French Joyce* looks at Joyce's position in French literary theory. Both show that Joyce's works have been considered important enough that almost every critical school has felt it necessary to deal with them. As a case study for the shifts of literary theory within the academy, Joyce can find few equals.

Segall notes that Joyce was largely excoriated by the far left and right in the nineteen-thirties, although for different reasons; particularly in the Soviet Union, Joyce was castigated for being bourgeois and apolitical. It was not until the New Critics, with their definition of literature as outside politics, that Joyce began to find more than a scattered approval (and the erroneous assumption that Joyce was apolitical was spread outside of Communist circles). While the New Critics, as a whole, largely ignored Joyce, some influential critics in the movement did find Joyce's work compelling. Segall looks at critical essays on Joyce by John Crowe Ransom, Cleanth Brooks, Allen Tate, and R.P. Blackmur, and finds that these New Critics (or, in the case of Blackmur, neo-New Critics) were the "ideal readers of Joyce" because of their attention to technical detail and because they studied the text with "deliberateness and detachment" (135). Segall states,

> [T]hey fostered a criticism that set the substance and tone for much of the Joyce criticism that followed. What today has become a Joyce industry consists almost entirely of exegetical analyses of the sort pioneered by the New Critics. . . . [They] began the process of extricating Joyce's work from the crossfire of cultural politics in order to place it instead within the confines of the academy. . . . Joyce became less of a cultural threat and more of a technical problem. (136)

But for the New Critics to say that the academy is somehow outside of cultural politics is problematic. By positioning themselves that way, the New Critics in fact define themselves within a cultural politics of elitism, which fits nicely into Pound's definition of art. Far from depoliticizing literature, the New Critics were reacting to the calls of socialist and Marxist critics for proletarian literature, one that would depose a bourgeois literature concerned only with aesthetics and decadence. By 'removing' literature from the concerns of politics, the New Critics reinforced the view that literature should only be judged on its aesthetic value. Under this agenda Joyce's oft-reviled lack of political purpose (a charge brought by socialist critics in the 1930's, and which later critics debunk) is of no consequence to his worth as an artist.

Lernout differs from Segall on Joyce's fortunes with the New Critics. Lernout sees various "periods" of Joyce criticism: the early years, when Joyce directed, inspired, and/or supervised "almost all of the major studies on his work that were published during his lifetime" (21). The second period Lernout dubs "symbol hunting" and occurred during the forties and fifties with works by William York Tindall, Joseph Campbell, Marvin Magalaner and Northrop Frye. The next occurred with the publication of Ellmann's biography in 1959 (it was revised in 1982), and a wave of explication relying on biographical material, which Lernout surmises "impeded the influence of New Criticism, [and] which was responsible for another shift toward a more novelistic and scholarly approach" (23). The 1960's begin "the institutionalization of Joyce studies" with the start of the *James Joyce Quarterly* and the International James Joyce Symposia.

Lernout further lists differences between Joyce studies and the New Critical paradigm; first is the vast number of reference books devoted to Joyce's works, especially *Finnegans Wake*. Adaline Glasheen's *Third Census of Finnegans Wake* and James Atherton's *Books at the Wake* are just two of the better-known examples of literature devoted to cataloguing references in Joyce's work. The second difference is the large number of non-academic Joyceans, which Lernout cites as "another reason why New Critical doctrines such as the intentional fallacy have had little influence" (24–25). Lernout also cites a third difference "destined to hurt New Critical sensibilities": the "growing importance of genetic studies of Joyce's texts" with an emphasis on "the process of creation instead of on the finished product," which he also dates from the 1960's (25). Genetic studies continue to remain at the forefront of Joyce studies, with the publication of the *James Joyce Archives* in 1977 making Joyce's manuscripts available in facsimile. And the appearance of Hans Walter Gabler's edition of *Ulysses* was a crucial moment in the confrontation between authorially based humanist theory and textually based poststructuralist theory, particularly since Gabler's editorial project wedded author-centered editorial practice with document-based editorial theory (see Chapter Three). Curiously, the divergent strains of criticism—New Critical and biographical—seem to come together in a genetic critical program: genetic studies must, like New Criticism, be based in the documents at hand, and yet it must, like biographically-based criticism, also take into account the materiality of the author's life and its effects on the composition of the text. But the force which cemented Joyce into the academy was first the New Criticism.

The aesthetic aim of the New Critical project was continued in the first waves of structuralist literary theory which began to wash to American shores from France in the 1960's. When Barthes declared the death of the Author in 1968, it was a logical extension of the New Critical exercise of divorcing the literature from its historical moment of production (and Barthes himself has been characterized as an aesthetic critic[10]). Yet even this declaration relies on the principle that Foucault calls the "intransitivity of literature":

> [t]his was . . . the first step by which we were able to get rid of the idea that literature was the . . . expression of totalities. . . . [But] by keeping analysis at this level, one runs the risk of not unraveling the totality of sacralizations of which literature has been the object. On the contrary, one runs the risk of sacralizing even more. . . . [A] number of themes originating in Blanchot or Barthes were used in a kind of exaltation . . . of literature as a structure of language capable of being analyzed in itself and on its own terms. Political implications were absent from this exaltation. ("Functions" 5)

For example, in Barthes' famous essay, "The Death of the Author," he declares that the ultimate producer of a text's meaning is the reader, that "[t]he reader is the space on which all the quotations that make up a writing are inscribed without any of them being lost; a text's unity lies not in its origin but in its destination. . . . [T]he reader is without history, biography, psychology; he is simply that someone who holds together in a single field all the traces by which the written text is constituted" (171). Barthes is positioning the reader as a *tabula rasa* for the structures of language to play upon, denying that readers are themselves loci of political, historical, and social forces which shape their interpretations of a text. The discourse event of declaring the Author dead, while also denying any political implications for what Barthes called "the birth of the reader," could be quickly accommodated within an aesthetic discourse about Joyce, since Joyce's writing was always seen as removing the author from the foreground, and had traditionally been distanced from the political realm. Neither the New Criticism nor early structuralism questioned the central place of the text itself within their discourse, nor did they question the sacralizing impulse which kept it there. This impulse is simply part of the larger dominant discourse about the function of literature in our culture, and Foucault describes

> . . . two ways of characterizing writing, namely, the critical and religious approaches. Giving writing a primal status seems to be a way of retranslating, in transcendental terms, both the theological affirmation of its sacred character and the critical affirmation of its creative character. To admit that writing is, because of the very history that it made possible, subject to the test of oblivion and repression, seems to represent . . . the religious principle of the hidden meaning (which requires interpretation) and the critical principle of implicit significations, silent determinations,

and obscured contents (which gives rise to commentary). To imagine writing as absence seems to be a simple repetition . . . of both the religious principle of inalterable and yet never fulfilled tradition, and the aesthetic principle of the work's survival, its perpetuation beyond the author's death, and its enigmatic *excess* in relation to him. ("What is an Author?" 104–105)

This religious impulse appears throughout Joyce criticism. Indecd, the language used to describe Joyce's position in the discourse tends in much of that criticism to sacralize the writer more than the text in a peculiar reversal of the discourse of literature which Foucault describes here, but one that fits the operations of biographically based, "man-and-his-work" scholarship. An example of this exaltation can be found in an article by Richard Lehan, entitled "James Joyce: The Limits of Modernism and the Realms of the Literary Text" in the Spring 1994 issue of *Arizona Quarterly*. Lehan's language elevates Joyce to the status of creator-god, beginning with the first sentence: "James Joyce oversaw the modern novel through its evolution of various narrative modes." The essay displays numerous other examples: "Joyce is the paradigmatic modern" (87); "Joyce had in effect created what we mean by modernism" (94); and a sentence which bears quoting in full: "He is, to use a metaphor apt to his work, the father of us all, the man who saw the way before there was a way to see, the man who both made and unmade the modern novel, and the man who has taken us into narrative realms that we are only now learning how to read" (98–99). It seems significant that this last sentence echoes Ellmann's opening sentence of Joyce's biography: "We are still learning to be James Joyce's contemporaries, to understand our interpreter" (3).

Lehan's own position in this essay is that of traditional humanist attempting to save Joyce from "[c]ritics like Derrida [who] turned literary criticism on its head by coöpting Joyce, the premier modernist" (106); he firmly places himself within a discourse that centers human subjectivity in opposition to a postmodern discourse on Joyce, which decenters that subjectivity. The entire essay is taken up with carefully attacking postmodernist readings of *Ulysses*, such as Karen Lawrence's *Odyssey of Style* (1983) and Patrick McGee's *Paperspace: Style as Ideology in Joyce's 'Ulysses'* (1988), by invoking Joyce as icon: ". . . what Lawrence takes as non-referential language . . . takes on a totally different meaning once we see it as a kind of urban consciousness at work in the novel. . . . What Joyce gave us in *Ulysses* was a language to go with that consciousness—a language which became a literary legacy for writers like Dos Passos" (102).

The traditional critical discourse on Joyce has shaped Lehan's own readings of postmodernist Joyce criticism, and his language shows him to be firmly locked within the dominant discourse of Joyce as icon/creator. He is perfectly willing to allow that postmodernist literature can operate on principles of self-referentiality, and briefly discusses *Finnegans Wake* as an example of this literature, calling it "almost a pure example of what postmodernism means by differal, dispersal, and *différance*"(98). He then dismisses any attempt to read Joyce's other works through postmodernist means by again invoking Joyce:

> While Joyce in *Finnegans Wake* may have been moving away from some of the elements of modernism, he never moved completely away from his belief in the power of nature to speak directly to a receiving consciousness. Nature was always there in the process of flow and life force— always acting upon our minds. Language gave us insight into such processes rather than substituting its own reality for such meaning. Thus any attempt to read Joyce beyond the limits of modernism creates a literary reality separate from its own special mode of textuality. (99)

Lehan puts *Finnegans Wake* into its special category of postmodernist literature, then goes on to defend Joyce's other work from postmodernist readings. Significantly, however, he does not attack any postmodernist readings of *Finnegans Wake*; he restricts his critique to postmodernist readings of *Ulysses*, which he spends the first half of his article positioning as the seminal modernist novel. He criticizes Lawrence's study for moving us from "a text based upon the creative process to a text based upon the reading process" and posits a repressed subjectivity in postmodern language. He then discusses what that subjectivity is: the city of Dublin itself, the "urban consciousness" which speaks in the various stylistic modes of the second half of *Ulysses*. He questions "whether or not language can escape the forms of subjectivity that bring it into being" (103), and this statement, taken with his language which positions Joyce as the creator of modernism, leads us to the understanding that for Lehan, the true subjectivity in this case belongs to Joyce. The author/subject is centered once again. He does allow that "there is no *Ur Ulysses*, no essentialized text to which we can return for stabilized meaning" (106), but he rejects any notion of textual meaning which does not refer back to the central consciousness of the author. This position seems precariously balanced between traditional humanist and poststructuralist readings. Lehan's discourse, however, places it firmly in the former category.

## THE STRANGE CASE OF FINNEGANS WAKE

While *Ulysses* has traditionally been seen as a modernist classic, *Finnegans Wake* met with little more than incredulity on its publication, or (perhaps more patronizing) an earnest attempt to *want* to understand it simply because it was by the writer of *Ulysses*. Beginning with early reviews when the book was still called *Work In Progress*, Joyce encouraged a great deal of critical machinery to promote his last achievement, no doubt in anticipation of its difficulties for his readers. A full ten years before *Finnegans Wake* appeared, Joyce directed the publication of *Our Exagmination round His Factification for Incamination of Work in Progress*, a collection of twelve pieces on *Work in Progress* from twelve writers, and two letters which Ellmann describes as "hostile and humorously illiterate" (613). These letters, by a G. V. L. Slingsby and a Vladimir Dixon, are suspected to have been written by Joyce himself as a joke; but doubt has been cast on Joyce's presumed authorship of the Dixon letter, which follows—or rather, shows a writer attempting to follow—Joyce's style in the *Wake* while criticizing the book. Thomas Goldwasser has offered evidence that Dixon was indeed a real person living in Paris at the time *Our Exagmination* was being compiled (*James Joyce Quarterly* 16 [Summer 1979]: 219–223). The twelve writers were all part of Joyce's circle of admirers: Samuel Beckett, Marcel Brion, Frank Budgen, Stuart Gilbert, Eugene Jolas, Victor Llona, Robert McAlmon, Thomas McGreevy, Elliot Paul, John Rodker, Robert Sage, and William Carlos Williams. According to Ellmann, "Joyce admitted to Larbaud [that] he had stood behind 'those twelve Marshals more or less directing them what lines of research to follow,'" and Joyce also "saw to it" that the collection answered the leading critics of *Work in Progress*, particularly Wyndham Lewis and Rebecca West (613). Most of the essays had already been published in *transition*, but Joyce commissioned Williams' essay as a specific response to Rebecca West's negative review in *The Bookman* (Henke 76). Williams' essay places Joyce within a tradition of American revolution against British insularity, and he cries out that "this is the opportunity of America! To see large, larger than England can" and ends by making a prophetic statement, in light of the growth of Joyce studies in the United States: "America, offering an undeveloped but wider criticism, will take this opportunity to place an appreciation of Joyce on its proper basis"(*Our Exagmination* 180–185). Williams spoke more presciently than he knew.

   Beckett's essay is perhaps the best known of all those appearing in *Our Exagmination*. It is at once a brilliant analysis of Joyce's method and a diatribe against its critics. Beckett, himself a central figure in avant-garde literature, continues the program to place Joyce's work in an elitist *milieu*, and does so with characteristic wit: "Must we wring the neck of a certain system in order to stuff it into a contemporary pigeon-hole, or modify the dimensions of that pigeon-hole for the satisfaction of the analogymongers? Literary criticism is not book-keeping" (3–4). He continues with a sharp retort to those who find *Work in Progress* incomprehensible: "Here is direct expression—pages and pages of it. And if you don't understand it, Ladies and Gentlemen, it is because you are too decadent to receive it. You are not satisfied unless form is so strictly divorced from content that you can comprehend the one almost without bothering to read the other" (13).[11] With such apologists, it is easy to see a theme emerging that either one 'gets' *Finnegans Wake* or one doesn't—a position which might have amused Joyce, with its overtones of 'getting' a joke, since he found pleasing the comment by Oliver Gogarty (the real-life model for Buck Mulligan in *Ulysses*) that *Finnegans Wake* was "the most colossal leg pull in literature since Macpherson's *Ossian*" (Ellmann 722).

While writers like Beckett, Edmund Wilson, Eugene Jolas and, later, Joseph Campbell would praise *Finnegans Wake*, it was not always so; even those who had heretofore-championed Joyce's earlier works were at best puzzled by *FW* and at worst offended by it. Edmund Wilson, while calling it "one of the boldest books ever written," also stated that there was a "miscarriage" in the book because "the more daring Joyce's subjects become, the more he tends to swathe them about with the fancywork of his literary virtuosity" (*Wound and the Bow* 266). Ezra Pound saw little redeeming value in it: "I will have another go at it, but up to present I make nothing of it whatever. Nothing so far as I make out, nothing short of divine vision or a new cure for the clapp [*sic*] can possibly be worth all the circumambient peripherization" (*Pound/Joyce* 228). William Faulkner stated of *Finnegans Wake* that "James Joyce was one of the great men of my time. He was electrocuted by the divine fire. . . . He was probably—might have been the greatest, but he was electrocuted. He had more talent than he could control" (in Dettmar 280). Even Joyce's brother Stanislaus wrote: "I for one would not read more than a paragraph of it, if I did not know you" (*Letters III* 102). It took a shift in literary criticism to entrench the *Wake* firmly as a sacred text on a scale with *Ulysses*; Kevin Dettmar states that

> If ever there was a book written for the postmodern moment, it would seem to be *Finnegans Wake*. Indeed, one begins to suspect that had Joyce not written *Finnegans Wake*, contemporary literary theory would have had to invent it: for in its willfully overdetermined structure and self-conscious Babel of languages, poststructural theory finds the ideal proof-text for every aspect of postmodern *écriture*. (*The Illicit Joyce of Postmodernism* 210)

Indeed, Margot Norris writes that poststructuralist theory canonized *Finnegans Wake* in the seventies and eighties "by replacing obligation to read or understand the text with exploration of the way its language problematizes, and thus defers, its own reading and understanding . . . the same compulsory deferral of the *Wake*'s reading that had been vexing and frustrating critics for over thirty years came . . . to constitute its unique textual significance" (346–47).

## POSTSTRUCTURALIST LITERARY THEORY

Poststructuralist readings of Joyce, while denying an author-centered subjectivity, claim Joyce as one of the forefathers of postmodernism and his specter hovers over their anti-authorial project from the beginning. Most poststructuralist Joycean critics follow a particular formula within their writing: they explain their own subject positions in reference to their object of study, and then launch into the study itself. As Kevin Dettmar points out, these explanations often take the form of "traditional narratives of religious conversion":

Those who write about *Finnegans Wake* seem compelled to give us their testimony; for once they stood unbelieving outside the fold, before experiencing the novel in its full power—something of an epiphany, I suppose. . . . The second salient feature of most writing on *Finnegans Wake* . . . suggest[s] . . . an unshakeable belief in the novel's unique status in the canon of world literature. Thus reading *Finnegans Wake* is not, we are to understand, like reading any other book. . . . And as a pseudosacred text, *Finnegans Wake* requires a specialized vocabulary as well. The novel is not consistently referred to as *Finnegans Wake*—a manageable enough title, one would have thought—but is regularly called "the *Wake*," or . . . simply "*FW*." It has accrued its own adjective ("Wakean"), and is said to be written in its own language ("Wakese"); it apparently requires its own citation format (*FW* 3.20), as if it were a sacred text, or an epic poem . . ." (215–216)

While Dettmar's own analysis hinges on his conviction that *Ulysses*, rather than *Finnegans Wake*, is Joyce's real postmodern triumph, his description here of the rhetoric which surrounds the latter text points to that sacralizing impulse which Foucault describes.

Even when *Finnegans Wake* criticism does not take such an overtly religious tone, it makes claims for Joyce's project which position Joyce as an all-seeing prognosticator of the coming of poststructuralist literary theory. Even Norris, who would later decry the ahistorical way which poststructuralism would valorize the *Wake* (and thus blunt our understanding of its historical impact during its moment of production), shows in her earlier work on the *Wake* the same impulse. In the influential "The Consequence of Deconstruction: A Technical Perspective of Joyce's *Finnegans Wake*" (1974), she writes: "By writing *Finnegans Wake* as he did, Joyce attests to the impossibility of metalanguage, that is, the failure of making a critique in language of the epistemology embedded in language" (Benstock 219). Norris's evaluation of the *Wake* in terms of Derrida, Lacan, and Levi-Strauss are incisive and convincing; but the Joyce being validated here wrote books for academics rather than a general reading public. She "believe[s] that Joyce recognized the problems inherent in *Wake* criticism, and that as a result he planned critical studies as a kind of sequel to the work" (in Benstock 219). She lists *Our Exagmination*, as well as references Joyce made to a further study divided into four parts to correspond with the four old men-historians-commentators in the *Wake*, as evidence of Joyce's critical project. Norris seems to dismiss the possibility that Joyce's hand in these critical explications of his work served a more commercial purpose as well: to explain and publicize the work prior to publication in order to boost interest and sales. In essence, Norris continues the project of claiming Joyce for the professors and ignores other, more public dimensions of Joyce's writing. That her later work attempts to "retreat from [the *Wake*'s] narrowly postmetaphysical and self-reflexive teleology in the interest of restoring the text more broadly to its specific moment in history" is admirable and overdue ("The Postmodernization of *Finnegans Wake* Reconsidered" 358).

## BIOGRAPHICAL CRITICISM

Joyce the man stood behind some of the seminal criticism of his works, which almost every Joyce scholar today still consults at some point. Frank Budgen, Stuart Gilbert, and the essayists in *Our Exagmination* were guided by Joyce in their understanding of his writings. And the Ellmann biography remains, fifty years after its first publication, a Rosetta stone which every serious Joycean must read, and keeps Joyce the man in view when deciphering his texts. Ellmann's biography is a rich, detailed, and exacting work. Indeed, the back cover of the 1982 revised edition quotes Frank Kermode: ". . . Mr. Ellmann . . . fixes Joyce's image for a generation." Combining literary analysis with a prodigious amount of anecdotal information culled mostly from Joyce's brother Stanislaus, Ellmann intertwines Joyce's life and his art seamlessly and perpetuates an anti-New Critical stance for interpreting Joyce's works.

But Kelly points out that Ellmann's biography is not without its flaws, and it had its critics. Some, Kelly notes, found Ellmann biased, and Kelly himself agrees with Hugh Kenner and others that one of the chief faults in Ellmann's biography is its over-reliance on Stanislaus Joyce's recollections, with a concordant lack of cross-checking to sift the truth from Joyce's brother's own biases.[12] Kelly criticizes Ellmann's biography for concentrating on how the fiction illuminated Joyce's life: "Ellmann was interested in what *Ulysses* revealed about Joyce, not what Joyce revealed about Dublin. As a consequence, Joyce appears as an autonomous artist, and his fiction has not excoriated Dublin since 1959" (175). Kelly would reassert "historically verifiable politics" by looking at "Joyce's work as public utterances in an already well-defined public discourse," and asking the questions, "Who reads Joyce? And in what context?" (179). While Kelly makes a good case for reassessing Ellmann's biography and its influence on Joyce studies, the biography itself is an interesting document, simply because it enabled a biographically based critique which impeded New Critical methods. Further, Ellmann's biography of Joyce is simply a pleasure to read and some critics have even likened it to a novel.[13]

Herbert Gorman wrote the first biography of Joyce, published in 1941 after Joyce's death. To most critics, Gorman's biography is "tainted" by its being the "authorized" (hence, bowdlerized by Joyce) biography. Gorman sent the proofs to Joyce, and in an interesting move, Ellmann devotes three pages to documenting Joyce's interventions in Gorman's manuscript prior to publication, changing Gorman's portrayal of Joyce's father to a more flattering one and insisting on perpetuating the fiction that Joyce's marriage to Nora in 1931 was their second, rather than their first, ceremony. Ellmann states that "Joyce also used Gorman's book to pay off old scores" and that Gorman, "scarcely dar[ing to] touch upon" Joyce's family after 1922, removed references to the troubled marriage of Joyce's son Giorgio and made no mention of daughter Lucia's mental illness. The effect of Ellmann's recounting of this bowdlerizing from the Joyce family serves to further paint his own biography as being free of such interference and therefore more reliable and scholarly.

An interesting dynamic exists between the Gorman biography and Ellmann's: Gorman's work shows a persecuted genius, beset by squalid surroundings, often philistine friends, and an often shrewish wife; Ellmann's portrays a rounder, more complex human being (though still a genius), a circle of patient, understanding friends, and (still) an often shrewish wife. Taken together, these works give us an almost "inside-outside" look at Joyce's life, with Gorman providing (between the lines of often melodramatic prose) a glimpse of how Joyce perceived the world around him, and Ellmann providing one look at how the world perceived Joyce. In addition to these biographies of Joyce, Brenda Maddox's *Nora: A Biography of Nora Joyce* attempts to reconstruct what life was like for Joyce's wife, and gives a resoundingly different portrait of both of them. Maddox portrays Nora Barnacle Joyce as heroically putting up with James Joyce's drinking, whining, jealousy, and radical shifts from penury to prodigality. But none of these works on its own shows a full portrait of Joyce, and it is significant that the one written by the scholar is the one most often consulted by scholars (including this study).

## JOYCE'S PLACE IN THE ACADEMY NOW

As we have seen, Joyce's reputation began, like most writers, outside of the academy; in the shift of literary criticism from a public profession to an academic one, Joyce moved into his place as exemplar of High Modernism. But Joyce the author looms large over all critical enterprises dealing with his work, even those which profess to eliminate the author from their purview. *Pace* Segall, much of the primary work on Joyce being done today is not exegesis based on New Critical foundations but New Historicist, Marxist, and postcolonial critique which position Joyce's works within specific discourses; further, the genetic projects begun by textual scholars have influenced current Joyce criticism in ways which twenty years ago would have been unheard of, and the controversy over the Gabler *Ulysses* is directly responsible for this phenomenon. Similarly, work on other authors has engendered such meetings between textual scholarship and literary criticism (the Cambridge editions of Lawrence's works are one example[14]), so Joyce studies is not unique in this regard. The debates over editions of Joyce's works are interesting because of Joyce's position in popular culture as a master of twentieth century literature: the Gabler controversy occurred in popular periodicals as well as scholarly journals, and moved Joyce out of the academy briefly and back onto a more public stage.

Involved in this shift is Joyce's position in commodity culture, and this position can be traced back to the same place where the academic Joyce got his start: the censorship trials. The next chapter examines the development of this public Joyce and its position at the end of the twentieth century.

## NOTES

[1]See Morris Beja's "Synjoysium: An Informal History of the International James Joyce Symposia," *James Joyce Quarterly* 22 (2) Winter 1985: 113–129. Beja is one of the founders of the International Joyce Symposia, and his account is a personal recollection of the evolution of this gathering through the mid-1980's.

[2]This figure from various articles about the Joyce Wars dating from 1986 forward. Random House was unwilling to release specific sales information. However, David Ebershoff, Publishing Manager of The Modern Library/Random House, did state that "interest in *Ulysses* has remained just about even from where it was ten years ago" until the publication of The Modern Library's list of 100 Best Novels of the Twentieth Century, which ranked *Ulysses* number one. Ebershoff wrote: "Demand for our edition shot through the roof with the announcement of the list of 100 Best Novels . . . In 2 days we sold about what we typically sell in 4 months. I expect the regenerated interest to have impact over the next several months" (electronic correspondence with the author 24 July 1998).

[3]See Hugh Kenner's *Ulysses: Revised Edition*, Baltimore and London: Johns Hopkins University Press, 1987, pp. 2–4. First published in 1980.

[4]See *Letters II*, 87–177; Ellmann, 328–332; Forrest Read's *Pound/Joyce: The Letters of Ezra Pound to James Joyce*, "A Curious History" 20–23.

[5]For an interesting look at the role of censorship in the popularity of modernist works, see Joyce Wexler's "Selling Sex as Art," in *Marketing Modernisms: Self Promotion, Canonization, Rereading*, ed. Kevin J.H. Dettmar and Stephen Watt (Ann Arbor: University of Michigan Press, 1996) 91–108. Also discussed in Chapter Two.

[6]See Moscato and LeBlanc, 78–98, 111–112.

[7]Hugh Kenner, in his "The Making of the Modernist Canon," states that the New Critics felt just the opposite of Eliot: "*Ulysses* had been blighted, ever since 1930, by Stuart Gilbert's heavy-handed crib. Nothing as mechanical as that could be organic. Frank Budgen's 1936 book . . . was too biographical to survive New Critical scrutiny" (58).

[8]Of course, as this anthology appeared the year after Joyce's death, the urge to see his work as a unified whole is perhaps understandable, although Joyce also fostered this idea by using characters from *Dubliners* and *Portrait* in *Ulysses*. *Finnegans Wake*, however, is not so easily placed as a continuation of *Ulysses*, as none of the earlier characters are present in the *Wake*.

[9]For a more complete view of the influence this study had on scholars, see Morton P. Levitt's "Harry Levin's *James Joyce* and the Modernist Age: A Personal Reading" in *Re-Viewing Classics of Joyce Criticism*, edited by Janet E. Dunleavy. Urbana and Chicago: University of Illinois Press, 1991: 90–105.

[10]See Susan Sontag's introduction to *A Barthes Reader* (New York: Farrar, Straus & Giroux, 1982), particularly pp. xxii–xxxii.

[11]For another perspective on how Beckett has shaped our perceptions of Joyce, see Kevin Dettmar's "The Joyce That Beckett Built" in the *James Joyce Quarterly* 35.4 (Summer 1998)/36.1 (Fall 1998): 605–620.

[12]See Kelly 155–175 for a complete analysis of the major flaws in Ellmann's biography. Kelly looks to reviews and letters by William Noon, S.J., William Empson, J.F. Byrne, Hugh Kenner, Ira Nadel, and Phillip Herring as dissenting voices in the reception of Ellmann's biography.

[13]See Melvin J. Friedman, "Ellmann on Joyce," in *Re-Viewing Classics of Joyce Criticism*, ed. Janet Dunleavy (Urbana and Chicago: University of Illinois Press, 1991): 131–141). Friedman states that "Even [Ellmann's] most unforgiving critics must pardon him for writing well" (139).

[14]For an excellent summary of the major issues in the debate over the Cambridge Lawrence, see the collection *Editing D. H. Lawrence*, edited by Charles L. Ross and Dennis Jackson (Ann Arbor: University of Michigan Press, 1995).

# CHAPTER TWO

# JOYCE.COM,
## in which
# IMAGE IS EVERYTHING

*I was trying to work out when and why I got interested in reading Joyce.
In my early teenage years, I saw a copy of* Ulysses *owned by a friend's
mother, and my memory of the book was that it didn't contain punctuation (I must have seen Molly Bloom's monologue!). . . . The overall reason for reading Joyce, particularly* Ulysses, *was to accept the challenge of
reading (and understanding) a "difficult" novel . . . the same reason I
tackled Umberto Eco's* Foucault's Pendulum. *Many people had said*
Ulysses *was the most important novel in the 20th century, which I
thought was a good reason for reading it.*
—*Charles Cave, non-academic Joycean*

Charles Cave's web page, "James Joyce" (www.ozemail.com.au/
~caveman/Joyce/) indicates that his profession is computer software, but
that "Joyce is one of [his] favourite authors" (18 Mar. 1998). His recollection associating *Ulysses* primarily with Molly Bloom's monologue, and his
confession that he read the book as a challenge and because of its reputation for being the "most important novel in the 20th century," indicate
many of the ways people know of or come to read *Ulysses.* Its reputation,
built on an academic foundation, is that *Ulysses* is "the most important"
work in this century. Further, Cave states that he "joined the International
James Joyce Foundation" and the "Sydney based James Joyce Foundation"
in 1995, which illustrates that there are non-academics within the Joycean
world. Cave's web page shows the elements of the public Joyce as constructed in the late twentieth century. He does not mention the pornographic reputation of *Ulysses,* but his earliest remembrance of
encountering the novel centers around Molly Bloom's monologue and its
lack of punctuation. This emphasis on "Penelope" also exemplifies the
way that *Ulysses* exists in the public discourse of the late twentieth century: "Penelope" is the chapter most associated with Joyce's radical style in
the popular press, but the sensual aspects of the chapter are usually repressed when the chapter is used metonymically as representative of

Joyce's difficulty. The radical nature of *Ulysses* was centered around its obscenity in much of the early public discourse about the novel; now, this aspect is rarely (if at all) mentioned in conjunction with the radical—and
difficult to read—nature of Joyce's writing. Popular press articles usually
focus on one aspect or the other, and for American audiences the difficulty
of the writing style is more often the dominant way that *Ulysses* is discussed.[1] This repression is not an unusual state for American readers of
*Ulysses* at this historical moment. The stylized representations of Joyce's
image in popular culture, such as his likeness reproduced on the shopping
bags in Barnes & Noble bookstores, tend to efface the radical beginnings
of Joyce's career, much as his canonization in the academy did. It is easy to
forget, in this era of Madonna, how vehement the reaction was to Joyce's
"pornography" and "dirty words" during the early twentieth century. Certainly, his position as a canonized writer has been solid for the last three or
four decades: his short stories (particularly "Araby" and "The Dead") are
regularly anthologized, giving him inarguable status as a writer to know
of, if not to know. And H. G. Wells' famous lament about Joyce's "cloacal
obsession" has little meaning for most undergraduates (and even gradu-
ates) encountering *A Portrait of the Artist* in the university classroom of
the late twentieth century. Can anyone be shocked by Joyce after hearing
Howard Stern?

## THE JOYCE OF SEX

As discussed in the previous chapter, the legal strategy followed by Ernst in
the censorship trial of *Ulysses* relied heavily on positioning Joyce's work as
a literary classic. Such a strategy countered the evaluation of *Ulysses* as
pornographic with a literary parallel to the concept of *noblesse oblige,* in
which a classic could not be obscene by definition: it was high art, and
such art was above lewdness.[2] But, to be sure, Joyce became known to the
wider American public as a writer of scandalous prose—through the trial
of the *Little Review*'s editors, Jane Heap and Margaret Anderson, upon the
book's publication in 1922 to loudly denunciatory reviews in the press,
and in America with the appearance in 1927 of a pirated version generally
accepted to have been published by Samuel Roth, a convicted pornogra-
pher. In fact, one famous photograph shows Joyce and Sylvia Beach seated
in front of a placard proclaiming in large letters "The Scandal of *Ulysses,*"
the title of an article excoriating Joyce's novel which ran in *The Sporting
Times* in 1922.[3]

Pornography played a strong role in marketing modernism; as Joyce
Wexler states: "Explicit sex [in modernist works] was a protest against mate-
rialist social values, but it also increased sales. . . . Censorship advertised the
work of Joyce and Lawrence far beyond the avant-garde audience" (91).
Wexler's thesis is that modernist writers, particularly Lawrence but also
Joyce, were responding to "contradictory ideologies of authorship" in which

money and serious art were antithetical. She places this antithesis squarely in the context of a conflict between Romanticism and Victorianism:

> On the one hand, the Romantic artist as genius was expected to express an inviolable inner vision without regard for its rhetorical effect or market values. On the other hand, the Victorian author as professional was expected to earn a living by writing . . . In this conflict, art was aligned with writing for oneself, martyrdom, and self-expression, while sales were aligned with writing for an audience, professionalism, and rhetoric. The characteristic difficulty and obscenity of modernist fiction were formal responses to this situation. (91)

Wexler further states that "many modernists disavowed financial aims while benefiting materially from the erotic aspects of their work" (91), but it is highly arguable whether Joyce fits easily into this formulation. As early as *Dubliners*, Joyce was highly concerned with financial aims and with reaching a wide audience. Further, as Kelly has shown, Joyce's primary concern was to show Ireland its own face in his "nicely polished looking glass," surely an admission of rhetorical aims. And throughout his career, he was greatly interested in the reviews and sales of his work; in fact, he agreed to a publicity shoot for *Finnegans Wake* with photographer Giselle Freund for *Time* magazine in 1938. Joyce's appearance on the cover of *Time* was a calculated effort to boost sales for his last book, which had met with mixed reactions in serialization. A letter from Adrienne Monnier, partner of Sylvia Beach, specifically points to Joyce's concern with money; she mentions that André Gide found "something saintly" about Joyce's indifference to publishing success but that "[w]hat Gide doesn't know—and like the sons of Noah we put a veil over it—is that you are, on the contrary, very concerned about success and money" (Ellmann 651–52). Joyce was willing to trade on the reputation of *Ulysses* in order to help sales of *Finnegans Wake*, asking Freund in their first session to photograph him with Sylvia Beach at Shakespeare and Company, even though the friendship between Beach and Joyce had been strained by this time over his decision to publish *Ulysses* in America.[4]

This decision led to the censorship trial that defined *Ulysses* for the twentieth century as a literary classic—and a difficult work. The inclusion of Judge Woolsey's decision as the foreword to the American edition of *Ulysses* further ensured that it would also be forever linked to its early obscene reputation, by positioning the book's formerly banned status as the initial pronouncement on *Ulysses'* significance. The trial simultaneously established that *Ulysses* was too difficult for the less educated to understand and reinforced the link to pornography by acknowledging the graphic nature of the work. Judge Woolsey states that *Ulysses* is "emetic" rather than "aphrodisiac" (Moscato and LeBlanc 38), but the end result of printing his decision in the American edition of 1934 is that readers were (and continue to be) reminded of the prospect of titillation.

Decades later, *Ulysses* is no longer viewed as pornographic. But the book continues to be associated with pornography, albeit in a more subtle fashion. Of the portions of *Ulysses* that entered the public discourse as being obscene, the primary offending chapter was "Penelope," with the "Nausicaa" and "Circe" chapters also reaffirming Joyce's "filthy" reputation. It was during the typing of the "Circe" episode that the famous incident took place of the typist's husband flinging the typescript into the fire, a story that gets repeated often in general interest articles.[5] But it is "Molly's soliloquy" (as "Penelope" came to be known) that became the defining portion of *Ulysses* within popular culture, and explanations of Joyce's work in popular newspapers and magazine articles continue to underscore this relationship. The current emphasis is on the chapter's stylistic innovations, but the frequent mention of this episode in defining the importance of *Ulysses* to literature hearkens back to its early, obscene reputation. The other chapters of the book exhibit equally revolutionary narrative techniques, yet it is Molly's monologue that continues to serve as the representative for Joyce's impact upon modern fiction. The link to pornography, then, is suggestive rather than distinct in the general discourse surrounding the book, and yet the Woolsey ruling continues to foreground such a link upon reading the 1961 edition. In 1984 that edition no longer became the only one available in America, and as a result of the Gabler *Ulysses* and the ensuing controversy this pornographic connection became secondary to the discourse of difficulty that continues to define the book within popular culture. The prurient reputation of Joyce's prose continues to exist, however, as a semiotic Other within that discourse, somewhat repressed but never fully erased.

## KISS ME, I'M IRISH

Including Judge Woolsey's decision as the foreword not only reinforces the pornographic elements of *Ulysses*, but with his reminder that readers must bear in mind that Joyce's "locale was Celtic and his season Spring," it also functions to re-insert Joyce into an Irish tradition. Such a reminder subverts the trend within academia that follows Pound's move to "de-Irish" Joyce (to use Kelly's phrase), and points toward the divergence of the academic Joyce and the public Joyce. While currently there is a counter-trend within academia to reassert Joyce as an Irish writer first and an international one second (particularly in post-colonial studies), for over half a century Joyce's connection to Ireland was secondary to his place as pre-eminent Continental modernist. Ireland, in this formulation, merely served as fodder for Joyce's genius rather than as a formational matrix for it. This view is losing currency as the ideal of a "universal" literature gives way to an understanding of literature as localized, historicized, and politicized.

But this theoretical shift is a fairly recent trend in academia; for the public, Joyce has long been intimately connected with the "Celtic locale" of

Woolsey's decision. Joycean iconography in popular culture almost always links him to his nationality; in fact, as the article accompanying Freund's 1938 photo-essay in *Time* states, "No observer of his life and works can fail to note that James Joyce is a typical Irishman" ("Night Thoughts" 84).[6] Freund's photographs, as Maurizia Boscagli and Enda Duffy have shown, function both to efface Joyce's Irishness in favor of presenting a more cosmopolitan image and to semiotically retain "as its haunting uncanny, a trace ... of ... Ireland" (145). Boscagli and Duffy offer a Barthesian reading of the photo-essay's presentation of Joyce as cosmopolitan modernist, noting that the "contradiction that exists here . . . between Joyce's representation as transnational exile and the retained traces of his Irish origins, is precisely what enables us to envision him as an exile" (145). On a more conscious level, all of Joyce's writings are, quite simply, about Ireland, and therefore the connection between the writer and his Irishness is continually emphasized for the general reader. Ireland's own reclamation of Joyce as a favored son achieved a peculiar state when his likeness was printed on the Irish ten-pound note in 1993.[7] This blend of Joyce, Irishness, and commerce juxtaposes several strands of Joycean iconography: the sacred nature of literature, money, and the author are combined into a bold statement of Ireland's growing importance on the European stage. Ireland can no longer be considered provincial with such proof that her prodigal son has returned home.

Of course, in the United States the Irish ten-pound note is not widely circulated, and Joyce's Irish roots strike other chords there. Americans seem to have a fascination with all things Irish; witness the present craze for the touring Irish musicals "Lord of the Dance" and "Riverdance." Such "stage Irishness" has entered the popular imagination before, but as if to prove how mainstream this most recent transformation of the Celtic twilight has become, a television commercial for Folger's instant coffee features a Celtic dancer at a rehearsal, presumably for one of the two touring extravaganzas mentioned. Another example of this fascination with Irish culture arises in the popularity of Frank McCourt's novel, *Angela's Ashes*, a book which (however factual) reinforces the discourse of the repressed, poor, and Catholic stereotypes of Irish culture. Further evidence of America's Irish obsession is found in three television programs, all appearing in 1998 on each of the major networks: "Costello," about a South Boston waitress and her Irish-American family; "Trinity," about an Irish-American family with all the stereotypical Irish-American roles (police officer, priest, drunk); and "To Have and To Hold," about a young Irish-American couple and their families.[8] The examples listed here do not begin to catalogue the importance Ireland plays in the American imagination, but they do point to that importance being predicated on stereotypes of Irish nationality. One reason for this fascination, of course, stems from the large number of Americans who can claim Irish descent, and the distance that Americans have from the actual Irish forces the stereotypes to function in place of a more accurate understanding of Irish culture. The Irish often say that these Americans are "more Irish than the Irish themselves,"[9] and this popular phrase attests to the American identification with those stereotypes, which exaggerate (like all stereotypes do) the features of actual Irish culture.

But Joyce's relationship to this American attraction to Irishness is problematic, as indicated by Boscagli and Duffy's reading of the Freund photographs. Joyce's reputation as modernist literary master relics on the transcendent quality ascribed to his works—they are about more than just Dublin. The identification of Joyce with Irishness contradicts his own rejection of Ireland throughout his life. However, Joyce's principled rejection of his homeland is contravened by the fact that he wrote about little else. Even *Finnegans Wake*, arguably a book that attempts to transcend boundaries of history and nationality, brings us by "commodius vicus of recirculation back to Howth Castle and Environs" (3). For the general reader, unconscious of the duality of Joyce's face vis-à-vis Boscagli and Duffy, the identification of Joyce with Irish culture has rarely been suppressed. This continued identification of Joyce with his Irish origins works directly against the kind of transnational Modernism espoused by Pound, and functions to position Joyce within an Irish *milieu* in the general public. In effect, the identification with Irishness moves Joyce back into the tradition H. G. Wells placed him in, as a specifically Irish writer: "Like so many Irish writers from Sterne to Shaw Mr. Joyce is a bold experimentalist with paragraph and punctuation" ("James Joyce" 23). This quote further identifies Joyce's experimentalism with Irishness, not Modernism, and underscores a curiosity: Ireland is excoriated by the Modernist Irish writers as provincial and stifling; yet it produced some of the greatest literary experimenters of the twentieth century, like Joyce and Beckett. Perhaps the provincial Ireland of the early twentieth century functioned as the Other against which these writers measured their own achievements, and explains at least in Joyce's case why, although he left Ireland, he focused all of his major literary achievements on the very culture he avowedly turned his back upon.

FACE KNOWN TO ALL MEN?

Joyce's use of early twentieth century popular culture in *Ulysses* has been well documented, and continues to be of interest to cultural scholars.[10] To date, though, there are few scholarly discussions of the uses to which current popular culture has put Joyce. One of those few instances occurs in the compilation of essays entitled *Joyce and Popular Culture*, edited by R. B. Kershner (1996). In one of four essays grouped under the heading of the same title, Vincent Cheng looks at numerous examples of Joyceana in popular culture. Cheng notes that the "'conscious Joyce'—that is, what Joyce means, if anything at all, in mass culture . . . [is] mostly negative in connotation and attitude: obscure; obscene; esoteric; formidable; weird; degenerate; even insane" (180). Cheng proposes that an alternate Joycean unconscious "exists and operates even within those who . . . have never heard of James Joyce and his works at the conscious level"; he appears to find this unconscious Joyce to be a more positive construct than the conscious Joyce (182). In an interesting example of what Cheng sees as a "moment of Joycean consciousness via a mass-culture experience," he discusses a scene in *Back to School*, a 1986 film aimed at high school students and young adults. This film starred Sally Kellerman as a college English professor and Rodney Dangerfield as a successful businessman who returns to college for the degree he never pursued. In Kellerman's introductory scene, she approaches the lectern of her class and begins reciting the last part of Molly Bloom's soliloquy, ending with an impassioned and sensual "yes I will Yes." Dangerfield, caught up in the emotion of the monologue, jumps up and cries, "Yes! Yes!" to the laughter of the other students. Kellerman replies: "Oh, thanks for the vote of confidence. I think Joyce is pretty hot, too . . . . And now that I've got your attention, I'd like to run down the reading list for the semester, see what else turns you on" (in Cheng 191). The message Cheng sees presented in this scene is that "Joyce is sexy and fun stuff . . . . Hollywood has immense power to get high school students interested in Joyce . . . . Now a teenager viewing *Back to School* and hearing of Joyce for the first time is likely to be more interested in reading such a radical dude" (192).

While Cheng's supposition that such filmic references to Joyce in mass-marketed movies can advertise his work to a larger audience outside the university is arguably correct, the scene also operates within a cultural understanding of Joyce already present and depends on that understanding for characterization. Kellerman's character in the film is a free spirit, sexually uninhibited and self-confident. Choosing to open a class on the first day of the term with a sexually charged *frisson* is an indication of her role in the film as Dangerfield's love interest. She begins the film dating a stereotypically stuffy Ivy League professor but later leaves him for Dangerfield, an uneducated lower East side man who has followed the Horatio Alger track to success. Such a socially unacceptable move (within the film) is foreshadowed by her reading of Molly's soliloquy: for an audience unfamiliar with Joyce, it shows her unconventionality and sensuality; for an audience familiar with Joyce, it provides a nice way to parallel one unlikely couple with another (Kellerman/Dangerfield and Molly/Leopold). Further, for the first audience, an exposure to Joyce as "hot" subtly invokes the association of Joyce with pornography.

Cheng's essay catalogues other appearances of Joyceana in mass culture, including popular songs, television shows, commercials, and t-shirts; he writes, ". . . if imitation and even parody are the sincerest forms of flattery, even if sometimes unacknowledged or perhaps unconscious, then [appearances of Joyce in popular culture] suggest that Joyce is obviously getting a good deal of flattery and respect"; he suggests that "a Joycean Unconscious is getting the culture to Say Yes to Joyce—and that, in this way,

Joyce *is* getting some respect" (192). He ends on what can only be read as a note of hopefulness, and this subtext can be analyzed in part by understanding the perception of Joyce both inside and outside the academy. Cheng alludes to the uneasy relationship the non-academic world has with Joyce's works, in that these novels *stand for* something elite and intellectual, which cannot be understood without some kind of specialized knowledge. Respect and suspicion (the latter often disguised as derision or parody) have long been strange bedfellows in American thought about the academy, and they find themselves partners once again in the popular culture's estimation of Joyce's works. As Cheng demonstrates, parody and imitation of Joyce's works exist, but whether they are evidence of "flattery and respect" is arguable. Still, Cheng's theorizing of a "Joycean Unconscious" is suggestive; students at the end of the twentieth century are immersed in mass culture at an unprecedented rate. They are therefore presumably exposed to this "Joycean Unconscious" long before they get to university classrooms, whether or not their English professor reads Molly's breathless words on the first day of class. Still, if this Joycean Unconscious exists, it remains unconscious, and therefore repressed by the discourse of inaccessibility that surrounds the work, a discourse which leads to popular utterances like the Allan Sherman song, "Hello Mudduh, Hello Fadduh (A Letter from Camp)": "And the head coach wants no sissies/So he reads to us from something called *Ulysses*."

BLONDES PREFER *ULYSSES*

Primarily, Joycean appearances in popular culture underscore his value as an intellectual commodity, a value based on academic ownership of the works' meaning (the idea that only academics with specialized knowledge can really understand the works). The "snob" appeal of Joyce, based on this commodification, shapes the subtext of all appearances of Joyce or *Ulysses* in popular culture. A fascinating example can be found in a photograph of actress Marilyn Monroe reading *Ulysses*, a picture that first appeared in 1955 (reprinted in *Joyce and Popular Culture* 170). This photograph in part subverts the "dumb blonde" image of Monroe while subtly reinforcing the sexuality of Joyce's text by linking it with another icon of sexuality in American popular culture. Richard Brown has succinctly stated the unusual paradox of the photograph: "How can one imagine Marilyn Monroe, prime cultural symbol of a certain kind of 'dumb blonde' stupidity, reading *Ulysses*, equally potent cultural symbol of demanding literary genius, a kind of Everest for readerly intellectual achievement?" (172). Simultaneously, Monroe's status as a sex symbol becomes entwined with the pornographic reputation of *Ulysses*; as Brown notes, Monroe appears to be reading the last chapter—the Molly episode—which was "reviled by the censorious as the 'dirty book's' most 'dirty part'" (172). This shorthand for titillation would have been far more pronounced in 1955 than it is today, because the photograph appeared only some twenty years after the Woolsey decision.

Brown briefly explores how readers would bring to the photograph "certain assumptions about *Ulysses* as a famous 'dirty book'," and offers a semiotic reading of the photograph in this eroticized light (172–73). He spends little time discussing the paradoxical question of the "dumb blonde" reading the "Everest" of literature, except to say that in this reading the book would serve as a prop for a joke at Monroe's expense—and thus privilege the text over the reader in the photograph. The erotic connection between Monroe and *Ulysses* cannot be denied—and further accentuates the book's pornographic reputation within popular culture—but the equally strong reputation for difficulty exists as another layer of semiotic meaning in the picture, perhaps overshadowing the sexual association. *Ulysses*' image has become as stylized a representation of intellectualism as Monroe's has of sexuality. The derision raised by the juxtaposition of the two—the joke on Monroe that Brown points out—also indicates that, for readers distanced from the cultural moment of *Ulysses*' reception as pornographic, neither Monroe nor *Ulysses* can be read outside of their stylized images. While Monroe continues to be associated almost exclusively with her "blonde bombshell" image in the popular culture, *Ulysses* had already by 1955 shifted from its pornographic reputation into the canon of sacralized literature. A more recent example that underscores this shift occurs in an episode of the situation comedy *WKRP in Cincinnati* which aired in the early 1980's.[11] The station's secretary, played by another blonde bombshell, Loni Anderson, is seen reading *Ulysses* at her desk. The subtext here clearly points to the intellectual association of *Ulysses*, as the secretary's actions in the series always show her to be quite intelligent and provide a marked contrast with her outer appearance as a sexual object. *Ulysses*, in this instance, provides a clue to the viewer that Anderson's character is not what she is visually coded to be. The association of sexual titillation in the Monroe photograph, or in the *WKRP in Cincinnati* episode, is primarily a subliminal one for the late twentieth century viewer. Molly's soliloquy is no longer primarily associated in the popular press with its "dirty" language, but rather with its stylistic technique—the lack of punctuation and stream-of-consciousness narrative. For those who have read *Ulysses*, of course, the association with sexuality will be stronger, although it is uncertain whether the graphic language of Molly's sexual ruminations would be seen as shocking in a post-Erica Jong age. For those familiar with *Ulysses* only through its current reputation, however, neither the photograph nor the television show would raise the association of pornography with *Ulysses*, since the association of sexuality would belong to the voluptuous blonde, not the book she is reading. Complexly, *Ulysses* may function in the Monroe photograph and the television show to move the women from their sex-symbol status into a carnivalesque opposition, bringing the social

codes for sexual desirability and intelligence together in a society that de-
nies their co-existence in its female representations.

Brown offers the Monroe photograph as an example of Lyotard's *differend*, an "almost irresolvable [form] of discursive border dispute in which
both parties seem to have equivalent forms of justification with their parallel but apparently mutually exclusive discursive practices" (176). But the
photograph is part of the larger *differend* that is Joyce's book itself; existing on the border between academia and popular culture, *Ulysses* functions in exactly the same way that Brown describes for the Monroe
photograph. As a part of academia, *Ulysses* exemplifies the qualities valued by that institution: complexity, linguistic virtuosity, self-conscious
artistry, and irony (among others). These are the qualities that contribute
to *Ulysses*' reputation for difficulty, as they are associated with the very elements of "literariness" that distanced it from being pornographic in the
censorship trial; in effect, it was these qualities, associated with academically canonized literature, that began to strengthen barriers between
*Ulysses* and the non-academic reader. *Ulysses* is, without doubt, a book
that requires the reader to invest more effort into the reading than a traditionally written novel does. The academic discourse surrounding the book,
however, valorizes this aspect over any other and thus reinforces the academics' own position as interpreters.

But popular discourse around *Ulysses* emphasizes the book's affinity
with more accessible elements of fiction that do not call for specialized
training in close reading to understand, such as content rather than literary
style. The book is marketed to the general reader under the rubric of more
plot- or character-driven concerns like comedy, tragedy, psychological real-
ism, and thematic treatment of human sexuality. In fact, the front flap of
the dust jacket for Danis Rose's *Reader's Edition* summarizes *Ulysses* as
telling "the sadly comic story of Leopold Bloom, a good man led by love,
attempting to come to terms with loss: the deaths of his son and of his father, the departure of his daughter from home, the passing of his youth and
the adultery of his wife." There is no mention of the book's revolutionary
style, its experimentation with representation, its exploration of discursive
practices, or any of the other elements which are indicative of its greatness
to academia. Nor is any mention made of Stephen Dedalus; in this formulation *Ulysses* is about a simple man having a long and troubling day, not
about the nature of art or consciousness, two intellectual concerns that
Stephen represents. Dust jacket summaries, of course, are notoriously reductive, but the plot summary, while not incorrect, functions to erase any
of the revolutionary potential seen by scholars in Joyce's narrative or thematic practices. In effect, the two discourses of academia and popular culture produce two *Ulysses*, and the reading of each one is shaped by the
discourses themselves—what is valued in the book diverges when viewed
through the distinct lenses of the academic and the general reader. The discourse of the popular *Ulysses* is complicated, however, by its dependence

on the academic *Ulysses* for continued validation as a literary masterpiece. In effect, the public *Ulysses* works both within and against what Janice Radway describes as the academic culture's "affirm[ation of] the validity and preeminence of [a] single set of criteria against which all works are measured, and [the insistence] that there is only one appropriate way to read" (260).

## ULYSSES FOR DUMMIES

While the Monroe photograph subtly sustains both the erotic and intellectual aspects of *Ulysses* within popular culture, the intellectual challenge of the book has almost completely overridden the pornographic understanding of Joyce's novel at the web site "*Ulysses* for Dummies" (http://www. bway.net/~hunger/ulysses.html). The site yokes the book's reputation for difficulty with an icon of anti-intellectualism, the highly successful ". . . for Dummies" series of reference books published by IDG Books Worldwide, Inc. This web site's satiric reinterpretation of Joyce's complex novel through cartoons and reductive chapter summaries exhibits the dual nature of the parody: it is both exaltation and effrontery. The home page of the web site reinforces Joyce's contradictory status of popular appeal and inaccessibility. Beneath the title of the page, a bold-faced statement proclaims, "As seen on the July 20, 1998 edition of ABC's *World News Tonight!*" This statement serves to reiterate Joyce's importance in the culture at large, points to the apparent public need for a "stripped-down, revved-up version" of *Ulysses,* and plays upon the ubiquitous "as seen on TV" blurb for products of dubious quality sold in drugstores. The text introducing "*Ulysses* for Dummies" highlights the book's status as "masterpiece," but points out that

> . . . the common reader has been reluctant to face Joyce's great panorama. Laden with obscure references and dogged by an ever-growing body of secondary literature, the book's reputation as a "difficult" work has placed a barrier between the book and its potential audience. This is a shame, because Joyce was writing for a general readership, and his novel offers a remarkable experience even for the reader with no prior familiarity with Joyce's world. (21 Oct. 1998)

The paragraph pits the Joyce Industry against the common reader, and claims Joyce for the non-academic audience by pointing out Joyce's intent to write for that audience; the academics "dog" the book with secondary literature, and it is this imposition by academia rather than Joyce's own obscure references or nontraditional writing style that places barriers between *Ulysses* and readers. Further, the commodification of Joyce's work as symbol of Literature is emphasized in the next paragraph:

> *From Hunger* [the web magazine that publishes the page] smells an opportunity when we step in it. Herewith, our stripped-down, revved-up

version of Joyce's great work, which we, with one eye on the marketplace, have called *Ulysses* for Dummies.

By mentioning the "marketplace," the authors are reinscribing the popular appeal of *Ulysses* (as well as blatantly coöpting the successful "For Dummies" series) while simultaneously trading on its opposite status as inaccessible: they have, ironically, positioned themselves as being indispensable to readers, just as the critic claims to be, and become part of that "ever-growing body of secondary literature" that "dogs" *Ulysses*. As such, the site offers these summaries of the novel's high points in the form of a sales pitch:

> Now you can thrill to the discussion of Shakespeare in chapter 9; weep with Simon Dedalus at Dignam's funeral in chapter 6; frolic with Bloom and Stephen in chapter 15's dreamscape of Nighttown; and join in Molly's optimistic vindication of the world in chapter 18.

The site's characterization of the "Circe" chapter as a "frolic" for Bloom and Stephen is not only reductive but also implies that the Nighttown episode is a happy romp rather than the phantasmagorical weaving of all the major themes of betrayal, loss, and reconciliation in the book that it is. Further, the sexually graphic nature of both "Circe" and "Penelope" is completely elided in this description, indicating that the book's status as "difficult" has completely overridden the book's earlier reputation for pornography. Of course, for the audience familiar with *Ulysses*, the description is humorous and ironic, but for our imaginary reader, the description functions to shape the way she will view the book upon reattempting it. The illustrations for each chapter represent some of the graphic elements of the book—for example, Bloom and Stephen are shown, backs to the screen, urinating in the garden in "Ithaca"—but the child-like simplicity of the illustrations precludes any but a humorous response. The stylized representations of the three major characters reduce them to metonymic symbols: Bloom with his mustache and bowler hat; Stephen carrying a baton-shaped stick, representing his ashplant; and Molly, completely absent from the illustrations and captions until her soliloquy chapter, where she is shown in bed (Figs. 1–3). While the drawings of Stephen and Molly are generic representations of male and female figures, Bloom's representation evokes Charlie Chaplin's "Little Tramp," and this identification reinforces the comic aspects of the novel conjured by the introductory page's flippant style.

Each chapter's illustration is captioned with a one-sentence summary of the plot taking place and the time of day. For example, the opening "Telemachus" page shows a picture of Stephen and a robed Buck Mulligan on the balcony of the Martello Tower, overlooking a child-like drawing of the sea, complete with triangular sailboat, shining yellow sun, and flying birds represented by a curled "V." The caption reads: "**June 16, 1904. 8:00 a.m.** Stephen Dedalus, a young schoolteacher, speaks to his friend, 'stately,

Bloom

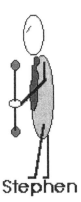

Stephen

Figures 1–3. Illustrations from the website, "*Ulysses* for Dummies." Figure 1 is Leopold Bloom; Figure 2 is Stephen Dedalus; and Figure 3 is the complete illustration of Chapter 18, showing Molly Bloom in bed with Leopold Bloom as the day breaks.

plump' Buck Mulligan, in the disused Dublin watchtower where they live"
(boldface in original). All of the captions for each episode are similarly
structured. The Homeric parallels are not mentioned in any of the captions, with the sole exception of "Aeolus." The site's authors stated that
they had no ulterior motive for excluding the Homeric titles, nor did they
have any particular reason for including "Aeolus" (Hunka and Tzanis
5 Nov. 1998). Whether or not it was a deliberate move, the sole reference
to "Aeolus" points to the Homeric parallels' importance to the novel, and
repeats the kind of interpretive stance taken in much of the secondary literature. The Homeric schema was printed in Gilbert's 1936 book on *Ulysses*,
although Joyce had for years attempted to suppress it from critics. Eliot,
too, pointed out the importance of the Homeric structure in his 1922 essay,
"*Ulysses*, Order, and Myth" which helped shape so much critical attention
to *Ulysses*.

Lost in the web site's summary of the novel's plot is Molly's adultery, a
curious erasure of one of the major elements of the story, and a further repression of the novel's link to sexuality. The emphasis for each chapter is the
relationship between Bloom and Stephen; Molly is not even mentioned until
her appearance in the final chapter. Further, the summaries are disjointed;
for example, Chapter 4 ("Calypso") shows Bloom at the breakfast table,
with a black cat and a dialogue bubble showing Joyce's onomatopoeic
"Mrngkao" over it. This chapter is crucial to developing the relationship
between Leopold and Molly, yet the caption merely states, "8:00 a.m.
Leopold Bloom, an advertising salesman, eats breakfast" (boldface in original). The tragic nature of Bloom's wanderings—in essence, Bloom intentionally stays away as long as possible in tacit acceptance of his wife's
adultery—is completely lost in this rendering. The next illustration, of the
"Lotus Eaters" chapter, shows Bloom at the post office, "get[ting] a love
letter addressed to his alter ego, 'Henry Flower.'" Without knowing that
Bloom is even married at this point, the love letter loses its significance. Further, there is no explanation of why Bloom even requires an alter ego. In
Joyce's text, Bloom is dabbling in his own flirtatious liaison, although it
never progresses beyond letter-writing; the letter to "Henry Flower" is a pa-
thetic echo of Molly's letter from Blazes Boylan confirming their own after-
noon consummation. If Molly is to be erased from the summary of
"Calypso," surely the resulting loss of the letter's significance dictates that
some other action from "Lotus Eaters" would be more appropriate, perhaps Bloom's wandering into a Catholic church and musing on religion, or
his taking a bath at the bath house. The effect of this kind of disjointed plot
summary is that Joyce's work becomes even more inexplicable—the plot
makes no sense here.

The web site, therefore, while claiming to make *Ulysses* palatable "for
Dummies," in reality further confuses Joyce's text for the uninitiated. In
fact, the site is humorous only to those who have read *Ulysses* already and
can fill the gaps left in the text by the summaries. The illustrations posit

someone knowledgeable about the details of *Ulysses*: for example, in the "Nestor" chapter where Stephen is seen teaching, the blackboard in the illustration reads, "TARENTUM," a reference to the lesson Stephen is teaching on Pyrrhus with which the chapter opens. The caption simply explains that "Stephen teaches at Mr. Deasy's school. God is 'a shout in the street,' Stephen says." This caption implies that Stephen utters these words to the children in his classroom, rather than in his sparring with Mr. Deasy as in Joyce's text. Much of the impact of the Joycean scene is, of course, lost in such simplification, but the knowledgeable reader of *Ulysses* can fill in such gaps and find humor in the illustration's animation, which depicts a dialogue bubble with the word "HEY!" appearing and disappearing at the open window. The real audience, then, of "*Ulysses* for Dummies" is not the general reader afraid to tackle Joyce's text because of its reputation for difficulty, but rather those readers who have already achieved some level of comprehension of *Ulysses*, perhaps by wading through the very material the site's introductory page scorns as "dogging" Joyce's novel. Once again, the book's difficulty is highlighted in spite of the site's simplification of the plot of *Ulysses*, although the questions raised by it may prompt a reader to delve once again into the text itself.

The final illustration at the site shows Molly and Bloom in bed, with the sun rising outside the window. Molly is sitting up in bed, with Bloom lying down next to her, his head at her feet. The word "YES" appears and disappears over her head, without a dialogue bubble, merely a line connecting Molly to the word, presumably to indicate that the word is not spoken aloud. The caption reads, "**Sunrise.** Bloom goes to bed, waking his wife Molly, who thinks about how much she loves her husband" (boldface in original). The effect of this caption, combined with the illustration, completely erases the pornographic elements of Molly's soliloquy and emphasizes the comical (in the classical sense of the word) element of the novel—the happy couple is united. The web site therefore functions to repress the pornographic reputation of *Ulysses* in favor of the intellectualized one, clear indication that the dominant trope associated with *Ulysses* is the one of the novel's difficulty.[12]

## MODERN'S MASTERSTROKE

Reputation for difficulty or no, sales of *Ulysses* have remained steady over time, hovering around 100,000 copies per year (see *n*2 Ch. 1). This is a surprisingly large figure for a book deemed too difficult, too obscure, and too intellectualized for the average reader. It is unclear how much of this figure is fed by class reading lists and scholarly research (Random House would not divulge such sales information), but these are not the only avenues of sale for *Ulysses*. Commercial booksellers keep the book on their shelves as a literary classic; if the book did not sell at all, this practice would surely cease. *Someone* is buying all those copies. But at the end of the twentieth century, as the clock wound down on Random House's copyright, those steady sales apparently were not enough. In the general list-making fervor that strikes at the end of decades (and now, of course, at the end of the century), Random House's Modern Library division delivered to the press a list of the "100 Best Novels of the Twentieth Century" that placed *Ulysses* in the number one position. The response to this list in the press revealed a great deal about the public's perception of Joyce and his most famous novel, as well as revealing even more about the sacred role of literature in our culture.

The Modern Library's list, an admitted publicity stunt to "bring the Modern Library to public attention" (Gates and Sawhill 65), gained such attention more for its omissions than its inclusions. While novels from the first eighty years of the twentieth century were well-represented, those written in the last fifteen were not; the most recently published novel included was William Kennedy's *Ironweed* (1984). Women and minorities were underrepresented on the list; most notably omitted was Toni Morrison. It does seem odd that the Nobel Prize-winning writer of *Beloved* and *Song of Solomon* was not included on the list, and genre fiction like Hammett's *The Maltese Falcon* and Cain's *The Postman Always Rings Twice* were. But the judges, composed of the board members of the Modern Library, never ranked the books. According to *The Washington Post*, the "board members merely checked off books from a master list of 440 titles supplied by the classics publisher, without putting them in any particular order. . . . In interviews, the judges do not even agree on what they were ranking—the best-written books, or the most important, or the most influential. One judge acknowledges that he voted for books he has not actually read" (Streitfeld). Further, the master list was weighted toward authors who were published by Random House: for example, Gore Vidal had 21 titles listed of the 440, "more than William Faulkner, Henry James and Joseph Conrad put together" (Streitfeld). The *Post* revealed that many of the judges did not actually contribute 100 books; one, historian Edmund Morris, stated that he only contributed around 37, and author William Styron admits to only submitting 50 or 60. But the books in the top five of the rankings—including *Ulysses* at number one—were all selected by at least nine out of the ten board members. These five books were the only ones that the judges were actually asked to rank, and the strange result is that two of the five novels would not have individually been ranked that high had the list been compiled in a more straightforward manner. Joyce's *Portrait* was ranked number three, but two of the judges would have placed it in the low thirties (Streitfeld).

Comments on the list in popular periodicals confined themselves to criticisms of the list's methods; the placement of *Ulysses* at number one rarely seemed to raise an eyebrow, although the *Post*'s article did mention that the "inscrutable *Ulysses* has become, of all things, a bestseller" (Streitfeld). The implication in this statement, clearly, is that *Ulysses* ought not to be; it is "inscrutable" and therefore not fodder for the bestseller lists. Another comment, one that also questioned Joyce's place at the top of the list, is presented in the August 3, 1998 *Newsweek* in the manner of a joke, complete with set-up and punch line:

> After rattling off a bunch of omissions—including his own "Mumbo Jumbo"—Ishmael Reed said he was pleased to see James T. Farrell on the list. "I'd put *Studs Lonigan* before *Ulysses*." Why? "Homer did it already." (Gates and Sawhill 65)

While it is arguable whether or not Reed was joking, the presentation of this passage by the writers functions to puncture Joyce's image as Great Modernist Master chosen by the Establishment: he's a plagiarist, or at the very least, unoriginal. Such an opinion serves as a counterweight to the academic reputation of *Ulysses* as a masterpiece *sui generis*.

The Reader's List, compiled over the Internet via voluntary and anonymous input from visitors to the Modern Library site (www.randomhouse. com) between July 20 and October 20, 1998, offers a counterpoint to the Modern Library's list (and serves to position the Modern Library's as the "establishment" opposed to the "people"). This list, of course, cannot be considered any more scientifically accurate than the "official" list, because there is no way of knowing whether anyone voted more than once for any particular works; nor does the list contain only non-academic contributions (this author confesses to voting herself for *Ulysses* on this list). The list does, however, diverge significantly from the Modern Library's. With 217,520 votes cast, the number one novel chosen by readers was *Atlas Shrugged* by Ayn Rand.[13] *Ulysses* placed eleventh and *Portrait* fifty-eighth to the Modern Library's first and third, respectively. While *Ulysses* placed relatively high on the Reader's List, it still dropped ten spots, and *Portrait's* drop of fifty-five spots further indicates that the voters do not share the Modern Library's admiration for Joyce's work.

However, the Best 100 Novels list was a rousing success for the publishers of *Ulysses*. David Ebershoff, publishing manager of the Modern Library, stated that once the list was published, demand for *Ulysses* skyrocketed: "In two or three days, we sold what we typically sell in four months" (electronic correspondence with author 24 July 1998). In August, online bookseller Amazon.com listed *Ulysses* as number two on its paperback bestseller list and attributed this "instant comeback" to the Modern Library's rankings (Streitfeld). At the Modern Library's web site, a listing titled "Modern Library in the News" publishes various mentions of the list in the press, including one from the August 3, 1998 *Time* magazine which listed Joyce as a "winner" in its "Winners & Losers" column. But clearly, the real winner is Random House through the increased sales of literary "classics." Plainly, whatever the suspect nature of the listings, the surrounding publicity resulted in a windfall for Random House and, in the process, Joyce's *Ulysses*.

Further, the list and the controversy over it point to the sacred nature of literature in our culture. Readers became incensed over the inclusion, placement, or exclusion of particular works, some of which are reprinted at the "Modern Library in the News" page. These comments invoke an ideology of literature that illustrates Foucault's statement that writing's "primal status . . . retranslat[es], in transcendental terms . . . the theological affirmation of its sacred character ("What Is An Author?" 104). For example, the page quotes *The Chicago Tribune*'s editors: "Anything that gets Americans the least bit exercised about literature is a worthy effort," a statement which seems to position the list as an almost moral crusade to get Americans (who, the statement implies, are shirking their literary duty) to read great books. Another selection quotes a July 22 letter to the *New York Times*, in which the writer states that the list is a "good thing for several reasons, but the best is that it will result in more books being read." Such an ideology serves academics in that it validates the literate culture—and the educational system that fosters it. It is also apparent that certain kinds of books are being valorized within these statements, in that the Modern Library's list represents those books as being "literary." The large sales of paperback genre fiction would belie the impression that Americans do not read at all, as these statements imply on the surface. What the statements actually encode is a system of discrimination between high and low art, and a Leavisite disdain for those books defined as "low"—they do not actually count as books. This separation of the sacred literature from the profane is one of the reasons behind the many negative responses to such books as *The Maltese Falcon* or the *Studs Lonigan* trilogy, both seen in one response to the list as "potboilers" that "lower the bar" (Gates and Sawhill 65). Placing *Ulysses* at the top of a list that, in effect, "commands" that only certain books validated by the academic, critical, and economic machinery of the literary culture be read ensures that it will remain firmly entrenched within that culture, and that the "religious principle of the hidden meaning (which requires interpretation)" will continue to operate around it (Foucault, "What Is An Author?" 104).

## THE PUSILLANIMOUS READER

Publicity-driven sales or no, Joyce's reputation for inaccessibility continues to be the dominant trope within public discourse about *Ulysses*. In the October 26/November 2, 1998 double issue of *The New Yorker*, Rebecca Mead writes of an exhibition of inscribed first editions of Joyce's novel being held by a rare-book dealer. Mead's article, in a magazine aimed predominantly at the common reader, sustains the notion that Joyce's works are not readable:

> When, earlier this year, *Ulysses* was nominated by the Modern Library as the greatest novel of the twentieth century, it was simultaneously nominated by the postmodern public as the greatest unread novel of the twenti-

eth century. A forthcoming exhibition of personally inscribed first editions of the book seems to provide empirical evidence confirming at least the latter characterization: of the twenty-four copies that will be on display, several have what book dealers call unopened pages—pages that have not been sliced open by an eager reader. Could it be that even some of Joyce's intimates and supporters couldn't get through the thing? (54)

Mead lists five who did not get all the way through "the thing," including Sylvia Beach's mother (who apparently stopped at page 117) and Eleanor Rockefeller (page 381); Mead writes, "Even the volume belonging to Margaret Anderson, the editor of *The Little Review*, in which sections of *Ulysses* were published in serial form, remains uncracked" (54). Clearly, Mead implies that the book is unreadable even for those who presumably, like Anderson, were heavily involved in the novel from the beginning. The article focuses on the "several" unread copies without giving a more exact number which would indicate the proportion of read to unread books of the twenty-four being displayed. Further, there could be many reasons why Anderson, at least, did not open her copy; the proprietor of the bookshop holding the exhibition, Glenn Horowitz, points out that Anderson would have read the novel in manuscript, and therefore would not necessarily have had to read it in print. By focusing on the unspecified number of unread copies, Mead implies that "the thing" (a phrase showing a distaste for or frustration with Joyce's book) is unreadable for all, "even" Margaret Anderson. She quotes Horowitz: "Some people ran out of steam. But I don't think that they got to a particular part and thought, Oh! Leopold Bloom is counting stools in the toilet bowl! I think they got to the point where they said, 'Life is too short'" (54). This statement invokes Joyce's reputation for obscenity while also implying that the book is not worth the effort.

Further, the article implies that Joyce was more concerned with other writers than with ordinary readers. Joyce's inscriptions are unemotional and prosaic, except to fellow authors. Mead recounts the infamous story of F. Scott Fitzgerald's meeting with Joyce, in which he threatened to throw himself out of a window to prove his devotion to the writer of *Ulysses*, and then prints Joyce's "fulsome" inscription to Fitzgerald: "Dear Mr. Fitzgerald: Here with [*sic*] is the book you gave signed and I am adding a portrait of the artist as a once young man with the thanks of your much obliged but most pusillanimous guest" (56). Mead also includes Joyce's fascination with the Irish poet James Stephens, whose copy bears the inscription "from his twin-colleague and admirer" (56). Stephens shared the same birthday with Joyce, who was always impressed with such coincidences, and who at one time wanted Stephens to take over *Finnegans Wake* (Ellmann 591–92). While the notion *is* a little odd, Joyce was at the time experiencing deep doubt over his *Work in Progress*; his most ardent supporters were criticizing the book or saying that Joyce had finally gone mad. Mead's article makes it appear that Joyce's desire for Stephens to take over *Finnegans*

*Wake* was prompted simply by the coincidental birthdays. Further, Horowitz explains that Stephens "wasn't Joyce's birthday 'twin' at all. 'He had an extremely checkered upbringing, and he had no idea when he was born . . . But he did nothing to inform Joyce of the misapprehension'" (56). The effect of this story, combined with the apparent effusiveness of Joyce's inscriptions to writers and not others, is to paint Joyce as eccentric and uninterested in the reading public. Indeed, Mead ends her article by pointing out that Stephens' copy, at least, is opened to the very last printed page. Writers found Joyce's works worth reading, this ending implies, but the common reader did not. The public Joyce, as constructed yet again by this article, emphasizes his separation from the common reader.

## WHO READS *ULYSSES*?

The public Joyce remains embedded within a trope of difficulty, tied to the obscenity trial and Joyce's reputation for pornography, however subliminally, and separated from the academic Joyce through ridicule and satire. Simultaneously, however, the public Joyce's value as a commodity depends upon the very academic institution that serves as the object of ridicule. During the Joyce Wars this contradictory status reached an eruptive state that highlighted both discourses. Concurrent debates over the nature of the literary canon—often dubbed the "culture wars" in the press—were also taking place in both academic and non-academic circles. The confluence of the two found expression in the public organs of literary thought: Joyce, as shorthand for Literature, was seen as under assault by vaguely sinister forces that would seize authority over Joyce's words, rendering traditional notions of the author irrelevant (and by extension, the notion of the stable self). At the same time, anti-academic discourse appeared throughout the presentation of the debates themselves: at various times, the editorial disagreements were characterized as tempests in teapots, described as arcane, funny, trivial, or strange, and parodied as petty, personal, and preposterous, as the following chapters will discuss. The combatants themselves, in their letters to *The New York Review of Books* and *The Times Literary Supplement*, unintentionally contributed to such characterizations through their heated, sarcastic, and sniping remarks over matters which, to the public, seemed irrelevant to the act of reading. Further underscoring the alienation between the academy and the general public was the fact that the debate centered on a text deemed unreadable by much of the public, anyway. The outlines of the public Joyce and the academic Joyce were never clearer than during the Joyce Wars of the 1980's, when it became obvious that the two referred to the author of completely different texts, both titled *Ulysses* but being read for different purposes vis-à-vis Lyotard's *differend*.

This status as *differend* can begin to explain why an esoteric battle over editorial concerns found its way into the popular press. The "parallel but mutually exclusive practices" of the academic and the general reader briefly intersected, by virtue of the debate in the popular press, in a dispute over "ownership" of *Ulysses* between traditional editorial scholars and those espousing views of authorial intention as a chimera. *Ulysses* became a battleground within academia over the materiality of books. To the general public, this academic dispute advertised *Ulysses'* status as "special case" within literature, requiring specialized scholarly knowledge to even know what words Joyce actually wrote. The first Joyce War revealed that scholars, ostensibly explicating literature for the "lay people," were actually not concerned with readers at all. The Gabler *Critical and Synoptic Edition* of *Ulysses* was not produced in order to achieve, once and for all, what Joyce intended to publish for the reading audience, but rather to show, through careful editorial reconstruction, the pre-publication "ideal" text of *Ulysses,* a kind of Platonic and mystical origin for the imperfect material text. The reading text was secondary to such a project of scholarly mastery over Joyce's frustratingly haphazard writing and correcting process. The following chapter outlines the composition history of *Ulysses* and the editorial theories behind the disagreements over Gabler's edition.

NOTES

[1]Interestingly, in newspaper articles appearing in the *Irish Times*, it is the sensuality of Molly's monologue which becomes the dominant trope, and it is possible that because the ban on *Ulysses* was lifted there so much later than in the United States the sexual nature of the book at large is fresher in the public consciousness.

[2]Robert Spoo has argued that Ernst's strategy could have followed no other route in arguing the case of *Ulysses*. At the time, if a work was deemed pornographic in part then legally it was pornographic in toto, and so Ernst's strategy was "legally revolutionary; it was about contextualizing local bawdry within the larger achievement" (e-mail to the author 29 Apr. 2002). For Spoo, arguing (as Kelly does) that Ernst's strategy ignores the 'ethical potency' of a literary work is "abstract and unhistorical" and discounts the brilliance of Ernst's arguments. I would not disagree with Spoo's assessment of Ernst's strategy from a legal standpoint— but I maintain that Ernst's argument, as the general public came to know it through the trial's publicity and the inclusion of the decision in the American printing of *Ulysses*, fostered the status of *Ulysses* as *differend*: its obscenity exists as a separate discourse from its difficulty, and the trial strategy helped to make difficulty the dominant discourse of *Ulysses* for the American reading public.

[3]The fact that such a review appeared in a paper devoted primarily to sporting events parallels the Joyce Wars' appearance in popular periodicals seventy years later; both speak to cultural concerns over Joyce, albeit the earlier appearance indicates a concern with Joyce's pornography and the latter with Joyce's literary legacy. From the beginning, it is clear, Joyce's writing heralded something important for Anglo-American culture, although the historically determined nature of that importance diverged wildly.

[4]See Ellmann, 651–53; Beach, 201–06.

[5]See Beach, 64; Ellmann, 507–08.

⁶This photo essay and accompanying prose are also available in book form: *Three Days with Joyce, Photographs by Gisèle Freund* (New York: Persea Books, 1985).

⁷Curiously, the currency also prints the first line of *Finnegans Wake* rather than a quote from *Ulysses,* the work that brought Joyce to international prominence. Perhaps *Ulysses'* reputation in Ireland as primarily a "dirty book" made it inappropriate to include on the national currency. With Ireland's entry into the European Union the Joyce ten-pound note has been discontinued, although one can find them currently auctioned on E-Bay.

⁸These programs, however, were all cancelled in their first season, which may show that while Americans accept Irish stereotypes, they do not necessarily accept clichéd scriptwriting.

⁹Eamonn Slater, professor of Irish history and culture at Dublin's National Institute of Higher Education. Lecture on the relationship of Irish-Americans to stereotypes of Irish culture, Fall 1987.

¹⁰For recent examples, see R.B. Kershner, *Joyce, Bakhtin, and Popular Literature* (Chapel Hill: University of North Carolina, 1989) and (ed.) *Joyce and Popular Culture* (Gainesville: University Press of Florida, 1996); Cheryl Herr, *Joyce's Anatomy of Culture* (Urbana: University of Illinois Press, 1986); *and Joycean Cultures/Culturing Joyces*, edited by Vincent Cheng, Kimberly J. Devlin, and Margot Norris (Newark: University of Delaware Press, 1998).

¹¹Cheng mentions this appearance of *Ulysses* in a note as a parallel to the sexually-charged reading Brown gives the Monroe photograph ("The Joycean Unconscious" *n*2). Neither critic fully addresses the intellectual subtext of either the photograph or the television episode.

¹²An unintentional parody of the censorship and copyright issues plaguing editions of *Ulysses* occurs at the web site, as well. The authors include a disclaimer to the effect that the site is a parody, and invite readers to "[f]ollow the threatened litigation that engendered this disclaimer" by providing a hypertext link to letters sent by the legal firm representing the publishers of the "For Dummies" series, IDG Books Worldwide, Inc. The link leads to a page entitled, "Our Brush with Intellectual Property Litigation," which discloses that the authors received a notice of intent to sue for trademark infringement because they used the words "for Dummies." They also publish an earnestly sarcastic reply to this notice that includes threatened counter-litigation, in the form of a class action suit against IDG Books for defamation of character since the publishers "make such a significant buck by characterizing its readers as morons."

¹³Of the top ten, four were by Ayn Rand and three by L. Ron Hubbard. The remainder were *To Kill A Mockingbird* by Harper Lee, *1984* by George Orwell, and *The Lord of the Rings* by J.R.R. Tolkien. The only one of these books included on the Modern Library's list was *1984*.

# CHAPTER THREE

# EDITIONS IN PROGRESS,
## or,
# PREVENTING ACCIDENTALS
# IN THE TOME

*No matter what text Random House chooses to continue in print, from now on no edition can be definitive. We have lost our bibliographical innocence forever.*

—*Charles Rossman*

The incredibly tangled publishing history of *Ulysses* has been well documented in various books, scholarly articles, and reviews.[1] Such an interest in this history grew in relation to the explosion of genetic criticism in Joyce studies, and from the knowledge that, even from the first edition in 1922 published by Sylvia Beach's Shakespeare and Company, numerous errors were pointed out by Joyce himself. He put together a list of errata for the second printing, but by then he was absorbed with writing *Finnegans Wake* and left off doing further corrections himself. For the 1936 Bodley Head edition, Stuart Gilbert made corrections with Joyce's help, but corrections of *Ulysses* during Joyce's lifetime were sporadic at best. *Ulysses*, having never achieved error-free publication, remains firmly entrenched within the religious discourse of the sacred text—scholars quest to reach the true utterance of the author, the Holy Grail a definitive *Ulysses* as Joyce wrote it. Joyce becomes the unknowable consciousness that can only be located through a palimpsest, with the true word forever just out of reach. Such a subtext informs the editorial crusade called the Joyce Wars, and contributes to the fervor of the combatants. What follows is a recounting of that publishing history and the competing editorial theories of the first Joyce War.

### "A FUNNY LITTLE PUBLISHER"

Joyce composed *Ulysses* over a span of seven years, from 1914 to 1921. It was serialized in the American periodical *The Little Review*, beginning in 1918, and was subject to prosecution under American obscenity law. In fact, Jane Heap and Margaret Anderson, the editors of *The Little Review*,

were put on trial in 1920 and defended by John Quinn, who was later to
buy (at the urging of Ezra Pound) what became the Rosenbach manuscript.
In England, Harriet Shaw Weaver's magazine, *The Egoist*, serialized five
chapters in 1919, but objections from her printers and subscribers forced
her to abandon *Ulysses*. Weaver attempted to get Leonard and Virginia
Woolf's Hogarth Press to publish the book, but its size and Virginia
Woolf's own dislike for *Ulysses* blocked that avenue. Joyce, in the mean-
time, had been selling manuscript copies to John Quinn in America. When
Anderson and Heap lost their trial in 1921, Joyce went to Sylvia Beach in
Paris and sadly complained that his "book [would] never come out now."
She offered to publish *Ulysses* on the spot, and their long (and, for her,
sometimes exhausting) publishing relationship was established:

> All hope of publication in the English-speaking countries, at least for a
> long time to come, was gone. And here in my little shop sat James Joyce,
> sighing deeply.
>
> It occurred to me that something might be done, and I asked: "Would
> you let Shakespeare and Company do the honour of bringing out your
> *Ulysses*?"
>
> He accepted my offer immediately and joyfully. I thought it rash of him
> to entrust his great *Ulysses* to such a funny little publisher. But he seemed
> delighted, and so was I. (47)

There seems to be some discrepancy, though, over who asked whom to
publish the book; Noel Riley Fitch, in *Sylvia Beach and the Lost Generation*, quotes an early draft of Beach's memoirs: "I accepted with enthusiasm
Joyce's suggestion that I publish his book" (78). So it would seem that Joyce
might have planned to ask Beach to publish *Ulysses* for him. Fitch never offers an explanation for this discrepancy in Beach's drafts, but the thought
remains that Joyce, who was so adroit at asking for help from his friends
and patrons, had in fact found yet another soul to aid him in his literary
struggles and it seems likely that he did propose the venture to her first. It's
also entirely possible that he had mentioned it to Beach in some earlier conversation, and that when he learned of the trial's outcome (which virtually
assured that *Ulysses* would not be published at that point by anyone) she
was therefore prepared to offer her services as a publisher. These scenarios
are speculative, at best, but Joyce's known self-promotional abilities lead to
such speculation in light of the two versions of Beach's story.

The book was sent to a printer in Dijon named Darantiere. None of the
typesetters spoke English except the foreman, who edited Joyce's admittedly nonstandard text heavily throughout all eleven printings in the shop.
Joyce wrote a full third of the novel in the proof stages, and so the difficulties of catching errors in this situation proved enormous. Because of his
failing eyesight Joyce's handwriting was at times illegible, and while the ad-
vantages of typesetters not knowing the language (and thus not being able
to object to what they were setting) were great, this ignorance also affected

the accuracy of the typesetting process. Several of those who typed up the manuscripts (mostly women friends of Sylvia Beach, or even friends of friends) refused to complete them or, as in one story, the husband of one typist threw the manuscript of Circe into the fire when he read what she was typing.[2] John Quinn had to be cabled to make copies of his manuscript, and he at first refused; but he was persuaded to make photographic copies and, since it was a "fair copy," it was more legible than the prior manuscript. These manuscript copies were then typed and sent off immediately to Darantiere.[3]

*Ulysses* was being rushed through in order to comply with Joyce's wish that it come out on his fortieth birthday, February 2, 1922. Darantiere made sure that two copies were ready on that date (one for Beach and one for Joyce), and the rest followed some weeks later. The unusual printing situation, the rushed nature of the job, and Joyce's eye trouble virtually guaranteed that errors would occur in the first edition. In a letter to Harriet Shaw Weaver, quoted repeatedly throughout the Joyce Wars, he wrote: "I am extremely irritated by all these printer's errors. Working as I do amid piles of notes at the table in a hotel I cannot possibly do this mechanical work with my wretched eye and a half. Are these to be perpetuated in future editions? I hope not" (*Letters I* 176). Joyce made some corrections for the second printing and was involved with various translations of the book, but his growing interest in *Finnegans Wake* soon eclipsed further involvement in the printing fate of *Ulysses*.

The errors in the 1922 edition, while considerable, might have been tolerable had *Ulysses* not undergone further vicissitudes during its voyage toward publication in the English-speaking world. As its reputation grew, it became a highly demanded item that had to be smuggled into the United States. Its status as both banned object and work of genius gave it an almost fetishistic power, and it became a mark of literary sophistication to own one (even if the owner never actually got around to reading anything but the parts considered obscene, most notably "Circe" and "Penelope"[4]). Because it could not be reprinted in the United States within the prescribed period for securing a U. S. copyright, the first edition could not secure legal protection against pirating. Samuel Roth in New York began doing so in *Two Worlds Monthly*, a magazine he started for that purpose. This piracy, and the money lost to Joyce because of it, spurred Joyce's decision to get *Ulysses* published legally in America. Even more errors were introduced into the pirated edition and, extraordinarily, Random House used this version as the basis for the first American publication in 1934, once the favorable Woolsey ruling was in. Two years later, the Bodley Head version was published in Great Britain, and was reprinted in 1941, 1947, and 1949, and reset in 1960; the Random House version was reprinted in 1940 using corrected plates from the 1934 edition, and was reset completely in 1961. This 1961 version was called on the dust flap a "scrupulously corrected" text but errors still existed, as pointed out by Jack Dalton some years later (see below).

After a seven-year project in which he used computers to reconstruct *Ulysses* from the manuscripts rather than the printed editions, Hans Walter Gabler's *Critical and Synoptic Edition* appeared in 1984; the trade version derived from the critical text was published in 1986, which then became the only version available in the United States at that point. The ensuing controversy over the Gabler edition, initiated by John Kidd, finally prompted Random House to reissue the 1961 edition, and the Garland Press-issued *Critical and Synoptic Edition* went out of print in 1990 (a complete history of the Gabler edition is detailed later in this chapter). In 1997, the Oxford University Press World's Classics issued an annotated 1922 edition, and in the same year Danis Rose's *Reader's Edition* appeared. John Kidd's edition through W.W. Norton is reportedly embroiled in legal difficulties with the Joyce Estate over copyright.

While copyright may seem like an arcane tangent of the editing controversy, it is actually at the center of most of the furor. *Ulysses* is a lucrative property for the Joyce estate, and the estate's role in the Gabler edition's troubles cannot be overemphasized. The relationship of *Ulysses* to the copyright laws of the United States and Britain is unclear at best. In 1922, the copyright laws of Britain had established (since the 1911 Copyright Act) the length of the author's lifetime plus 50 years after his death as the copyright period, and this rule covered all published works. Substantial revision with new material added renews the copyright in the changed work, but the original edition's copyright is unaffected. Therefore, the copyright of the 1922 edition (and all other versions which appeared before the author's death, since they were based on this edition and not substantially revised) ran out on January 1, 1992. The Joyce estate currently has a copyright only for the Gabler edition and the reading text derived from it.[5] But the situation in the United States is completely muddled, in part due to the isolationist policies followed by Congress in the early part of the twentieth century.

In 1922, United States copyright law dictated that English-language works published abroad but seeking American copyright had to be deposited in Washington within 60 days of such publication, and the manufacturing clause required that the work then had to be published inside American territories within four months of the deposit of the original edition. This clause, obviously, benefited domestic book publishers. Once this requirement was satisfied, the work then had to be registered to confirm the copyright, which meant that a copy of the American edition had to be deposited. The difficulties of obtaining a copyright in America for *Ulysses* in 1922 under those terms are obvious. In 1976, Congress passed a Copyright Act which changed the copyright term to 75 years from first publication for works published before 1978; the original act gave up to 56 years of protection which, if *Ulysses* had been published in the U.S. in 1922, would have meant that the copyright expired at the end of 1978. But the 1976 Act, due to the length of time it took for the legislation to pass (14 years altogether), grandfathered those works which would have expired before the Act was passed; their copyright terms were extended to fulfill the new 75 year limit and *Ulysses* would then have been protected until the end of 1997. As it was, *Ulysses* was not published in the United States until 1934, supposedly giving it a copyright until 2009. But since *Ulysses'* copyright history is tangled up with its labyrinthine publishing fate in the United States, copyright protection for the American printing of Joyce's most famous work might not exist at all.

The copyright which Random House filed for in 1934 gives four dates: 1918, 1919, 1920, and 1934. The first three dates were added with the name Margaret Anderson, the editor and copyright holder of *The Little Review*. Thus, the portions which were published in *The Little Review*, covering thirteen full episodes and part of a fourteenth (those portions published before the *Review* was prosecuted), were claimed under those dates; the 1934 claim covered the unpublished balance of the fourteenth and the full remaining episodes. But the version published was typeset from a pirated setting of the 1922 first edition—which was not copyrighted in the United States at all—and was very different from those materials printed in the *Review*, since Joyce had revised all the episodes for the first edition. Therefore, the copyright claims are for a text posited as a satisfactory whole, but in fact is composed of portions which are nothing like what was claimed for copyright dates 1918–1920, and a corrupted remainder which was later corrected. According to Bruce Arnold,

> [t]he differences between the parts of *Ulysses* which were actually copyrighted and the version of *Ulysses* printed in 1934 are more substantial than the differences between the accepted, pre-Gabler version of the book and his revised version. . . . [T]here is . . . no justification for claiming that any earlier version of *Ulysses* . . . enjoys any copyright in the United States at all. *Ulysses*, as subsequently revised and now out in a reprint based on the 1961 edition, and offered by Random House as an alternative to *Ulysses: The Corrected Text*, is not copyright in the United States and never has been. ( 85)

While Arnold's conclusions are arguable, it is clear that a great deal of room for dispute exists for the copyright status of *Ulysses* in the United States.

When Gabler approached the Joyce estate in 1975 with the idea of editing the text from the manuscript up, copyright was not his main concern. But certainly such concern was part of the Joyce estate's motivation for approving such a project; the estate consulted "an eminent American lawyer" who advised them that "the 'new' material would be protected to December 31, 2027" (du Sautoy 72). Presumably, this information was based on the amendments made to copyright law in the United States prior to 1976;[6]

for works created before January 1, 1978, but not published or registered
by that date, the law had been changed to read as follows:

> These works have been automatically brought under the statute and are
> now given Federal copyright protection. The duration of copyright . . .
> will generally be . . . life [of the author]-plus-50 [years] . . . The law pro-
> vides that in no case will the term of copyright for works in this category
> expire before December 31, 2002, and for works published on or before
> December 31, 2002, the term of copyright will not expire before Decem-
> ber 31, 2027. ("Copyright Basics")

But this portion of the law only applies to works *created but not published* by 1978. The law clearly states that any work published before 1978
is protected only for a total of 75 years from the publication date, meaning
that *Ulysses* was not affected by this extension to 2027 at all. Presumably,
the new material in the Gabler edition was considered to be unpublished
before the required date, and it is on this supposition that the attorney advised the Joyce estate. As du Sautoy makes clear, the estate was well aware
that any new copyright secured would not affect the original: "it must be
stressed that nothing would affect the period of protection that already applied to the original text of *Ulysses*. The period of extension applies to
'new' material written by Joyce himself, extracted from proofs, manuscripts, etc., not to the rest of the text" (72).

Parts of the Gabler edition fall under the portion of the law covering
"works made for hire" and the copyright at the time extended on this
material for "75 years from publication or 100 years from creation, which-
ever is shorter" ("Copyright Basics").[7] A search of the United States copyright records reveals that Gabler holds two separate copyrights for his
edition: he received the 1984 copyright for the "foreword, acknowledge-
ments, presentation of genetic synopsis, and notes," and a copyright for
the "afterword" of the 1986 trade edition printed as *Ulysses: The Corrected Text*. The Trustees of the Joyce estate (listed as "employer for hire")
received a 1984 copyright for "draft texts, reading text, editing, and compilation." Random House, also listed as "employer for hire," holds the
copyright for "editorial revisions[,] new preface[, and] new afterword" to
the 1986 trade edition.[8] Thus the estate and the publisher received a copyright on the edited reading text, and here is where critics of the trade edition leveled serious charges at the estate, saying that the whole project was
rushed through to secure copyright and that the scholarship suffered as a
result. But it would seem that the copyright issues raised by critics of the
edition are simply a chimera; the estate was well aware that the 1922
*Ulysses*, flaws and all, would still enter the public domain as scheduled.

But with the Gabler reading text suddenly the only one available in the
United States in 1986, Random House and the Joyce estate essentially enjoyed copyright protection for a "new" text, for at least another forty-one
years. The imprimatur of being the "corrected" text of *Ulysses* was sup-

posed to guarantee the Gabler edition preeminence over any printing of the 1922 edition, virtually assuring the estate of income and making any other edition unworthy of scholarly study (and therefore unworthy of classroom use as well). The outcome of the Joyce Wars was that the Gabler reading text has now been changed to "The Gabler Edition" and Random House has reissued the flawed 1961 version. Furthermore, the Joyce estate is attempting to block the publication of John Kidd's edition, and has so far succeeded; they are in the midst of negotiations with Kidd's publisher, W.W. Norton, Inc., over permission and copyright status, with the estate claiming that *Ulysses* in America is copyrighted until 2009, based on the publication date of 1934. But as this edition is in essence derived from the 1922 version it possibly is only copyrighted until 1998, when the 1922 edition would have entered the public domain. The future of the Kidd edition is cloudy, at best. The Rose edition, published in Britain, took advantage of a change in British copyright law and avoided copyright claims by the Joyce estate: in 1995 British law became compliant with European copyright law which allows a 70 year term after an author's death, but this change occurred three years after *Ulysses* came out of copyright under the old law.[9] For three years, *Ulysses* was in the public domain in Britain, and the Rose edition—in progress while the text was out of copyright protection—was able to go forward without notifying the Joyce estate or paying a fee for permission.[10] The copyright questions in the United States, however, are still being debated between W.W. Norton and the Joyce estate, and as a result Kidd's edition remains unpublished.[11]

### PROBLEMS WITH THE 1961 RANDOM HOUSE EDITION

After its appearance the 1961 edition was the preferred text for scholars in the United States, until in 1966 a scholar named Jack Dalton gave a lecture at Cornell University on "Textual Criticism and James Joyce" (a lecture which later turned into a seminar, and thence into a paper delivered at the 1969 James Joyce Symposium in Dublin). Dalton's piece was published in the collection *New Light on Joyce from the Dublin Symposium*, edited by Fritz Senn, in 1972. In his lively essay, Dalton meticulously compares readings from several editions as well as the manuscripts, and calculates that roughly 4,000 errors occur in the 1961 text:

> . . . the old edition had been, of course, an early collateral descendant of the first edition, whereas the new edition was a lineal descendant. The new edition, far from being 'scrupulously corrected,' was merely a reprint, with some new errors, of the 1960 English resetting. It was the fifth successive resetting of type since the first edition; each edition had been copied from the one preceding. Some 1,700 errors had accumulated in thirty-five years of resetting, and most of these errors were, in 1961, already at least twenty-five years old and had appeared in at least three successive settings. And then there were well over 2,000 corruptions which

went back to the manuscripts, things which had *never* been printed correctly. (102)

Dalton further elucidates the reason for so many transmissional errors:
"many of the reprint transmission errors date from 1936, the first edition
set in England. . . . Before the limited 1936 edition was issued the following year in a trade edition, the publishers . . . did considerable proofread-
ing and correcting before photoreducing it. But when they came to reset it
in 1960 they chose as their copy-text the limited edition, no doubt because
its type was so much larger and more readable. Thus the 1937 proofread-
ing was bypassed and lost" (107). In short, Dalton points out that not only
was it the appalling conditions under which *Ulysses* was composed and
printed in 1922, but it was also the apparently haphazard resetting process
after the first edition that contributed to the error-ridden state of the book.

Dalton's piece exposed the mess of *Ulysses*' publishing history in detail—and more importantly, what it meant for interpretation—to literary
scholars for the first time in a wide forum. Until then most Joyceans, like
many other literary critics, felt that textual scholarship was somehow unrelated to the work of interpreting texts; the physical appearance of a work
seemed an arcane concern. This divide between textual and literary theorists was bridged decisively in the controversy over the Gabler edition,
when Joycean literary scholars suddenly found themselves needing a crash
course on editorial methodology in order to understand why this much-
heralded definitive text was suddenly being torn to shreds. The controversy
forced Joyceans to discard what Philip Cohen has called "a sort of willful
blindness" in "[p]ursuing foundational or antifoundational explanations
of literary phenomena without knowing about or attempting to account
for the varying material circumstances of the production of texts—their
composition, revision, dissemination, and transmission" (xii). Disregard-
ing authorial intentions (a project institutionalized by the New Critics
and further developed by structuralists and other postmodern theorists)
negates investigation of text-constitution because such investigation places
textual production firmly within social and historical constraints. The controversy over the Gabler edition forced Joyceans to "grapple with the onto-
logical implications of the fact that a literary work more often than not
exists in a variety of textual states" (Cohen, xiii). The unique method
which Gabler employed in his *Critical and Synoptic Edition*, actually a
combination of German editorial methods relying heavily on structuralist
theories and the eclectic school of editing in the Greg-Bowers tradition,
forced Joyce scholars for the first time to confront the fact that *Ulysses* as a
unified, stable text does not actually exist—theoretically or even physically.

EDITORIAL THEORY AND PRAXIS

In traditional editorial practice dating from the appearance in 1949 of Sir
Walter Greg's seminal "The Rationale of Copy-Text" (reprinted in *Studies*

*in Bibliography* 3: 19–36) the general rule is that if a variant in texts is directly attributable to authorial intervention ("active authorization") then it must be admitted into the edited text; if a variant is obviously due to transmissional errors (typographical misspellings, miscopying, etc.) then it is to be corrected; if a variant is not known to be attributable to the author ("indifferent variants") then it must be determined whether or not it satisfies two requirements: "(1) whether the original reading is one that can be reasonably attributed to the author, and (2) whether the later reading is one that the author can reasonably be supposed to have substituted for the former" (Greg 32). If the answer to the first question is yes, and the second no, then the earlier reading should be kept. If the answer to the first is no, and the second yes, then the later reading must be assumed to be authorial revision and kept. If the answer to both is yes, then the variant must also be considered authorial revision and kept (Greg 32). This formulation merely stated in methodological terms what editors had been doing all along, and places authorial intention as something that can be divined and followed. Greg also makes distinctions between "substantives" and "accidentals" in variations: a substantive is that which affects "the author's meaning or the essence of his expression"; an accidental is that which affects "mainly its formal presentation," such as "spelling, punctuation, word-division, and the like" (Greg 21). An editor must follow the accidentals of a base text, using the one which comes earliest in the stemma (or linear history of textual descent) and therefore is closest to the original manuscript; but the editor must be free to exercise judgment on substantives in the case of what he calls an "indifferent" variant, i.e., one for which there is no clear evidence of authorial intervention. In this way, the editor is not bound by versions of a work which repeatedly transmit incorrect (non-authorial) variations, and can produce a text that most closely resembles what the author presumably wrote.

Greg's principles were further refined by Fredson Bowers, editor of *Studies in Bibliography* until his death in 1991, and with whom Gabler worked as a post-doctoral fellow at the University of Virginia. Bowers points out that Greg's rationale was mainly concerned with the peculiar editing difficulties present in the sixteenth- and seventeenth-century English texts which were Greg's field, and that dogmatic application of the rationale to later literary works was not the intended outcome of Greg's project:

> Greg himself visualized only a Renaissance textual situation; nevertheless, . . . most of his conclusions are . . . pertinent to texts of any later period . . . whenever the transmissional conditions are the same.
>       . . . Throughout Greg's discussion he never mentions the relative authority of a holograph manuscript as against that either of a scribal manuscript or the printed book that ultimately derived from the holograph with or without the author's supervision. Since Elizabethan authorial manuscripts of works that saw print can be counted just about on the fingers of

one hand, it seems evident that Greg saw no point in considering a contin-
gency that was unlikely to arise. (94)

Bowers points out that Greg's distinctions apply to collateral manuscripts, and that the choice of copy-text was necessarily an expedient one
for Renaissance scholars; because of the attempts, over time, of editors to
modernize the spelling (by either changing it to conform with current
practice or simply trying to make it consistent within the document), the
choice of a copy-text must be made based on accidentals, i.e., that text
which comes earliest in the stemma must summarily be closest to the author's own text, and therefore this text must be used as a base. But editors
must be free to choose substantives from any of the texts on the stemma,
based on the three-pronged rationale outlined above. Being confined to
the substantives of a particular version is what Greg called the "tyranny of
the copy-text," and what he was attempting to find a systematic way to
escape.

Bowers discusses some chief differences in editorial decision-making
when confronted with works published in later periods, most notably for
our understanding of Gabler's methods those dealing with "multiple authority"—those texts which exist as branches of the same tree of textual
descent. Editors of modern works have far more pre-publication materials
to consider than editors of Renaissance works, including holographs, typescripts, proofs, and serialized published versions of works, all of which
may show some evidence of authorial revision in both substantives and accidentals. Bowers lays out three principles for editors of modern works as
corollaries to Greg's rationale:

> First, evidence must exist, or be conjectured with major probability, that
> the author revised his text not only in the substantives but with more than
> casual attention to the accidentals; second, evidence should be sought that
> the printer of the revised text was relatively faithful to his copy, or was
> made so by scrupulous authorial proofreading, so that the author's acci-
> dental texture has not been restyled in any thoroughgoing way. If these
> two criteria are met, then . . . an editor needs to examine his collations of
> the variant accidentals to determine what categories are manifestly autho-
> rial and what are manifestly compositorial. . . . [T]he probability . . . that
> a majority of the generally unassignable accidental variants is authorial or
> compositorial should be the ultimate determinant in the selection of a
> copy-text as between two authorities, whether an original and a revised
> edition, or two collateral editions. (146–149)

Bowers develops Greg's rationale in terms of authorial intention, believ-
ing that most variants needing emendation are transmissional in nature
and therefore a copy-text should be chosen based on substantives (what
comes closest to what the author intended, which is not necessarily the earliest text). Greg's rationale was developed in a context where no manuscripts were available; Bowers attempts to modify Greg's rationale to deal

with the specific historical situation of nineteenth- and twentieth-century texts, when manuscripts, proofs, and the like are usually readily available. G. Thomas Tanselle, a prominent editor in the Greg-Bowers tradition who comes to figure in the Gabler debate, elucidates this tradition clearly:

> . . . an editor has less to go on when judging variants in punctuation and spelling than when judging variants in wording, and for that reason the text chosen as copy-text often supplies most of the punctuation and spelling for the critical text. But the editor is free, of course, to make rational decisions regarding [these] when evidence permits; . . . a copy-text is simply the text most likely to provide an authorial reading . . . at points of variation where one cannot otherwise reach a decision. ("Recent Editorial Discussion" 64)

Thus was the state of Anglo-American editorial practice when Gabler came as a post-doctoral student to the University of Virginia. German textual editing practice followed much the same lines of the Greg-Bowers tradition, until the mid- to late-1960s. At that time, German editorial theory was influenced by structuralist linguistic theory, and the German school diverged from the Greg-Bowers tradition in fundamental ways. In an article translated into English by Gabler (1975), Hans Zeller delineates these differences and the reasons for them. The root of the disagreements over the 1984 *Ulysses* is Gabler's method, which combined elements from both schools and therefore led to charges of inconsistency.

Zeller raises three questions in relation to traditional editing practice: "(1) Is contamination admissible, that is to say, may the editor transfer variants from one authorised version to another, as . . . the Greg-Bowers principles require? (2) What is meant by the (final or non-final) intention of the author, and how may it be determined? (3) What should be regarded as textual error?" (236). The first question, and the most relevant one to the Gabler *Ulysses*, he answers by discussing his definition of "version," which is informed by structuralist and formalist linguistic theory: "the text [is] a complex of elements which form a system of signs, both denoting (*signifiant*) and denoted (*signifie*). That it is a system means that the work consists not of its elements but of the relationships between them" (240). This definition then determines that

> a version is a specific system of linguistic signs, functioning within and without, and authorial revisions transform it into another system. . . . [I]n principle, a new version comes into existence through a single variant [which] has an effect on invariant sections of the text. In considering different versions one must therefore not confine one's attention to the variants. . . . Fundamentally, therefore, whether the variants are numerous and of far-reaching effect is not a necessary condition for the constitution of a version. A new version implies a new intention. (240–41)

Zeller describes the textual history of a work (the actual documents which an editor has access to) as "a 3-dimensional cylinder standing upright [where] the different versions are horizontal planes perpendicular to the axis of the cylinder" (244). He states that a historical-critical edition must create a reproduction of this cylinder by giving the complete textual history, and that a critical edition creates a reproduction of a particular plane, or an individual version. Projecting one plane upon another would constitute what Zeller calls "contamination" (244). He declares that a historical-critical edition's editor

> selects one version (or, when there are substantial differences between the versions, more than one) for reproductions as the text in his edition, and he presents the remaining textual history (or possibly all of it) in the apparatus. From a historical point of view the different versions are in theory of equal value. . . . For the editor there is no "best version." In selecting the text to be edited he is not bound by the final intention of the author. . . . As long as the editor sees his function as that of a historian, he has a wide range of freedom in the selection of the version for the edited text, but this version he must reproduce without contamination. (244–45)

Gabler followed this theory in creating the synoptic edition of *Ulysses,* which shows all variants in the manuscript documents and thus creates the cylinder described by Zeller. But the largest innovation in his edition of *Ulysses,* what he calls a "continuous manuscript text," was assembled by the computer from the existing fragmentary pieces of *Ulysses.* This text was created by the computer from the sequence of the manuscript documents showing the genetic development of *Ulysses* as a whole, going from fair copy to what Joyce wrote on the typescripts to what he wrote on the proofs. This "continuous manuscript text" is, in some ways, similar to what might have been produced if Joyce had written out *Ulysses* on one long piece of paper, à la Jack Kerouac's typing of *On the Road.* It is this assembled simulacrum of a continuous manuscript for *Ulysses* that Gabler chose as his copy-text to produce the reading text which, in Gabler's claim, comes closest to what Joyce actually wrote. While it would seem on the surface that such a procedure contaminated one plane with another, contrary to Zeller's principles, what Gabler in effect did was create an entirely new plane that never actually existed in any concrete sense.

Gabler's own explanation of his rationale can be found in the edition itself:

> The first edition of 1922, then, is *Ulysses* as Joyce allowed it to go before the public. . . . Yet, as Joyce himself was the first to be aware, the text it carries is corrupt. Joyce's helpers, as well as many a conscientious later proofreader in the course of the book's publishing history, attempted . . . to mend it at the surface. For the critical edition of 1984 we chose a different approach, endeavouring to *attack the corruption at the roots.* . . . The rich array of surviving documents that record the work's development made it possible *to catch the text before these corruptions occurred and to rebuild* Ulysses *as Joyce wrote it.* . . . The core of [the critical edition] is an edited synoptic analysis of the growth of the text through all

stages of composition and revision from the fair copies or final working drafts to the first edition. *The synopsis represents an innovative method of displaying a text as it constituted itself in the process of writing.* Jointly with a conventional scholarly apparatus, it records the documentary evidence and explains and justifies all editorial decisions. It is also a critically relevant text of *Ulysses* in its own right. Its final extrapolation is a reading text which in the critical edition accompanies the synopsis, but which in the present edition is set forth by itself, to stand on its own merits. (649; my emphasis)

The emphasized phrases point to a subtext of reverence for the "true" text from Joyce's hand, an exaltation of the writing process itself, and thus enters the discourse of the sacred text and the sacralized author. This subtext works against the kind of structuralist, text-centered theory which Zeller promotes and points to a fundamental conflict between Gabler's methods and his overall aim, which was to produce an ideal text that reproduces the word according to Joyce, free from imperfections.

The critical edition indeed does follow Zeller's dictum for such editions: it presents a historical view of the development of the text, the collected version of the continuous manuscript text. As Gabler states in his explanation, the synoptic text shows all variants available, and "justifies" the editorial decisions made. For Gabler, the heart of this project was the synoptic text; as a view of the "cylinder" of *Ulysses*, it is breathtaking. Yet most of the vehement criticism leveled against the Gabler edition is not aimed at this synoptic text but rather at the reading text on the recto, later published alone to "stand on its own merits" as *Ulysses: The Corrected Text* in 1986. Without the critical apparatus on the verso, the reading text is presented as the definitive edition of Joyce's work.

WONDER DID HE WROTE IT HIMSELF?[12]

Many poststructuralist textual scholars hailed Gabler's critical edition as a breakthrough.[13] Jerome McGann called the *Critical and Synoptic Edition* "*prima facie* important," and analyzes Gabler's achievement in terms of its "methodological significance . . . in its immediate historical context" ("*Ulysses* as a Postmodern Text" 284). McGann's own prominence as a poststructuralist textual scholar was established with his book, *A Critique of Modern Textual Criticism*, which appeared a year before Gabler's *Ulysses: A Critical and Synoptic Edition*. McGann's book is a thoughtful and provocative critique of the Greg-Bowers-Tanselle school of editing, and helped change the face of textual scholarship: "while intention and authorial presence are still important topics in textual debate (how could it be otherwise?), in the last decade there has been a shift in attention to those social, institutional, and collaborative models of creation and production emphasized by McGann" (Greetham x).

McGann criticizes the belief, developed by Tanselle following Greg-Bowers, that "the theory of copy-text will ensure an edition that 'reflects [the author's], rather than someone else's, intentions' [and] assumes that any editorial intervention at the work's point of origin constitutes a contamination of the authoritative text" (*Critique* 34). This belief, according to McGann, disregards the historical facts that book production in the later modern periods can involve a close relationship between the author and the publishing house (*Critique* 34–35). He blames this misreading of the historical situation of book production on traditional textual editorial adherence to the principles developed from Greg's theory, which Greg developed from his study of Renaissance texts. McGann states that Greg set aside the issue of an author's final intentions because, without a manuscript or revised proofs as evidence, such intentions could not be determined (*Critique* 40). Bowers took Greg's theory beyond this understanding of authorial intentions because he was dealing with texts for which there was ample, and often contradictory, evidence of such intentions in the form of proofs, typescripts, and other revisions in addition to the printed texts (which sometimes exist in variant forms as well). Such evidence, though, also points to the intervention of publishers, particularly in accidentals. Publishing house rules often dictated changes to an author's punctuation and spelling, and such changes were usually agreed to by the author. Other kinds of intervention in the text exist as well; for example, editors frequently made revision suggestions to the authors before going to print,[14] and McGann offers the example of Mary Shelley making alterations to texts she copied for Byron, with these alterations being approved or changed by the author. McGann's challenge to the traditional editing establishment is based on his own ideology of the literary work as a social text:

> Authority is a social nexus, not a personal possession; and if the authority for specific literary works is initiated anew for each new work by some specific artist, its initiation takes place in a necessary and integral historical environment of great complexity. Most immediately—and this is what concerns us here—it takes place within the conventions and enabling limits that are accepted by the prevailing institutions of literary production—conventions and limits which exist for the purpose of generating and supporting literary production.
> 
> ...When we speak of the working relations which exist between author and publishing institutions, we obviously do not mean to suggest that final authority for literary works rests with institutional persons other than the author. . . . The point to be emphasized, however, is that those relations of production do not sanction a theory of textual criticism based upon the concept of the autonomy of the author. "Final authority" for literary works rests neither with the author nor with his affiliated institution; it resides in the actual structure of the agreements which these two cooperating authorities reach in specific cases. (*Critique* 48–54)

McGann states that the choice of a version to edit from, contrary to the Greg-Bowers-Tanselle school, does not need to rely on the concept of author's intentions because such a concept "hypothesizes two related phenomena which do not and cannot exist: an autonomous author, and an ideal ('finally intended') text" as a heuristic device to focus the editing task (*Critique* 56). In short, McGann theorizes that the ideal of a definitive text is unreachable, a supposition which Gabler supports.[15] This conclusion has been gaining ground in textual editing circles and importantly, through controversies like the one surrounding the Gabler edition of *Ulysses*, in literary criticism as well.

Indeed, the appearance of Gabler's edition of *Ulysses* provoked McGann to hail it as a step forward in textual editing: "[m]ore clearly and practically than any of the recent spate of theoretical work in criticism and hermeneutics, this edition raises . . . all the central questions that have brought such a fruitful crisis to literary work in the postmodern period" ("*Ulysses* as a Postmodern Text" 284). McGann analyses the *Critical and Synoptic Edition* based on Gabler's stated goal of elucidating the compositional process of writing: "Gabler's 'continuous manuscript text' is a hypothesized reconstruction of a text which displays Joyce working out what Gabler seems to regard as his final authorial intentions"; the reading text "reconstitutes, in a completed rather than genetic form, the text of 'the author's final intentions'" (289). McGann points out that Hugh Kenner's 1984 review of the Gabler edition incorrectly advertised the reading text as "a final version that would have been arrived at if no one had made any mistakes" (*TLS* 13 July: 771; qtd. "*Ulysses* as a Postmodern Text" 290). McGann rightly says that Gabler's conception of *Ulysses* is entirely different from that of an editor who was aiming for a corrected version of the 1922 edition:

> . . . such an edition would represent a "correct" text of *Ulysses*. Would such a text mean that Gabler's text is "incorrect"?
>
> The answer is no, for the simple and obvious reason that we are dealing with two different conceptions of "the text of *Ulysses*." Gabler's is an imagination of Joyce's work and not its reconstruction. . . . Gabler's edition does not give us the work which Joyce wanted to present to the public; rather, he gives us a text in which we may observe Joyce at work, alone, before he turns to meet his public. Given his purposes, then, Gabler is entirely correct to declare the synoptic text to be the most important feature of his edition. The "reading text" is of secondary importance. (290–91)

McGann states that Gabler's synoptic text reveals "in a precise and concrete way" the "idea of textual instability" and shows

> that another text of *Ulysses* can be imagined and concretely rendered—a text that does not simply offer a large mass of minor textual variations from the previously conceived text, but that completely overhauls *the way*

*we might think about the text as a whole.* . . . A number of different
*Ulysses* begin to occupy the space of critical possibility [and] some of
these *Ulysses* will represent themselves, at the surface, as more stable than
others. (291; original italics)

McGann hails the synoptic text as a visible rendering of the postmodern
idea of textual instability while acknowledging that the reading text seems
stable because "certain conventions of reading" allow us to see it that way.
McGann postulates that once the diacritical language which marks the
synoptic text is mastered, we can immerse ourselves in a protean *Ulysses*
which truly shows the fluid act of writing. He also states that he imagines
that a completely different genetic text of *Ulysses* might be conceived
which would show "the history of the work's initial production rather than
its initial composition—the author's rather than the writer's *Ulysses*"; such
a work would serve as a copy-text for a critically emended 1922 edition
(292). Such distinctions between the "writer" and the "author" are a hall-
mark of postmodern thinking, in which the act of writing is separated from
the act of publicly presenting the written work, and show McGann's own
ideological assumptions about the nature of texts in general.

   McGann further differentiates the Gabler edition from a traditional editorial project: "In an earlier edition the 'clear text' on the rectos would
have been the editor's ultimate object of interest. In Gabler's work, on the
contrary, it has to be regarded as a supplementary aid in the reading of the
synoptic text, which is this edition's chief goal and ultimate concern"
(297). This distinction is a crucial one, and it is the misunderstanding
about the reading text's role in Gabler's project which caused the Joyce estate and the publishers to label the 1986 edition "The Corrected Text." Divorcing the reading text from the synoptic text is equivalent to publishing
an appendix or set of endnotes without the text which it elucidates, and as
a result the reading edition was presented to the world as a traditionally
edited critical edition, with the attendant impressions that it was "definitive." McGann's essay appeared before the reading text did, and does not
wrestle with the implications of such a procedure. His essay is significant,
however, in that it examines Gabler's project on its own terms and was an
early postmodernist champion of the Gabler editorial method.[16]

   Of course, as Geert Lernout has pointed out in an essay supporting
Gabler's work as an example of postmodern European editorial methods,
"McGann's support for Gabler's edition seems to be motivated more by
tactical reasons than by real sympathy, given that the basic thrust of
Gabler's approach runs counter to McGann's own position" ("Anglo-
American Textual Criticism"). While Lernout's analysis here of McGann's
motives is probably correct, when he goes on to conclude that McGann
"was so keen on accepting an edition that went beyond Greg-Bowers-
Tanselle that he was blind to some of its real features," he does McGann a
disservice. McGann was well aware of the differences in textual orienta-

tion between his own position and Gabler's, namely that of emphasis on post-production and pre-production genetic editing; he calls in his essay for "close studies of its methodology, its execution, and its archival basis before we know how well and carefully Gabler has carried out his work," and in a note appended to this statement he mentions John Kidd's paper, "Errors of Execution" as an "important critique," and that "[s]cholars have yet to assess fully the lines of criticism which Kidd's paper has opened up" (284; *n*7). It is clear that, while certainly McGann was "keen" on Gabler's project as an advance over the traditional textual editing methods, he also exhibited scholarly caution. This caution, however, may be over-shadowed by his theoretical enthusiasm in the essay.

Another respected voice in editorial circles is that of Peter Shillingsburg who, like McGann, also does away with the idea of a definitive critical edition. Shillingsburg's *Scholarly Editing in the Computer Age* (1986) gives a comprehensive view of the history of textual editing and offers a useful schema for the competing camps. He names four categories of editorial orientation towards texts: the documentary, the authorial, the social, and the aesthetic (18–30). Each category will emphasize a different place for textual authority, and Shillingsburg notes that "[t]hese competing views cannot be melded into one as long as the underlying assumption about the goal of scholarly editions remains the establishment of a single finished-product text" ("The Autonomous Author, the Sociology of Texts, and the Polemics of Textual Criticism" 26). He offers instead the view that scholarly editions would "organize and present works primarily as *process* not primarily as *product*," and that scholarly editors are not guardians of correct texts ("Autonomous Author" 26–27). They would, in this paradigm, be historians of the text's various textual incarnations, from manuscript to printed edition (much like Zeller's definition of a historical critical edition), and offer what Shillingsburg calls a "comprehensive view of textual criticism" which would not allow literary critics to remain "blissfully ignorant" of the text's composition and production. In effect, Gabler's *Critical and Synoptic Edition* does just that; it is the reading text, which was offered as the "correct" text, that contradicts the postmodern editorial practice spelled out by McGann, Shillingsburg, Zeller, and even Gabler himself.

The crux of the contradictions between eclectic editors and poststructuralist editors (which term encompasses German structuralists and McGann/Shillingsburg New Historicists, among others) is simply that eclectic editors center the author's intentions and postmodern editors situate the author among many other factors involved in producing a text. It cannot be denied that authors produce texts, but editors like McGann and Shillingsburg make a strong case for the contextual framework of culture which also influences a text's production. An editor operating under the social theory of editing would point out that, even when errors were introduced by typists or printers, Joyce often used them as creative springboards, working these errors into the text during revision and making them integral parts of the finished product. In effect, the typists or printers became co-creators of the text of *Ulysses*. Such a textual situation involving a writer known for his strong control over even the paper used for printing leads to serious questions for the editor in the Greg-Bowers-Tanselle school. The earliest manuscript of *Ulysses* is incomplete, and the Rosenbach manuscript—the most complete extant manuscript—has an unclear position in the stemma. Fully one-third of the book was written during the proof stage, and Joyce often incorporated variants introduced by typists or the printer. The manuscripts are therefore suspect as copy-text. Yet it is known that the earliest printed edition does not represent the "final intentions" of the author, since Joyce complained about errors. Into such an editorial dilemma entered Hans Walter Gabler in 1977.

## THE GABLER EDITION: A HISTORY

According to Peter du Sautoy, Chairman of Faber and Faber until 1977 and trustee of the Joyce estate at the time, he was approached in 1975 by Viking Press and Hans Gabler simultaneously about publishing a new edition of all Joyce's works. The head of Viking, Marshall Best, consulted Richard Ellmann, who was enthusiastic about such a project "to provide sound texts of all Joyce's works" (du Sautoy 72); eventually it was decided in 1977 that Gabler would edit a new text of *Ulysses* only, under the supervision of an Academic Advisory Committee consisting of Ellmann, Clive Hart and Philip Gaskell. Financially, the Joyce estate was only involved with paying the Committee and minor administrative expenses; the bulk of the funding came in the form of a $300,000 grant from the *Deutsche Forschungsgemeinschaft* (the German equivalent of the National Endowment for the Arts). The publication costs would be covered by Garland Publishing, Inc., which would receive payment from the trade publishers (Random House and Bodley Head) if they decided to publish the Gabler text.

Du Sautoy's words on the estate's position in relation to copyright are cautious; he says that the estate "took account of the possibility" that Gabler's edition would be protected by its own copyright, since it was Marshall Best of Viking who emphasized this point (based on the copyright claims of the Cambridge University Press for a new critical edition of D.H. Lawrence's works). Du Sautoy states that a new copyright "was an additional point that the James Joyce Trustees had to weigh, but it was certainly not the mainspring of their decision," based as it was on Ellmann's interest in a critical edition of all of Joyce's works (71–72). The copyright question, du Sautoy maintains, was only raised for *Ulysses*, and he writes,

> [M]y personal view [was] that the revision of copyright texts should not take place till after the expiration of the copyright period, but I discovered that there was already more than one proposal being discussed, at least for *Ulysses*, so the problem had to be faced. On the general question of

> the copyright Ellmann mentioned for comparison that it was not unusual
> to have to pay for certain variant readings of even writers like Dickinson
> and Poe—not that he liked the idea—and at the time of publication of the
> first Cambridge editions of Lawrence there were strong objections in the
> literary journals to the copyright claim. (72)

But since there was the possibility that a competing edition of *Ulysses*
might be published, the estate took the advice of the unnamed American
attorney that the new material would indeed be protected, and went ahead
with their plan. Du Sautoy answers charges that the trade edition was
rushed through in order to secure copyright[17] by pointing out that the
copyright was issued based on the *Critical and Synoptic Edition*, and that
the trade edition, as reprinted from this edition, does not secure a new
copyright at all, but rather falls under the copyright claim for the *Critical
and Synoptic Edition*. This evaluation is borne out by the records at the
United States Copyright Office. He also points out that it would be in the
interests of the estate to postpone such an edition, since it would extend
the original copyright term for *Ulysses* for a longer period of time. These
explanations are hard to fault. The 1986 edition, in principle, secures nothing for the Joyce estate that the 1984 *Critical and Synoptic Edition* did not
secure. But postponing the edition would not "extend" a copyright for the
original, since any newly emended text would have its own copyright, and
the original on which it was based would still be subject to its original
copyright.

But enthusiasm for the project in 1975 was primarily over the prospect
of having a corrected *Ulysses*. Such enthusiasm was based on a misunderstanding of Gabler's editorial aims, and as Gabler's editorial theory became
clearer to those on the Advisory committee, disagreements broke out.
Philip Gaskell and Clive Hart left the project over such disagreements, and
Gabler became involved in many contentious arguments with the committee. None of this background discord was broadcast outside of the affected
parties, and as a result, Gabler's methods did not come under scholarly
scrutiny until the edition was actually published. It was only after the controversy began that this discord came to light in Charles Rossman's article,
"The New 'Ulysses': The Hidden Controversy," published in the *New York
Review of Books* (12/8/88: 53–58). Rossman gained access to Ellmann's
letters and uncovered the eminent Joycean's efforts to maintain harmony
on what was increasingly a fractious enterprise.

At the time Rossman's article appeared, it had been three years since
John Kidd's initial allegations had been made, and six months since his article "The Scandal of *Ulysses*" appeared in the *New York Review*. Kidd appeared to be a lone voice in the wilderness, judging by the tenor of the
public press articles on Gabler's edition. But there had been a conference
on the edition at Monaco in 1985[18] and as Rossman points out, "what became clear at the . . . conference was that the 'Academic Advisory Committee' and the Joyce estate had some serious disagreements with their own

edition" ("Hidden Controversy" 54).[19] His research into the Ellmann correspondence reveals that beginning in 1981, Gaskell and Hart wrote to Ellmann and proposed a meeting with all the advisers to have a "detailed
textual discussion" and try to reach an agreement over general editorial
principles. After this meeting, a letter to du Sautoy indicated that this disagreement over unspecified textual matters was resolved. Ellmann writes:
"you must have felt as I did that the objections to Hans Gabler's work were
surprisingly minor. . . . Hans was I thought quite tractable about everything. . . . I thought that Hans was quite willing to make concessions . . . ."
(in "Hidden Controversy" 54). But within a year, Rossman writes, tensions
mounted again and by 1983 Gaskell criticized Gabler's methods, primarily
the authority Gabler gave the Rosenbach manuscript over typescripts,
proofs and printed text. This disagreement, of course, stems from Gaskell's
sharply different conception of how to edit the text; he believes that the
first edition should have a primary place in making emendations, whereas
Gabler's project concentrated entirely on manuscript and revisions from
the author's hand prior to printing. Ellmann seems to have been somewhat
swayed by Gaskell's arguments against Gabler's methods at this point, and
he writes to du Sautoy in February 1983 that "it seemed to [him] that Hans
had several times preferred Rosenbach readings inferior to the typescript
readings. [Gaskell] objects on textual grounds, but I should add on an objection on artistic grounds" (in "Hidden Controversy" 55). At this point,
Gabler reversed his prior conciliatory stance and became adamant about
his position, and when the advisers met in June 1983, Ellmann found
Gabler intractable. He wrote to Gabler criticizing Gabler's "doctrinaire in-
flexibility" but also attempting to reach a compromise:

> I am not asking you to throw up your hands, but only to show an aware-
> ness of the pitfalls and a respect for the work as Joyce knew it from 1922
> until his death twenty years later. I very much hope that you will still see
> the possibility of modifying your rigid stance about the results of your ge-
> netic investigation, and of modifying your oppositely indulgent position
> about critical questions where changes must inevitably seem presumptu-
> ous. If you do so, the result will be much more widely acceptable, and the
> brilliant way in which you have prepared the genetic text and the final ver-
> sion would receive the accolade it deserves. ("Hidden Controversy" 56)

Here we see that Ellmann is operating under the traditional conception of a
critically edited text, in which the genetic material is supplementary to the
"final version." His knowledge of textual theory was slim, and his objections were, as stated in his prior letter, primarily artistic. Gabler remained
firm, and Gaskell and Hart withdrew from the project, as the Estate had
decided to proceed with the edition as it was. The clear implication, at least
from the Estate, was that the commercial interests took precedence over
any scholarly objections raised by the advisers.

Gaskell and Hart eventually rejoined the advisory committee, but the committee was advisory in name only at this juncture, as correspondence between du Sautoy and Gaskell and Hart make clear. They were still not happy with Gabler's methods and subsequent editorial choices, but they were "content that . . . the edition go ahead in its present form, as decided by the Estate" (du Sautoy 74; "Hidden Controversy" 57). Clearly, the estate had bypassed its own advisory committee and chosen to go with what they had. A further letter from Gaskell to du Sautoy shows that the publishers were also pressing for the edition to be published soon: "I confirm that we are now willing to be named and acknowledged in whatever way seems best to you and the others concerned. I am delighted to know that Gavin (Borden) [head of Garland Publishing] can keep to the timetable" (du Sautoy 74).

The plan was to allow two years of scholarly assessment of Gabler's edition before publishing a trade edition. But according to du Sautoy, "the Trustees were under immediate pressure from the trade publishers to release the reading text" but were well aware that even keeping to the two year timetable, "work on [the trade editions] had to begin some months earlier. We had no objection to that" (74). This position appears naïve, in that two years hardly seems adequate time for serious scholarly assessment; indeed, as Arnold writes, "If one considers the scale of the project [of bringing out an entirely re-set version in both hardback and paperback] . . . at the end of a two-year rights period for the special scholarly edition, then the concept of scholars actually *having* two years in which to debate is ludicrous" (147). What little scholarly debate there was occurred at the Monaco symposium in May 1985, convened specifically to assess Gabler's edition of *Ulysses*. Hart reported to du Sautoy after the conference that the kind of criticisms made about individual readings "were of the kind that Hans expects to be made and to which he is willing to lend an interested and at least partly sympathetic editorial ear," but that "in themselves [do not] seriously invalidate the edition" (75). Any chance for real academic debate over Gabler's methods was outweighed in 1985 by commercial considerations. Hart goes on to say that he did not believe the trade edition should be held up, and du Sautoy writes,

> I felt that the Estate should not change the arrangements we had already put in hand with the trade publishers. There was some doubt about the description of the Gabler text. I wanted to avoid words like "authentic" or "correct," and eventually we settled on "corrected edition" as, I hoped, a factual description. It may still have some ambiguity, however. (75)

Hart had convinced du Sautoy that there were no further serious qualms in the scholarly community other than what the committee had already quarreled over. It is obvious from both men's statements that honoring their contracts with the trade publishers was uppermost in their minds. Such a statement further reveals sidestepping by the Joyce estate around the issue of whether the *reading* text would take precedent over other editions. Du Sautoy's grudging acknowledgment that calling the reading text "the corrected text" may "have some ambiguity" does not mitigate the fact that, upon its appearance, the 1986 text was the only reading text of *Ulysses* available, and by default calling this one "corrected" suggested that it was indeed "authentic" under such circumstances. The implication was that prior editions were unworthy of purchase because they were "incorrect" and that the Gabler reading text replaced them as the "corrected" one. Du Sautoy further hedges when he closes his essay almost apologetically by saying that he does not believe in the existence of such a thing as a "final" text, but that the estate "considered the Gabler text at the time to be the best available, and . . . acted on the best advice they could obtain" (76). He follows this disclaimer with a rhetorical shrug: "Luckily *Ulysses* itself will survive any amount of textual controversy" (76). An air of *fait accompli* surrounds such a statement; given that these words were written in 1989, such resignation is understandable. But it is also clear that even in 1985, the estate felt that it was too late to undo what had been done. The reading text was published in 1986 as scheduled, and the consequences of this decision were to be long lasting.

AND IN THIS CORNER . . .

John Kidd's paper, "Errors of Execution in the 1984 *Ulysses*," was delivered at the April 1985 conference of the Society for Textual Scholarship. This paper exhibits little of Kidd's characteristic sarcasm which became so evident in his later writings; indeed, his position at that time as an unknown scholar rebutting the biggest names in the Joyce industry would seem to dictate an even tone. The paper itself is limited to some examples of flaws in the genetic material presented in the edition, not the reading text, and many of Kidd's criticisms are worthwhile. He summarizes them as follows:

> The errors of execution in the 1984 *Ulysses*, as I see them, begin with the decision not to examine Joyce's unpublished correspondence and the archives of his associates. Failure to collate three editions and at least twelve impressions during Joyce's life left the printing history incomplete. Nor were we offered an essay on the transmission of the work in print or an estimate of Joyce's role in corrections. Among the considerable facts which *are* gathered in the apparatus . . . I have noted errors in transcription, the absence of Joyce's instructions to the printer, and hundreds of variants not recorded in the historical collation. The synoptic left-hand pages do not represent the documents per se, because emendations are inserted and authorial readings are tucked away in the notes. (248–49)

Kidd's criticism of neglecting unpublished documents and corrections to printed editions is valid, if we were operating under traditional editorial theory. Such authorial intervention in the work once it had passed into the hands of the printers would indeed be necessary to consider. But that is not Gabler's intended project; he wished to reconstruct Joyce's pre-publication manuscript, in order to see an "ideal" version of *Ulysses* before it passed into print. In effect, Gabler viewed the printing process itself as part of the contamination of this "ideal" *Ulysses*, and did not feel it necessary to include it. Such a construct of Joyce's work is purely abstract, and owes a great deal to a Bowersian view of final authorial intentions. What it ignores is the material fact of *Ulysses'* existence as a text, and as McGann states in his *Critique*: "an author's work possesses autonomy only when it remains an unheard melody" (51). Once it passes into publication, it is subject to what McGann calls "interventions," only some of which may be contaminations through transmission errors. Kidd misconstrues Gabler's editorial intentions when he criticizes him for not using such post-publication documents, but is quite correct in noting that such final authorial intentions can also be found in post-publication documents. In fact, many emendations were made based on errata lists and resettings of the text which occurred during Joyce's lifetime. There seems to be a level of inconsistency here which Kidd is right in pointing out.

Kidd is also correct in critiquing Gabler's emendations of the synoptic text as "not represent[ing] the documents per se, because emendations are inserted and authorial readings tucked away in the notes" (248–49). If Gabler's intention was to show a full record of the variants within manuscript documents and authorially revised proofs and typescripts, then such variants should have been included in the genetic apparatus itself. Emendations should have been reserved for the reading text alone. In addition, Kidd takes the edition to task for not giving a complete printing history and for neglecting "an essay on variants occurring after 1922 . . . or . . . to establish authority for any of the two hundred readings it takes from the later editions" (245). These criticisms are solid, in light of Gabler's genetic project. Kidd tries to be fair: "the synoptic apparatus of 1984 is a very real innovation that deserves both praise and emulation. Its present state, however, still has some bugs" (246). He then gives some specific examples of these bugs, and his case is strong that further consideration needed to be given to just what Gabler had accomplished (which McGann also recommends in his essay on the edition, p. 284). Such an evaluation seems thoughtful and worthwhile.

But Kidd's refusal (or inability) to critique Gabler's text under any rubric but a traditional one apparently caused Gabler to dismiss his objections outright, much as he had done during the conflicts with his advisory committee. His response to Kidd's paper, unscheduled on the program and extending for a longer period of time than Kidd's paper itself, was scathing and condescending. Knowing the facts about his earlier confrontations with Ellmann, Gaskell, and Hart, this response is not surprising, but at the time it appeared well out of bounds and Kidd was visibly shocked.[20] In part, the article which appeared in the *Washington Post* just prior to the conference had a role in Gabler's high feelings, quoting Kidd that he would "blow the Joycean establishment wide open" (Remnick B1+). The article portrayed Kidd and Gabler as David and Goliath and, by inserting the rhetoric of war into the debate, helped frame the conflict as a personal vendetta (see Chapter Four for a complete analysis of this article).

Gabler's reply begins in full battle mode: "A defense of the critical edition of James Joyce's *Ulysses* against the allegations in Dr. Kidd's paper is not required. These allegations are all unfounded or misconceived" ("Response" 250–256). He then defends the edition "to reassure [the audience] that *Ulysses* has not been executed, or even erroneously executed—that is: decapitated, hanged, or quartered by mistake—in 1984" (250). He does acknowledge that mistakes and oversights are inevitable in any editorial enterprise. But he points out that Kidd's charges stem from a misunderstanding of Gabler's own project, albeit in combative language:

> the 1984 edition of *Ulysses* . . . establishes the text of the work that Joyce (successively) wrote, and not the text manifesting itself through the deviational forces of pre-publication transmission at the one particular moment in historical time marked by the work's first publication in book form. Perhaps it is a pity that neither principle was even remotely fathomed in its implications by what Dr. Kidd felt urged to put polemically before you. We might have had a fruitfully constructive debate on the wider issues of our common interests and activities. Instead, we have a shambles of undigested editorial lore in an argument that, for lack of stringency and incisiveness, collapses into triviality. (251)

Gabler then defends his emendation principles against Kidd's charges as outlined above, but he himself seems to have misunderstood Kidd's point. Gabler states that "[w]hat is used as copytext is a genetic assembly of the text of *Ulysses*. This is critically edited—so that once more, it makes no sense to complain that one doesn't get a 'straight' genetic presentation. Of course one doesn't—or one wouldn't need a copytext" (252). This argument appears circular: the genetic presentation is critically edited against itself. The reply further elucidates Gabler's claim that any post-1922 corrections were "carefully scrutinized" and where authorial revision was ascertained it was included in the genetic apparatus. Gabler plainly states his own editorial project as "the establishment of the critical text according to Joyce's autograph inscription and revision" and dismisses post-publication documents as outside the scope of his project. And yet, this clear statement of his intentions gets lost in a sharply worded, sarcastic and personal attack on Kidd:

> Surely, when the whole debate has shrunk to this point, it is acutely troublesome to discover that Dr. Kidd doesn't even appreciate truly bibliographical reasoning when he encounters it and actually badly bungles the issues when he claims himself to be setting out to argue bibliographically. . . . I wish I had the privilege of answering a worthier challenge. Beyond having taken the opportunity of airing some perhaps not altogether

unimportant points of editorial rationale, let me stress in closing that *nothing* has emerged from Dr. Kidd's paper to change the critical text of *Ulysses*. (253–54)

The text of Gabler's reply as printed in *Studies in the Novel* contained a postscript, in which he obliquely apologized for the strident tone: "Five years in retrospect, the response still rings with a strong note of irritation. The tone made listeners unhappy at the time. A present reader will perhaps more easily recognize that the irritation was caused in no small measure by the amateur critique presented to a professional conference of textual scholars" (255). Even while backing away from the tone of his reply, Gabler still manages to make it clear that bad feelings linger. He does call his final statement (that Kidd's paper had no implications for the edition) "an overstatement in the heat of the moment," and acknowledges that Kidd "was one of several contributors" whose corrections were included in the trade publication; but this is as close as he gets to an apology. It would appear that Gabler and Kidd, from that point forward, had stepped into the framework provided by the *Post* article and become mortal enemies in the Joyce Wars.

NOTES

¹For a summary of this history, see Bruce Arnold's *The Scandal of Ulysses: The Sensational Life of a Twentieth-Century Masterpiece*, New York: St. Martin's Press, 1991; also, Jack Dalton's "The Text of *Ulysses*," in *New Light on Joyce from the Dublin Symposium*, edited by Fritz Senn, Bloomington: Indiana University Press, 1972. For further perspectives on this publishing history, see Richard Ellmann's *James Joyce*, Oxford/New York: Oxford University Press, 1959 (revised 1982); Sylvia Beach's *Shakespeare and Company: New Edition*, Lincoln: University of Nebraska Press, 1956 (New Edition, 1991); Michael Groden, "Foostering Over Those Changes: The New *Ulysses*," *James Joyce Quarterly*, 22 (2): 137–159; also Michael Groden, *'Ulysses' in Progress*, Princeton: Princeton University Press, 1977; John Kidd, "The Scandal of 'Ulysses'," *The New York Review of Books* 30 June 1988: 32–39. Almost all of the articles about the Gabler controversy, whether in scholarly journals or popular periodicals, give a summary of Joyce's composition of *Ulysses* and its checkered publishing past.

²See Ellmann, pp.507–508; Beach, pp. 64–65.

³An interesting discrepancy about Joyce's composition habits arises between Sylvia Beach's account in her memoir and Hugh Kenner's 1980 article on Gabler's project in *Harper's* magazine. Beach describes Joyce using "blunt black pencils . . . and pencils of different colors to distinguish the parts he was working on. Fountain pens he didn't understand at all" (65). But Kenner states that Joyce used "a plain steel pen" (90), a description later repeated (without acknowledgment of Kenner's article) in the *New York Times* front page article announcing the publication of the Gabler edition. To my knowledge, no one has remarked on this discrepancy. It seems significant, because one of the criticisms that John Kidd leveled at Gabler was that Gabler's reliance on facsimiles did not allow him to tell the difference between pencil marks, pen marks, and some erasures. The fact that Beach remembers

Joyce using only black and colored pencils to compose *Ulysses* would seem, on the surface, to indicate that pen marks were inserted by someone other than the author—a fact which appears significant in making editorial decisions. But in Michael Groden's *Ulysses in Progress*, he describes the Cyclops chapter as being composed partly in pen, which contradicts Beach's recollection. The Rosenbach manuscript was also composed in ink. This discrepancy points out yet again that, as a source, Beach's memoirs are faulty in some respects.

[4]For various commentaries on this phenomenon, see pp. 3–73 of Moscato and LeBlanc, *The United States of America vs. One Book Entitled Ulysses By James Joyce*, Frederick, MD: University Publications of America, Inc., 1984.

[5]As stated in the Preface, this situation has changed with the alteration of copyright laws in the European Union. The 1922 *Ulysses* went back into copyright protection for an additional twenty years, and will now enjoy European copyright until January 1, 2012. This amendment to the law was passed in 1996, so the 1922 *Ulysses* was in the public domain for four years—allowing the Rose edition to be published in Europe without needing permission from the estate.

[6]Such amendments had been considered in a piecemeal fashion since 1962; the Copyright Act of 1976 combined these amendments into a single Act covering all aspects of copyright law, and made them retroactive.

[7]Now, of course, that time period is extended by the Bono act even further to "95 years from publication and 120 years from creation."

[8]Richard Ellman received the only other listed copyright of the Gabler edition, for his prefatory material.

[9]Sarah Lyall, "A New Edition Purges What May Have Been Joyce's Errors and Enrages Critics," 23 June 1997. *New York Times* Archive online, 20 Apr. 1998. In a bit of unintentional comedy, the online version of the article appended a paragraph dated four days after the original article appeared: two excerpts of Joyce's 1922 text and of Rose's *Reader's Edition* illustrating the differences between the two versions were printed incorrectly, and the small paragraph offers the needed corrections. Yet again, Joyce's text suffered from printing errors.

[10]This situation, too, has much changed since this study was first written. The Rose edition is currently unavailable anywhere, because of an injunction granted to the Joyce estate based on Rose's use of previously published manuscript materials (specifically, the Rosenbach Manuscript, published in facsimile in 1975). See the Preface and Conclusion for a detailed discussion of this new development.

[11]As of this writing, Kidd's edition is still awaiting publication. Norton is being coy about whether or not it will publish Kidd's edition at all. In an article appearing in the Boston *Globe* on April 9, 2002, Norton's president, Drake McFeely, is quoted as saying Kidd's edition cannot be published yet due to the Bono Act. McFeely says, "It's not out of the question we won't publish it then. But that's a long time from now, and we have a lot of other projects" (Abel B1).

[12]A paraphrase of Leopold Bloom: *Ulysses* 5. 268–69, 1986 Gabler edition; page 78, 1961 edition.

[13]For example, see Christine Froula's early review, "The Adventures of *Ulysses*," *Yale Review* 74 (1985):454–466. Froula later reversed her praise of Gabler's edition. See also, Michael Patrick Gillespie's "The *Finnegans Wake* approach to *Ulysses*," *Irish Literary Supplement* 4 (1985):36; Suzette Henke, "Reconstructing *Ulysses* in a Deconstructive Mode," *Assessing the 1984 Ulysses*, eds. C. George Sandulescu and Clive Hart, Colin Smythe and Barnes & Noble, 1986. Of course,

not all postmodern critics praised Gabler's edition; Paola Pugliatti situates Gabler's edition within post-structuralist theories of text but remains critical of its editorial methods as being influenced by "a static and inflexible notion of text" (113–14); in other words, Gabler's combination of the Greg-Bowers and German editorial methods lead to the edition's application of theory to be flawed, in Pugliatti's estimate. Pugliatti continued her criticism with "Who's Afraid of the 1984 *Ulysses?*," *James Joyce Quarterly* 27 (1): 41–68, in which she calls the synopsis a "faulty text" which does nothing to explain editorial decisions: "[t]he lefthand page of the edition . . . simply presents the text on which the editor grounded his decisions; it aims at showing *what* has been done but is structurally incapable of saying *why*" (42). It should be noted that the reply to this criticism was put forth not by Gabler, but by one of his assistants on the project, Wolfhard Steppe. Gabler has consistently refused to answer specific criticisms of the edition, instead confining himself to larger theoretical discussion. This policy fed yet more criticisms against him.

<sup>14</sup>For example, Maxwell Perkins often made such suggestions to F. Scott Fitzgerald, and Tay Hohoff, of the publishing house Lippincott, Inc., recalls the amount of editorial suggestions made to Harper Lee for *To Kill A Mockingbird*, which she willingly followed ("Mockingbird Publishing History," http://chebucto.ns.ca/Culture/HarperLee/publishing.html, 4 Nov. 1998). McGann gives the example of Byron actively seeking out his press editor's advice for help in the final revision stage, and there are numerous other examples. McGann agrees that each case requires its own historical investigation into the facts of production.

<sup>15</sup>See his "Afterword" to the 1986 reading text, *Ulysses: The Corrected Text*, pp. 647–650.

<sup>16</sup>Tanselle replies to McGann's assessment of Gabler's edition by saying that showing the variant readings in the apparatus is no different from what traditional editorial procedure has always done; Tanselle writes, "one may wonder why it interests McGann, for Gabler's aim is to trace the history of the composition of the work, and thus the focus is on Joyce as author, not on the collaborative forces of the production process," and he criticizes McGann's high claims for the textual apparatus: "the alternative system of reporting variants in footnotes or lists is also a 'language,' and when its conventions are mastered it tells us the same things." Tanselle misunderstands the relationship between the synoptic text and the reading text, and evaluates it accordingly; he acknowledges McGann's complaint that the conventional model of the critical edition subordinates the genetic record to a stable, privileged reading text. But Tanselle then rebuts this complaint in a way which shows one of the crucial problems within the debate: "although some editors have no doubt been so foolish as to think that their critical texts commanded 'unquestioned privilege' most editors—having laboriously worked through all the documentary evidence—recognize that any clear reading text is only one of the texts that can be derived from the evidence." It is indeed "foolish" for textual *editors* to believe in the privilege of the reading text, based on their specialized knowledge, but for *readers* without such knowledge, the appearance of a critical edition with variants recorded in footnotes or appendices leads to such a privilege. The very concept of a footnote or appendix is that of "supplementary" or "lesser" status, not deemed worthy by the author or editor to include in the text before the reader; it's interesting or illuminating, but not primary. This is the privileged position which McGann points out that Gabler's text is breaking away from, and asking readers to break away from as well.

[17]The first of these charges was leveled by John Kidd in his article, "The Scandal of *Ulysses*" (*NYRB* 30 June 1988: 32–39). Charles Rossman supported and enlarged these charges in the *New York Review of Books* (8 Dec. 1988) in an article titled, "The New '*Ulysses*': The Hidden Controversy" (53–58), in which he describes a letter from du Sautoy to Gaskell in 1983 and in another letter to Ellmann in 1985 in which du Sautoy mentions "the importance to the estate of establishing a new copyright" (58). This point, although not the main one of the piece, was also taken up in the *Times Literary Supplement* by Roger Shattuck and Douglas Alden; they made cutting remarks about the "commercial exploitation" by the estate and the publishers, and that "commercialism triumphed and almost cowed Joyce scholarship into silence" ("Searching for the True Text" *TLS* 10–16 June 1988: 640–641). This article provoked letters from the estate, Rossman, and Gabler among others, and remains a bitter point of contention on both sides.

[18]The proceedings of this conference were published as *Assessing the 1984 Ulysses*, edited by George Sandulescu and Clive Hart (London and New York: Colin Smythe and Barnes & Noble, 1986).

[19]In fact, as Fritz Senn recalled, "most of [those in attendance at the conference] had reservations" and "the general tenor was . . . critical" (personal e-mail, February 13, 2002).

[20]Kidd, "The Context of the First Salvo in the Joyce Wars," p. 240; Arnold, p. 160.

# CHAPTER FOUR

# TALES FROM THE FRONT,
## in which
# THE AMERICAN SHOOTS THE PRUSSIAN GENERAL

*For some time, at least, this [controversy over the 1984* Ulysses] *is likely to be known as the "Kidd issue."*

—*Clive Hart*

The primary battlefields of the first Joyce War were the *Times Literary Supplement* and the *New York Review of Books*, though various other popular publications served as alternate fronts with differing perspectives on the fray. The result of the often vitriolic exchanges over the Gabler edition was that, as Charles Rossman states, the Joyce community forever lost its textual innocence;[1] the acknowledged errors in all editions of *Ulysses* were, prior to what Hugh Kenner called the "Gabler Era," more often than not overlooked in favor of larger scholarly questions of meaning. Continuing in this vein proved unsustainable in light of the intense scrutiny that all the editions of *Ulysses* underwent, largely due to the efforts of John Kidd. As the *Miami Herald* reported of the 1989 conference on the Gabler *Ulysses* held at the University of Miami, "[i]n more genteel times, Joyce scholars served apprenticeships under masters such as Gabler, genuflecting until they were received as full members of the family, all in the name of scholarship. That was before John Kidd" (6 Feb. 1989: 4A).

The personalized nature of the disagreements disguised the fact that the debate wasn't just that of scholars quibbling over the placement of commas; the Joyce community as a whole during the 1980's was completing a shift (begun twenty years before) from looking at *Ulysses* as a unified masterpiece to viewing it as a multiplicitous text. Further, editorial scholarship was also undergoing a radical re-thinking of its own project, in light of theorizing by McGann, Shillingsburg, Zeller and Gabler, among others. The discourse of sacred literature surrounding Joyce erupted over the appearance of the Gabler edition of *Ulysses*, primarily because the Gabler edition repositioned Joyce's own intentions as somehow separate from what went before the public in the printed editions. Therefore, the author's relationship (manifested in the printed text) with the reading public—the "worshipers" of the word according to Joyce—was seen as secondary or, because it was corrupted, inferior to the "real" *Ulysses* that Gabler's *Critical and Synoptic Edition* professed to create. Further, the ownership of Joyce's "real" *Ulysses* was fully claimed by scholars, rather than the reading public, through the format and price of the Gabler edition: the edition itself spanned three weighty volumes at a price of over $200, and the diacritical markings appear as a mysterious code to the uninitiated. The reading text published in 1986 functioned as an interpretation of this mysterious utterance of Joyce, requiring faith that the scholar/priest had presented the word as Joyce wrote it. The Gabler edition functioned to claim Joyce fully for the scholars, and Kidd positioned himself in opposition to that claim. But close analysis of the public documents of the first Joyce War shows that the common reader found both sides of the debate alienating, and that the controversy served to make Joyce even more remote and mysterious than before.

### Haveth Computers Everywhere

Hans Walter Gabler undertook what was, undoubtedly, a monstrous editing task: using computers, he set out to give the world an edition of *Ulysses* free of printer's errors. At a time when computers were not so ubiquitous as they are now, Gabler's project seemed revolutionary—and so it proved to be, but not because he used silicon and motherboards to do it. At the time, however, the excitement generated over Gabler's project stemmed mostly from the novelty of using computers to speed up the onerous editorial task of cross-checking manuscripts. As early as 1979, the press was printing notices of this new methodology, and Joyce's cultural currency was clearly underscored. There were divergent reactions to using a computer to edit a literary work; in the March 14, 1979 issue of *Punch*, Allen Coren, in a column titled simply "Bloomers," takes satiric aim at using a machine to produce a version of *Ulysses*. Coren combines Joycean prose with examples of computer-generated messages:

> By lorries along Sir John Rogerson's quay, Mr Bloom walked soberly, past Windmill lane, Leask's the linseed crushers, the postal telegraph office, ping, whirr, clunk, We would draw your attention to the enclosed outstanding telephone account in the sum of £971,000,000,004.02 do not fold staple bend crease stick lick or touch and if paying by bank giro credit please state inside leg measurement when orduring; please state date of bath; police state all previous convictions on separate sheet provided (batteries not included) DO NOT detach, semi-detach, end of terrors bijou torn house, 3 bed 1 bth 1 ktch dwnstrs clks ample gge spce, patio patio bkrs mn, we have 7,000,000,000,002 fine examples like these on our flies. (Coren 417)

Coren offers no introduction to his purpose, only a small reproduction of a newspaper article entitled "Computer edits *Ulysses*" in the upper left-hand corner, showing the first paragraph as if torn out of a paper and pasted to the top of the page. The column itself is actually a clever blend of Joycean puns and computerese—note the "please state inside leg measurement when orduring" and the pun on stating convictions, "batteries not included"—and makes use of the Joycean style of onomatopoetic words and children's rhymes ("patio patio bkrs mn"). Clearly, the piece is intended for an audience familiar with Joyce's prose style, but it also reaches an even wider audience familiar with the impersonal nature of computer-generated form letters. In fact, the rhetorical strategy of placing the clipping at the beginning of the column explicitly serves to inform this wider audience who may or may not be familiar with Joyce's works. And placing the newspaper article's claim that *Ulysses* is "one of the most monumental works of modern fiction" prominently before the satire ensures that readers understand that *Ulysses* is considered a canonized masterpiece of modern literature, even if they've never read it, reemphasizing the academic Joyce's foundational relationship to the public Joyce. Further, by ridiculing a computer's ability to "create" literature (never mind that this enterprise is not Gabler's intended project), the column reassures us that computers make too many mistakes to "take over" human jobs requiring a creative and interpretive mind.

Compare Coren's mild suspicion with Hugh Kenner's early writing on the Gabler project. In April, 1980, his article "The Computerized *Ulysses*: Establishing the Text Joyce Intended" appeared in *Harper's* magazine, and was so influential in creating excitement over the Gabler edition that it bears close scrutiny. Kenner, a respected Joycean on a par with Ellmann in the Joyce world, was enthusiastic about Gabler's edition, to say the least:

> In Munich, for three years now, and with at least two years to go, an incredibly complex task of restoration has been in progress, entailing American photofacsimiles, international scholarship, and German computer programs. For the 260,000 words Joyce wrote with a plain steel pen so strained the primitive facilities of early twentieth-century book production—on the whole, an affair of hand-copying—that only technology, the movement of masses of information from continent to continent as well as from transistor to transistor, can now offer to untangle the mess. By mid-decade a sublimely accurate version will be available to the public. (90)

The religious subtext is unmistakable. Joyce is exalted by Kenner here, the "primitive printing facilities" overmatched by Joyce's "plain steel pen." Gabler's technological breakthrough, Kenner implies, will rescue Joyce's words from corruption, and the result will be "sublime." Further on, he addresses the fears which hide behind the *Punch* piece (though not in direct reply to it); after summarizing the publishing history and editing difficulties of *Ulysses*, he brings the article to a discussion of Gabler's project by invoking what the limitations of computers are:

> Already we need a computer to keep things straight. It needn't "com-
> pute," it need only not forget. It needs also to be capable of what a ma-
> chine can do best, the patient reliable comparison of long strings of letters
> to see if they are identical or not. That is no job at all for a human being,
> who needs to stay fresh and undistracted to deal with what comparison
> turns up. (93)

Again, Joyce's novel is given a supernatural status: it is so complex, "we
need a computer to keep things straight." The human ability to transcribe
by hand is "error-prone"; what Kenner fails to address is the error-prone
procedure of typing the information into the computer, which merely, in
essence, substitutes a typed copy for a handwritten one. What the computer did make more accurate was the checking for variants *between* versions entered into it, not the transcription of versions; they still had to be
"transcribed" into the computer. In fact, as Kenner points out, the computer program would only accept uppercase letters, and the typist had to
insert quotation marks prior to each actual uppercase letter for the computer to convert when printing. In other words, the manuscript "Mr
Leopold Bloom" had to be typed "MR "LEOPOLD "BLOOM. Kenner
points out that Gabler's team used quotation marks for this purpose since
Joyce never used them himself; the computer could easily distinguish them
from the actual text. Even Kenner calls this procedure "awkward" and
"complicated," but he ignores the implications of his own description and
forges ahead: "A man named John O'Hanlon copied the entire facsimile in
this awkward way; his work was checked three times by three different humans; whereupon, through its Optical Character Recognition unit, Com-
puter-Konstanz TR-440 ingested it, and purred, and took a nap" (93).
Though Kenner positions computerized procedure as a panacea for the
"primitive" hand-copying of earlier editing methods, and even though he is
careful to distinguish what the computer can and cannot do, the Gabler
project as painted by Kenner still seems mired in the very difficulties which
made Joyce's text such a publishing tangle in the first place. But Kenner's
enthusiasm for what the new computer technology could offer overshad-
ows these contradictions; indeed, as Charles Rossman would later write,
"Kenner's article is not an assessment of Gabler's procedures, but an awed
description of a scholarly miracle" ("Critical Reception" 162). Further,
John Kidd compiled a list of 200 errors specific to reliance on the computer, errors which resulted from faulty information being put into that
computer ("An Inquiry into *Ulysses: The Corrected Text*" 413; also in
Rossman, "Critical Reception, Part Two" 337). The computer, contrary to
what Kenner implies here, is not foolproof.[2]

Kenner distinguishes between the synoptic text, "a strange-looking page
on which every variant is accounted for in numbered half-brackets" that
can be read "with practice" (an enterprise more difficult than Kenner
makes it sound), and what Kenner calls the "comfortable text," i.e., the
reading text on the right-hand page. His description bears viewing in full:

> Simple. Instruct the machine by a button-push to ignore all its own half-brackets and delete all words between square brackets, and what it now prints out for the right-hand page is as close to what James Joyce meant us to read as eyes will ever see: prints out, moreover, not in bank-check characters but in any civilized type you want to specify.
>
> And prints out with no mistakes, with the lines numbered for convenience or reference; and the way of any rational publisher will be to photograph this golden text and circulate it by offset. No proofing errors.
>
> One of the unheralded virtues of the computer is that once it has things right there need never be another copying, another checking. And that is that. (95)

While it is not necessary to point out the abundance of praise couched in the adjectives Kenner uses, it is worthy to examine his claims that the "comfortable text" is the closest we can hope to get to "what James Joyce meant us to read," that any "rational publisher" would print this text by offset to avoid proofing errors, and that "there never need be another copying, another checking." These are large claims, and in fact, the procedure was not as simple as "pushing a button." Gabler was required to make many decisions on emendations once the manuscripts were assembled by the computer. But Kenner's enthusiasm at that time can perhaps be excused; the scholarly world long awaited a truly corrected edition of *Ulysses*, and it seemed then that Gabler's project indeed would answer all the editing problems attendant to Joyce's text. Kenner's article makes a strong case that Gabler's method was the cure to what ailed the publishing history of *Ulysses*.

The importance, though, of these early looks at the Gabler project is that they were printed in the popular press, aimed not at scholars but at the general public. Kenner's article in particular is noteworthy because of his position as a respected Joyce scholar, and his foray into the world of popular periodicals recalls the time when literary criticism was not primarily the property of the university and scholarly journals. Kenner's style, even in his scholarly articles, is witty, creative, and lively, eschewing a "scholarly" tone for an engaging one. But the center of the piece is not really *Ulysses* or critique in the usual sense; the piece instead focuses on the new method of using computers in humanities scholarship. This focus on computers taps into the zeitgeist of the late 1970's, a time when computer technology was just on the verge of making astonishingly fast inroads into daily life. Before the advent of cheap personal home computers, most people encountered them in connection with business and government, often in impersonal form letters much like what Coren parodies. The *Harper's* piece, however, carried the imprimatur of Hugh Kenner, which gave it some weight in critical circles and therefore served as advance advertising in the critical community. In fact, John Kidd points out in his article, "The Scandal of *Ulysses*," that Kenner's article was the only way that "most Joyceans . . . knew about the long-awaited but darkly-shrouded monument-in-progress," and called Kenner's writings a "relentless American campaign" (39). Kidd's polemical exaggeration cannot overshadow the fact that, indeed, Kenner's article was practically alone in discussing Gabler's project prior to its publication. Gabler did publish a few articles about his project, but they were confined mostly to journals in the specialized field of bibliography and textual studies.[3] Another early proponent of Gabler's project, Michael Groden (who was heavily involved in the edition as an advisor), published "Editing Joyce's *Ulysses*: An International Effort" in *Scholarly Publishing* 12 (1980) and in *Scholarly Publishing in an Era of Change* (1981). Notwithstanding these articles, which had a limited audience, most of the early attention to Gabler's project was primarily shaped by Kenner's article in the popular press, an article that reinscribed the sacralization of *Ulysses*.

## WE COME NOT TO BURY CAESAR

For Gabler, the synoptic edition was one that should take its place *alongside* other editions of *Ulysses*. This message was overshadowed by the reviewers and his own rhetoric;[4] it was completely lost in the furor which grew after John Kidd's "Errors of Execution," what Kidd called the first salvo in the Joyce Wars (*Studies in the Novel* 237). But prior to this shot heard 'round the world, Gabler's edition received a warmer welcome. Kenner continued his praise for the edition in the *Times Literary Supplement*, and Richard Ellmann reviewed it for *The New York Review of Books*. And the June 7, 1984 *New York Times*, on no less than the front page, heralded the appearance of Gabler's edition with the headline, "New Edition Fixes 5,000 Errors in *Ulysses*." All three articles take pains to promote the edition's restoration of Joyce's original intent, and outline some of the major emendations and their significance. It is worth noting, though, that the two reviews exhibit some room for doubt in their authors' praise of Gabler's methods and results; looking closely at them reveals that, even though both Ellmann and Kenner are supportive of the Gabler edition, they had some reservations as well.

Kenner's article almost repeats his earlier *Harper's* piece. He uses some of the same phrases, ideas, and examples, but the focus is, of course, not on the computer but on the edition itself. While the *Harper's* article was effusive, the *TLS* review is more restrained and scholarly. The difference in venue seems important in this regard, since *Harper's* is more firmly placed in popular culture than the *TLS*. The review is titled "Leopold's Bloom Restored" and appeared in the July 13, 1984 issue. Kenner begins by summarizing the composition and publishing history of *Ulysses* in greater detail than in the *Harper's* article, presumably because this history would be of more interest to the *TLS* audience. He backs away from stating outright that the text is error-free (as the *Harper's* piece implies) with a description of the proof-checking for Gabler's restoration of the "Ithaca" chapter. Apparently, the closing period which Gabler restored was missing when it was checked by Michael Groden of the University of Ontario (whom Kenner labels one of "two or three handy experts"). Kenner writes, "Uninformed human attention had had its carnival. The embarrassed printer explained that he'd whited the little dot out, thinking it was a dust spot. So much for good intentions. Computers have the merit of entertaining no intentions" (771). Yet again, Kenner valorizes the computer and its role in the edition, somehow implying that because the computer was used—not because the editorial method was better, or less open to debate—Gabler's edition is closer to perfect than prior ones.

Kenner summarizes traditional editing practice and where it has failed to give us Joyce's intended work: the "cautious bibliographical maxim that what the author has passed in proof has authority," and "that the latest reading we have in the author's hand is the one we are bound by." Kenner states that these two rules gave us a *Ulysses* with the dialogue dashes indented (a huge source of contention later) and other typesetter's errors intact because Joyce never worked from original proofs when he was checking the galleys. Gabler, working under the Greg-Bowers principles and German editorial theory, left these maxims behind, although Kenner does not discuss Gabler's mixed editorial theory in the review. What he does instead is to gloss over any criticism of Gabler's resulting emendations by saying parenthetically that if "you prefer [another] version, the evidence is preserved in the textual notes." He seems to be positioning the synoptic text—the "textual notes"—as secondary to the reading text here, indicating that Kenner has misunderstood Gabler's aim in the edition. Kenner is still operating under the traditional, author-centered "definitive text" tradition. As a result, he valorizes Gabler's scholarship in familiar editing terms: "behind Gabler's virtuoso performance lie reconstructed stories and his confidence in their details, a confidence he asks us to share" (772). As Kenner describes it, Gabler's method does not conflict with traditionally understood editing practice; all editors have to reconstruct the "story" of a manuscript and its relationship to the author's construction of a text, and all editors in effect ask their readers to share their confidence that they have got it right.

Kenner concentrates on Gabler's use of Bowersian methods of editing, rather than the potentially revolutionary project that McGann would later explain in his own evaluation of the edition. Kenner writes in the review's last paragraph an anecdote about Fredson Bowers responding to a complaint over an edition of Eliot's *The Four Quartets*. The story illustrates how Bowers relied on recreating the physical, material history of an edition; the complaint was that Eliot claimed the edition was the first copy off the press, but that there was an emendation in it which was inserted late in the press run:

> What, [Bowers asked], had become of the first sheet off the press? Yes, it rested at the bottom of the pile of printed sheets. Which sheet, then, did

the binder pick up first? The one at the top of the pile, therefore the last
one printed. . . . The first copy from the bindery is the last from the press.
What Professor Bowers did was to reconstruct a story, with agents manip-
ulating physical things. Bowers was Professor Gabler's mentor, and his
lessons have been taken to heart: however intricate the chain of reasoning,
see that it hangs together as a story. (772)

Kenner valorizes a type of editing practice grounded in the material existence of real documents; as a result he implies throughout his review that
Gabler's is the definitive *Ulysses*, even though Gabler's material copytext
exists nowhere but in Gabler's computer. Kenner does take issue with one
particular emendation:

> . . . I've found only one editorial decision I deplore. "—I wouldn't do any-
> thing at all in that line, Davy Byrne said. It ruined many a man the same
> horses." Into that beautiful unpunctuated sequence a typescript, allegedly
> "copied from a lost final working draft," introduced a comma after
> "man." The edition accepts this comma as authorial. Now there is one
> story I simply don't believe. (772)

There is no further explanation of *why* he does not believe Gabler's reconstruction, and the review thus ends on a rather curiously negative note—
curious, because up until this point, Kenner seemed to be nothing but
laudatory towards the edition. The disagreement Kenner seems to have
here is an aesthetic one; his evaluation of the sentence without the comma
as "beautiful" is subjective and arguable.

Earlier in the review, in another close look at Gabler's "reconstructed
stories," Kenner evinces nothing but confidence in Gabler's method; he
mentions a change Gabler made to the cost of a piece of Fry's Chocolate,
and the scenario Gabler presumed in making it:

> . . . in the text we've always had, Bloom's budget for the day puts the price
> of a cake of Fry's Chocolate at a penny, 0-0-1; that had been typist num-
> ber three's substitution for a shilling, 0-1-0. In making his list of errata for
> the second Paris impression, Joyce did not change the price of chocolate
> but instead altered the newly erroneous subtotal, to 0-17-5. Was Joyce
> conceding that Fry's chocolate sold for a penny? Should editor, like
> author, leave the price and change the sum? Gabler says not. "The sum of
> 0-17-5 which [Joyce] thereby leaves in Bloom's pockets would comprise
> pennies—and this cannot be, for Bloom has given his last coppers—liter-
> ally 'the last of the Mohicans'—in payment at the cabman's shelter." So in
> the new text the price of chocolate reverts to a shilling, and Bloom's
> pocket-money to 0-16-6.
>
> That overrides the author's latest inscription. I don't know how it
> agrees with 1904 chocolate prices. But it evidently corresponds not only
> with a *Ulysses* cross-reference but with a scenario whereby (1) the typist
> didn't correct an error of fact but simply made a mistake; (2) Joyce didn't
> see the error in the list but caught the resulting fault in the arithmetic, hav-
> ing (3), when he wrote of "the last of the Mohicans," and then made the

original list, had all his wits about him, whereas when he saw to the errata
the coal had faded. Confidence in such a story underlies the emendation.
(772)

In this story, we see evidence of Gabler practicing the Greg-Bowers rationale. The penny price interfered with a substantive (the "last of the Mohicans" and Bloom's budget), so Gabler reverted to an earlier reading which kept the text internally consistent, presumably something Joyce would have aimed for. This particular piece of editing drew a letter from Jack Elam of Suffolk, who wrote that Fry's chocolate did indeed cost a penny in 1904, and that the typist's correction was intended to correct Joyce's mistake (*TLS* 27 July 1984). Kenner replied on August 17, saying that he'd "suspected as much" and that letting the typist's correction stand "would be faithful to one criterion Joyce prized, the fit between his text and the non-textual world." But Kenner supports Gabler's emendation, citing that *Ulysses* is an internally consistent book and therefore Joyce's statement that Bloom spent the last of his coppers required that he have no pennies left at the end of the day. Even though Joyce "may or may not have noticed the typist's alteration of 1$s$ to 1$d$," he did notice that the sums came out wrong, and therefore corrected those while creating the discrepancy with the statement about the Mohicans, "which he may have forgotten. A less hurried Joyce would have had to choose one or the other, or (probably) contrive other alterations an editor is not authorized to envisage." Kenner ends the letter:

> In restoring the earlier readings, 1$s$ for the sweet and 0-16-6 for the balance, Professor Gabler was faithful to the textual editor's criterion of keeping the book consistent with itself while intruding minimally. Also he said in a note what he'd done and why. True, there is another world, not defined by texts though frequently coincident with them, a world in which we can sometimes ascertain the price of chocolate. But let editors start routinely invoking that world and Shakespeare's Bohemia will lose its seacoast, his Rome its chiming clock, his Ulysses all knowledge of Aristotle, his Shylock every objectionable trait, his Cleopatra her mastery of English, and his plays their picturesque integrity.

Kenner invokes the ghost of Shakespeare, as many people do in connection with Joyce, and foregrounds Joyce's status as a cultural icon. Gabler's editorial practice in this case draws no real fire, in Kenner's view; the fact that Joyce's text is now factually incorrect does not bother him as much as a textually inconsistent *Ulysses* would—*Ulysses* must remain intact as a created world. Later, Kidd would deplore this very factual inconsistency in his criticism of the edition. But for the time being, the matter was laid to rest, and the Letters to the Editor pages of the *Times Literary Supplement* were blissfully quiet for a while on the matter of the Gabler *Ulysses*.[5]

On the other side of the Atlantic, Richard Ellmann reviewed the Gabler *Ulysses* in *The New York Review of Books* (25 Oct. 1984: 30–31). Ellmann's review should have been wholly positive, given that he served as an advisor to Gabler during the editing of *Ulysses*, yet there is a sense of caution underlying the praise. On the surface this seems puzzling, but with the appearance of Charles Rossman's article four years later the reserved tone of Ellmann's review becomes clearly consistent with his growing unease over Gabler's project. At the time the review appeared, of course, none of the advisory committee's squabbling had come to light.

Like Kenner, Ellmann begins with a brief history of the problems which beset the publishing of *Ulysses*; unlike Kenner, he blames the errors not on the typesetters alone, but also on the well-meaning attempts of Stuart Gilbert at correcting the problems in the Odyssey Press edition of 1932, along with subsequent editors "with varying degrees of conscientiousness trying to correct misprints, and quite often adding more" (30). Ellmann relates that Gabler comes "nobly to the rescue," and he explains Gabler's rationale more clearly than Kenner does: "[w]hat Gabler aims at is an ideal text, based upon the evidence of existing manuscripts or upon the deduction from typescripts or printed versions of what the lost manuscripts must have contained" (30). The very next paragraph becomes negative, and stiffly formal, in a passive voice designed to avoid stating outright that Gabler may have made any mistakes:

> The undertaking has its perils. Deductions may not always be right, and the fact that many versions have not survived adds to the editor's difficulty. There is always the possibility that certain instructions to printer or typist were relayed by word of mouth or written down so casually that they were lost or discarded. Touchy situations arise when the printed text differs from all known manuscripts. In these the editor has to decide whether Joyce was responsible for the correction or not. Professor Gabler rejects the idea of "passive authorization," on the grounds that the majority of instances show Joyce, under pressure of time, spotting one error and missing another. (30)

Ellmann tiptoes carefully around possible disagreements with Gabler's method: "deductions may not always be right" and "touchy situations arise." This paragraph indicates that Ellmann had some reservations about the practical applications of Gabler's editing theory. But he quickly brushes away the doubts he raises: Gabler is called "happily conservative" in constructing his "ideal text," and it is "unlikely that the . . . changes he has introduced will excite great controversy," since they mostly involve accidentals (punctuation or spelling)—a prediction that proved utterly wrong. Ellmann cautiously approves the edition by calling the changes "subtle rather than earthshaking" and that *Ulysses* fans will want to have "the splendid new edition" but "need not expect to find it a new work" (30). Ellmann closes out his scrupulously lean praise by saying that "*Ulysses* has been given a commendably high polish and some of its small imperfections recovered" (30). None of this is gushing praise on the order of Kenner's

"wholly new *Ulysses*" which is everywhere "firmed up" by Gabler's "virtuoso performance"; given what we now know about the disagreements
behind the edition, Ellmann's review is a remarkably diplomatic one.

Ellmann's review does praise the restoration of the "love passage" in
"Scylla and Charybdis," basing his praise not on an adherence to editorial
practice but on literary interpretation. It is worth examining in full for two
reasons: it is this change which is repeated throughout articles and reviews
of Gabler's edition as an example of the momentous nature of the project,
in that Gabler had discovered a manuscript fragment that showed this crucial thematic statement; the fact that this one change was touted so frequently is also ironic, since Ellmann reversed his position later and said
that it should not have been included. In the initial review, he states that by
restoring the word known to all men as Love, the focus of the book becomes clearer and many ambiguities are eliminated:

> . . . allowing for the obliquity necessary to preserve the novel from didac-
> ticism, the word known to the whole book is love in its various forms,
> sexual, brotherly, paternal, filial, and is so glossed by Stephen, Bloom, and
> Molly. . . .The book revolts against history as made up of hatred and vio-
> lence, and speaks in its most intense moments of their opposite. . . . Like
> other comedies, *Ulysses* ends in a vision of reconciliation rather than of
> sundering. That it loses its force does not invalidate it. Dante says that
> Adam and Eve's paradise lasted only six hours, and Proust reminds us that
> the only true paradise is the one we have lost. But the word known to all
> men has been defined and affirmed, regardless of whether or not it is sub-
> ject to diminution. (31)

It should be noted that this restoration bears out a supposition Ellmann
made about the word known to all men in his 1972 work, *Ulysses on the
Liffey*, and the lukewarm praise for Gabler's editorial method appeared to
be overshadowed by the larger interpretive gains Ellmann found in the result. However, Ellmann recanted his interpretive rationale for including the
love passage in an essay for the *Georgia Review* ("The New *Ulysses*," 40
(2) 1986: 548–556): "It is extremely helpful to have Joyce confirm that the
word known to all men is *love*, and Gabler must be commended for un-
earthing this passage. But there are reasons for arguing that, however
much it may clarify Joyce's outlook, it should not be included in the final
text" (554). These reasons are not based on Gabler's editorial practice, but
rather on aesthetics: "By striking out the passage, [Joyce] could avoid
drawing undue attention to a weakness in Stephen's argument, and he
could save Stephen's celebration of love (of the selfless kind) until later in
the book, when in the *Circe* episode Stephen asks his dead mother, 'Tell me
the word, mother, if you know now. The word known to all men.' She will
not answer" (555).

It is certain that Ellmann did not wish to speak publicly against the
Gabler edition, given his intimate involvement with it from the beginning.
Indeed, in the *Georgia Review* article, he calls Gabler's edition "a great gift

to Joyce's readers" (548), and repeats almost verbatim the conclusion of the *NYRB* review. Ellmann did not weigh in again on the controversy which began to grow around the Gabler edition, save for participating in the 1985 Monaco conference, at which he read a modified version of the *Georgia Review* article.[6] And although he never admitted to them publicly, it is clear even in his initial review that he entertained doubts about Gabler's methodology in reconstructing *Ulysses*. His reversal of position on the love passage would not reach the general public, however; a shortened version of his initial review was included as a preface to the 1986 trade edition and, as such, remains in the public eye as an endorsement of Gabler's edition.

NEW AND IMPROVED!

Both Ellmann and Kenner's words hold some prestige in the world of Joyce studies, and their reviews spurred even more interest in Gabler's edition. And it would be expected that the readers of the *Times Literary Supplement* and the *New York Review of Books* would take an interest in a new edition of a literary work; after all, one of the functions of those two publications is precisely to publicize new works of literature or literary analysis. But the fact that the *New York Times* devoted a front page story to the appearance of the Gabler *Ulysses* shows that there was more than scholarly interest in Joyce's work. The article, of necessity, approaches *Ulysses* from a vastly different perspective than these two reviews—yet, remarkably, it begins to echo Kenner's review in some ways, and quotes both Kenner and Ellmann. The article makes little attempt to overtly praise the Gabler edition, but the idea that the 1984 *Ulysses* is not only *new* but *new and improved* comes across loud and clear in the title: "New Edition Fixes 5,000 Errors in *Ulysses*."

The article begins by discussing the "international team of scholars" who "[correct] almost 5,000 omissions, transpositions and other errors in previous editions of the seminal 20th-century novel" (1A). It is in this article that the phrase "stunning scholarly achievement" is first attributed to Ellmann,[7] and the writer, Edwin McDowell, takes great pains to give Ellmann's credentials before he does so: ". . . Richard Ellmann, Goldsmith's Professor of English Literature at Oxford University and author of the definitive biography of Joyce" (1A+). In fact, Ellmann's title is given repeatedly as "Professor Ellmann of Oxford," presumably because such an affiliation would act as a shorthand for an American audience unfamiliar with Joyce studies: anyone with an impressive title at such an impressive school must be worth heeding. While Ellmann himself was giving less effervescent praise in his review (and privately refuting that he'd ever used the word "stunning" in relation to Gabler's edition[8]), the *New York Times* article quotes him as saying that "[s]ome of the corrections are substantive . . . and at least one is of such importance that it will have a considerable effect upon the interpretation of the whole book" (C19). This kind of front page advertising helped the early reputation of Gabler's work in the non-academic world.

Kenner is also quoted in the article, and he is identified as "a professor of English at Johns Hopkins University and an authority on Joyce." His words are positive, and echo his review in the *TLS* that "so many things are sharpened and firmed up." In fact, Kenner is given the last word in the article, through his recounting of an anecdote:

> . . . Professor Kenner . . . recounted the time some years ago when he was in Taiwan and had spoken to a Chinese who venerated the writing of Henry James. "He'd read James in translation," he said, "but the Chinese language has no system for subordinate clauses. When I asked him what held it together, he replied, 'Reality holds it together.' That's the answer to the case of *Ulysses*—reality holds together a terribly imperfect text. (C19)

The effect of this last comment is curious; it leaves the phrase "terribly imperfect text" in the reader's mind as the last thing they take away from this piece. Yet the article's main point was that Gabler's text is now the "perfect" text, since it now has corrected the faults introduced by typists and printers. So there is a subtle double consciousness occurring here, in that the article simultaneously implies that Gabler has "fixed" *Ulysses*, a text that the anecdote implies can never actually manifest as anything but an "imperfect" text. Overall, however, the fact that the publication of this edition found its way to the front page of a widely circulated daily newspaper was extraordinary, and speaks to the position Joyce holds as master of the modern novel in our culture.

But not all the reviews were as generous as these three articles suggest. In a column called "Between the Lines," Craig Raines of the *Sunday Times* (London; 12 Aug. 1984: 39) gave a less than glowing response to Gabler's edition. The piece is sardonic, witty, and positions itself clearly as a non-scholarly response; after quoting Gabler's foreword that "any given text of *Ulysses* is erroneous at least seven times per page," Raines continues:

> Dear, dear. Learning this, who can suppress the picture of a great masterpiece fallen on hard times? Diaphanously thin in the seat of its pants, zip like a dentist's nightmare, out at the elbows, down at the heels, frayed at the cuffs, seams agape, *Ulysses* mumbles incoherently to itself, while we strain to catch the drift of its genius. In a trice, our wallets are open and the necessary £163 note gladly bestowed. Anything to accomplish the feat of restoration. (39)

The tone of the article rarely leaves this humorously sarcastic mode, and we get further skepticism about the point of undertaking such an editorial task:

> Is it the basest ingratitude to cite the example of Stephen's talkative ashplant as it trails noisily along in the first episode? In my Bodley Head edition and in the Penguin text, the stick addresses its owner thus:

> "Steeeeeeeeeephen." Professor Gabler, quick to pounce on such an obvi-
> ous solecism, informs us that Joyce intended a more sycophantic charac-
> terisation of the stick: it now whines, "Steeeeeeeeeeeephen." Ah yes. Just
> so. (39)

Further on, Raines sums up his view on the issue by saying that he believes
that misprints "are inevitable in any text and, on the whole, . . . [he]
couldn't give a fupenny tuck." Clearly, Raines finds that such errors do not
interfere with the actual practice of reading, and implies that the scholarly
preoccupation with them is pointless.

Raines also takes issue with Gabler's inclusion of the love passage which
Ellmann initially supported; Raines states that he doesn't think that these
lost lines need to be in the text, thus anticipating Ellmann's own retraction.
Raines objects to their inclusion on both editorial grounds (in that Joyce
may have either actively removed the lines or passively authorized the omis-
sion), and on aesthetic ones, in that his own interpretation of the library argument allows for Stephen's thoughts to be incoherent: "Gabler's addition
makes the argument more coherent, but that isn't Joyce's point about
Stephen's theory of Shakespeare. It shouldn't make sense and by omitting
the five lines Joyce is serving the idea of verisimilitude. Accordingly, I retain
my scepticism and I advise other readers to do the same." But even after all
of his sarcasm, Raines ends the article with an approval of the Gabler edition, based on its illustration of the process of Joyce's composition:

> The real reason for buying this edition is not to acquire a final, perfect
> text of the greatest book of the century, but to follow the moves of a bril-
> liant writer at work, however partially since not all the documents sur-
> vive. The final text will always be argued about: Professor Gabler is too
> often willing to accept readings from the fair copy of the Rosenbach man-
> uscript for his edition to be beyond question. However, the left-hand page
> of this edition shows us the work in progress—the way Joyce added,
> deleted, re-wrote extensively in proof—and for those with the patience
> this is worth £163. (39)

The effect of this last paragraph is to bring the discussion back to Joyce,
rather than the Gabler edition (and curiously enough, Raines seems fully
cognizant of Gabler's focus on process rather than final product in his editorial, a point which seems to have escaped Kenner and Ellmann in their
reviews). Joyce's status as the author of "the greatest book of the century"
and as a "brilliant writer" makes it worth exercising patience and spending
a substantial sum of money to see his work as it took shape. By finalizing
his article with these sentiments, Raines privileges the author over the
scholar, and reinforces stereotypes that scholars concern themselves with
minutiae that have no real bearing on the process of actually reading the
novel. Contrast the almost reverent tone of Raines' last paragraph on Joyce
with this passage about Gabler: "There are . . . a great many unruly commas who don't know their place. One or two colons have played hooky.

Gabler ticks them off and gets them into line." Even more scathing is Raines' discussion of an error in Gabler's edition "despite the aid of two assistants, computers and collation machines":

> At a certain point, the correction of mistakes merely leads to new mistakes. God seems to have written this into our contracts, lest we suffer the sin of *hubris*. So, on page 403 of volume one, Professor Gabler has corrected a "howler": some *incredibly* careless individual (possibly the author himself, but unspecified in either the historical collation chart, or the synoptic apparatus) has added a dash to signify new dialogue when all that is needed is paragraph indentation because the same person is speaking. The dash is, therefore, eliminated. However, the indentation continues mistakenly for the next six lines. And the error is mirrored in the synoptic text on the opposite page. I hope Professor Gabler doesn't have too many sleepless nights over it. It isn't *that* important, like so many of his own corrections.

Repeatedly, Raines names Gabler as "Professor," which may serve in his rhetoric to further alienate Gabler from the "real world" to which Raines' readers presumably belong, and he also mentions "Professor Richard Ellmann" in connection with scholars who "have expended many hours trying to identify the word known to all men." The *New York Times* article also refers to them as Professor, but the effect of the title in Raines' piece is less than honorific due to his sarcastic tone. Raines makes it clear that the people behind this new edition of *Ulysses* are somehow removed from the world he assumes his readers inhabit.

In another publication aimed at the general public, *Time* magazine's Paul Gray reviewed Gabler's edition (2 July 1984: 83–85), in which he called the printing situation for *Ulysses* a "palimpsest of confusion" (83). Gray mistakenly states that, upon its publication, *Ulysses* was "instantly recognized as a classic" whose subsequent editions added more errors while correcting others, and that a "nagging question arose and persisted: How to distinguish the novel's intentional complexities from accidental garbles" (83)? Gray goes on in the next paragraph: "The whole world has not been waiting for an answer, to be sure, but here it is anyhow." The unmistakable impression is that the edition was foisted upon the world by scholars whether it needed a new *Ulysses* or not. Gray continues, describing Gabler's project using computers and repeats the claim of 5,000 errors corrected in the edition. Then he again undermines the importance of the project:

> [5,000 errors], in isolation, sounds horrendous; indeed, any botching of a written word in an acknowledged masterpiece is one too many. But *Ulysses* consists of well over 400,000 words; so the margin of error has hovered somewhere under 2%. Furthermore, the vast majority of corrections made by Professor Hans Walter Gabler of the University of Munich and his colleagues involve spelling and punctuation; word changes or ad-

ditions amount to a fractional percentage of the text that transformed
20th century literature. (83)

It seems curious to reduce errors to a negligible percentage of total
words; the use of such statistics renders each error the equal of any other
error, as if the dropping of a comma were of the same order as the dropping of whole lines of text. Gray offers an apparently contradictory assessment of Gabler's edition: "There may thus be less in this expansive and
expensive production than meets the eye. But the result, even with a price
tag of $200, is by no means negligible." After reducing all errors in the
book to a fractional percentage of total words (and thus implying that all
words are equal), Gray calls the correction of these errors substantial
enough to justify a $200 price tag. But the contradiction is on the surface
only; the subtext of sacred literature justifies the "$200 price tag." It is the
special status of *Ulysses*, an "acknowledged masterpiece" which dictates
that, whether the errors are negligible or not, the reader must have the one
true text regardless of the price.

Gray repeats the example of the love passage (with accompanying sidebar illustrating the change) as an instance where the change was worthwhile. He also gives examples of clarified passages where the Gabler
edition restores words and lines of type that were dropped in prior editions. The review ends with the prescient observation that the edition "will
give scholars plenty to talk and quarrel about for years to come," and lays
this state of affairs squarely at Joyce's door by quoting the oft-repeated line
about keeping the professors busy for centuries. Gray closes out with a
blanket acceptance of Gabler's claim of producing a *Ulysses* as Joyce wrote
it: "Now, thanks to this herculean labor of scholarship, the disputes and
the enjoyment will encounter not unintended riddles but the very words
that Joyce chose for his posterity" (85). It is a curious sentence grammatically ("the *enjoyment* will encounter"?), but it is clear that while Gray
seems to have some doubts about the relative interest such a project raises
generally, he has accepted without question the premise that the Gabler
edition gives us *Ulysses* as Joyce intended it to be. There is no mention in
the review of Gabler's editorial theory, not unexpectedly; it is clear that the
scholarship is to be accepted on faith, unmentioned except as a "herculean
labor" which took the same length of time that it took Joyce to write the
book. Neither is there mention of the synoptic apparatus or its difficulty; it
would appear that Gray reviewed the results apparent in the reading text
on the rectos, and the choice is clearly indicative of the fact that the general
reading public is not interested in the scholarly aspect of the edition. This
kind of attention to the reading text at the expense of the synoptic text
plainly stems from the differences of perspective on the nature of text between the academy as represented by Gabler and the common reader.
These reviews for popular periodicals were unusual in that the edition they
were reviewing was not one aimed at the commercial market; the high

price and the limited press run of 2,000 copies from a specialty publishing house like Garland firmly place the edition outside the realm of commercial booksellers. But such is the currency of Joyce in the general literary culture that a scholarly edition found its way into *Time* magazine.

## THE WILD RUMPUS STARTS

For the time being, Gabler's edition enjoyed a fairly positive reputation in the public eye—until an article appeared in the *Washington Post* on April 2, 1985 announcing John Kidd's intention to "blow the whole Joyce establishment wide open" (Remnick B1). This article, contrary to Kidd's characteristically self-aggrandizing assessment of his own paper, "Errors of Execution," was in actuality the "first salvo" in the Joyce Wars (at least publicly). In fact, the very title of the piece casts the debate in terms of battle: "The War Over *Ulysses*." The first paragraph portrays Kidd as a "brash, young scholar" going up against the "titans of international James Joyce studies," primarily "Kenner and Ellmann" (B1+). Kidd appears as slightly obsessed in the portrait Remnick draws of him: "Kidd says he has gone $10,000 into debt in order to travel and buy old editions of Joyce. He sold his 800-volume personal library and furniture last year to finance trips to Europe and drives a 13-year-old car. 'All I've got left are my Joyce books,' he said" (B4). Remnick even quotes Kenner as saying that "Kidd is a man who obviously has a bee in his bonnet" (B4). The result of this portrayal is that Kidd becomes the embodiment of the slightly odd academic, out of touch with the real world.[9] Remnick continually casts the debate in urgent terms, calling Kidd's criticisms a "crusade" in which he "will stake his reputation": "As a young academic, the stakes for Kidd are high. . . . [he] risks alienating the Joycean establishment, such as Kenner and Ellmann"; "The coming weeks are crucial for Kidd, the time he has been anticipating for years"; "This could all lead up to a veritable war at a Joyce symposium to be held" in 1986 (B1+). At the same time, Remnick maintains a slightly bemused tone about the entire enterprise: "Like biblical scholars who continue to haggle over versions of the New Testament, Joyceans see nothing arcane or funny about wars waged over punctuation and other linguistic nits" (B1). This comparison speaks to the religious subtext of hermeneutical scholarship, and calls upon the discourse of sacred literature. He calls Joyce studies an "odd industry" but at the same time valorizes it: in acknowledging that other fields have their share of disputed editions, he claims that the "sheer immensity of Joyce's work, however, dwarfs other disputes" (B4). Here again is evidence of the popular Joyce, an appeal to Joyce's status as preeminent modern writer which invariably rounds out any discussion of this debate in the popular press.

Remnick quotes Gabler as well, but the quotes are less a response to Kidd's charges than an airing of personal grievance: Gabler states broadly that Kidd's objections are "misconceived or trivial" (the same words he would use in his reply to Kidd at the conference), and that "[w]hat I'm watching with some sadness is that John Kidd is fascinated with the popular appeal of the edition and has tried to catch some of the limelight for himself"; he further states that "I've tried to be helpful to Mr. Kidd at all times and I respect his intelligence greatly. But I suppose it's all about the old motto: 'No good deed goes unpunished'" (B4). As a result of Gabler's statements and the article's portrayal of Kidd as a David to Gabler's Goliath, the Joyce Wars took on a personal tone. Gabler's response to Kidd's paper was less a measured critical rebuttal than an angry reply. Because of the *Post*'s wide circulation, this article publicized the cast of characters in the Joyce Wars to a broad audience of Joyceans and non-Joyceans alike, working within stereotypes of academics as picking "linguistic nits" and being so obsessed with literature as to sell their furniture to buy books.

The *Post* did not follow up on this article by covering the conference, but *The New York Times* did. In "Textual Scholars Make Points About Points in Books" (29 Apr. 1985: B2), Isabel Wilkerson covers the conference in its entirety, but concentrates most on the Kidd-Gabler dispute. The article opens with a reference to the disagreement Kidd had with the size of the closing dot at the end of the "Ithaca" episode; Kidd is described as "Dr. John Kidd, an Andrew W. Mellon scholar from the University of Virginia" who "confronted Dr. Hans Walter Gabler, a professor from the University of Munich" and the editor of a new *Ulysses* (with, perhaps appropriately, a typographical error—"editor" is spelled "editior"). By using the lowercase "p" for "professor," the article leaves Gabler in a seemingly lesser position than the very impressive-sounding (to the public outside of academia) "Dr. Kidd" who is an "Andrew W. Mellon scholar." The article quotes Kidd's contention that Joyce wanted a larger dot, and that Gabler "is rejecting the authorized form made public by the author and proofread by the author four times." The quote from Gabler sounds reasonable and accommodating: "If it is true we have overlooked one phase of Joyce's final instructions, the point will become somewhat larger in later editions." This calm-sounding scholarly exchange is a far cry from the heated response evident in Gabler's rebuttal. The article's overall theme is that the disputes of textual scholars are an arcane world of obsessed fanatics "who speak of their authors as they would an uncle whose shortcomings they know all too well" and who "toil for decades in search of the definitive *Hamlet* or *Ulysses*, trying to perfect the work of an author whose final intentions . . . usually can never be known for certain." The comparison to biblical hermeneutics cannot go unnoticed, and in fact the article quotes one scholar attending the conference as joking that he knew "of only two great creative artists who, according to orthodox interpretation, never revised their work. . . . One, of course, is Shakespeare. The other, of course, is God."

But the article also portrayed the Kidd-Gabler dispute as simply one of generational change. Donald Reiman, chairman of the conference, cast the debate as a "war of generations, . . . with the younger scholars trying to improve the work of their predecessors to make a place for themselves in the profession." The next sentence makes it clear who is being cast in these roles: "Such was the case on Friday with Dr. Kidd and Professor Gabler." Wilkerson does mention the acrimony of the exchange between Gabler and Kidd, but curiously implies that the heat was all on Kidd's side:

> In the end, some scholars questioned the tone of Dr. Kidd's criticism. "He didn't win points," Dr. Reiman said. "He would have been better off simply presenting a better paper, building on Gabler's work, rather than singling him out."
> Others, like Dr. Thomas Berger, a Shakespearean at St. Lawrence University, seemed content to meet with colleagues and present their papers. "It gets lonely out there," he said. "This gives you a chance to talk to people who do the same crazy thing you do." (B2)

These final words of the article leave the very solid impression that this "crazy thing" that textual scholars do is irrelevant to the rest of the world, and that debates over the size of full-stops are entertaining events where people "earn points." The article gives no indication of the bitterness engendered and does not mention the *Post* article which preceded the conference. It makes no mention of Gabler's innovative textual theory, but leaves an impression that Kidd, by charging that Gabler ignored the author's wishes, is operating under the correct assumption of what textual editors are engaged in: in the words of the article's subtitle, they are "seeking perfection." This piece was the last article in a major daily newspaper which mentioned the earliest dispute, and it manages to convey the impression that the debate wasn't all that earth-shattering. The reality, though, is that the strident tone was set early and the press played a role in setting it—the gauntlet had been thrown.

In 1986, the reading text was published in paperback by Garland, and the trade edition derived from it was published by Random House as *Ulysses: The Corrected Text*; the flawed 1961 edition was discontinued. An interesting review of the trade edition appeared in *The Atlantic Monthly* (September 1986), written by Martin Amis—son of the novelist Kingsley Amis and a respected novelist in his own right—which casts a different light on the edition than many of the prior reviews in the popular press. As a dissenting opinion on the value of Joyce's most highly acclaimed novel, it is worth examining as a glimpse into the wider public's view of *Ulysses*, one that can get overshadowed by the deference to Joyce (and established Joyce scholars) in other popular press articles.

Amis briefly describes the new edition's corrections of "gremlins," such as "slips and skips" and "previously unretrieved corrections," before stating flatly:

> . . . the new edition will not reverberate far. It will scupper the odd doctorate, embarrass a few commentary footnotes, upend one or two learned

articles, and that's about all. If, like me, you have tried *Ulysses* before and got about halfway through (it's a common fate with the common reader), then the refurbished text simply provides another excuse to try again. Take my word for it: you won't notice the difference. (96)

Amis asks, "What, nowadays, is the constituency of *Ulysses?* Who reads it? Who *curls up* with *Ulysses*" (96; italics in original)? The answer for Amis, clearly, is not the general reader. Further, he describes *Ulysses* as "not reader-friendly. Famously, James Joyce is a writer's writer. He is auto-friendly; he is James Joyce-friendly" (96).[10] But Amis also calls Joyce a genius: "he makes Beckett look pedestrian, Lawrence look diffident, Nabokov look guileless" and that throughout the course of his books we can see Joyce "washing his hands of mere talent." Amis places this genius, however, firmly in a world inaccessible to the common reader, and diagnoses this tendency in Joyce as a condition of his modernity: "The exemplary genius, he is also the exemplary modern—fanatically prolix, innovative, and recondite, and utterly free of any obligation to please a reading public . . . he wrote to please himself" (96). Amis is here describing Pound's—and the academic—Joyce.

Amis fills the article with examples of Joyce's genius in *Ulysses*, culminating in the often-quoted "The heaventree of stars hung with humid nightblue fruit" sentence from "Ithaca" (*U*86 573.1039). But Amis also gives examples of "hideous prose" in the book, saying that "[b]eautiful prose came so naturally to Joyce that he often indulged a perverse attraction to its opposite: . . . mirror-cracking, clock-stopping prose"—this description calling to mind Joyce's own style of compound words—and that "most of the parodies feel like a deliberate strain on the reader's patience" (98). As an evaluation by a novelist, these criticisms carry some weight, but this structural deficiency does not completely mar the book's worth for Amis. The article, as a critique of *Ulysses*, joins a long line of critics who, while impressed with Joyce's virtuosity, found the book lacking any concern for readers.[11] However, Amis's critique of *Ulysses* ends with a dig at scholars and a resounding statement on what Joyce's place in the literary world is as a result of being a "writer's writer"; the last paragraph bears viewing in full:

> The critics have assured us that *Ulysses*, like *Finnegans Wake*, "works out." This is nice to know. The good reader, pen in hand, makes a little mark on the page when he encounters a significant passage; the ideal reader of *Ulysses* can run his nib down the length of every margin, all 644 of them. We like difficult books, Lionel Trilling said, and the remark has become one of the battle cries of modernism. Yet who are *we*, exactly? Academics and explicators like difficult books for obvious reasons, and Joyce helped create the industry they serve; with modern geniuses, you must have the middleman. The reader, I contend, remains unconsulted on the matter. Joyce could have been the most popular boy in the class—the

funniest, the cleverest, the kindest. He ended up with a more ambiguous
distinction: he became the teacher's pet. (99; italics in original)

The entire article hinges on this last statement: that Joyce is the property of
academics, that he wanted it that way and that he deliberately wrote that
way. Amis, looking at the dichotomy between academics and non-
academics, clearly finds that Joyce is not accessible to the common reader.
Calling Joyce the "teacher's pet" establishes that, as of 1986, Joyce's works
had completely become the property of academics. This review, appearing
as it did in a widely circulated magazine, does not concern itself with the editorial issues surrounding the Gabler edition, but rather with whether or not
Joyce is worth reading at all. Plainly Amis regards the kind of errors in
*Ulysses* which the Gabler edition claimed to have corrected as inconsequen-
tial to the common reader; as Raines had written two years earlier, such errors are "irritating but inevitable" and not worth worrying about (39).

These two writers seem to imply that academic concerns are not the
concerns of the general reader, but those involved in the editorial debate
would certainly not agree. In fact, Kidd was quoted in the 1985 *Post* article
that "When you read a book, you have a right to as good and accurate an
edition of the book as possible and an honest statement from the publisher
about what you're getting" (Remnick B4). Kidd casts his own campaign
against the edition as being on behalf of the reader, and because his primary attacks on the Gabler edition were printed in journalistic forums, he
continued to appeal to this reader throughout the Joyce Wars. But was the
Gabler edition really aimed at the general reader? What was the purpose of
issuing review copies of a three-volume critical edition to reviewers at daily
newspapers? Gabler himself saw the synoptic text as the primary point of
his project, a thoroughly theoretical enterprise which would employ the
latest views in editorial theory; the reading text served, in his estimation, as
an aid to reading the synoptic apparatus. Releasing the trade edition on its
own, without the critical apparatus, was the decision of the Joyce estate
and, as indicated by an announcement in *Publisher's Weekly*, primarily an
economic one. The announcement in the June 13, 1986 issue quoted figures from Random House stating that "from 1971 to mid-1985, the company sold 13,000 hardcover copies, 177,101 Modern Library copies and
530,000 Vintage copies" (Frank 25). The article further states that the first
printing of the trade edition of Gabler's text was set at 50,000 paperback
and 10,000 hardback copies (26). *Ulysses* was a substantial source of income for the Joyce estate. As outlined in Chapter Three, the decision to release a trade version without the critical apparatus (which was the heart of
Gabler's edition) was initially based on a misunderstanding of Gabler's theoretical project—that he was not giving them a corrected text in the traditional sense—and by the time such an understanding was reached by du
Sautoy and Ellmann, among others on the advisory committee, the con-
tractual obligations with the trade publishers took precedence over any

misgivings they might have had about what the public was going to be buying. Naming the trade edition *The Corrected Text* continued to foster the
illusion that this version was a definitive text, a decision which was made
by the publishers rather than Gabler. Allowing the 1961 edition to go out
of print made Gabler's trade edition the only version available to students,
teachers, and the general public. The editorial debate had more or less sunk
out of the public view (if not the scholarly one) at this point—until
June 30, 1988, when John Kidd went once more into the breach.

### "IS NO ONE AWAKE AT THE WHEEL?"

By the time Kidd's article "Scandal of *Ulysses*" appeared in the *New York
Review of Books* the pump was primed, so to speak, in the scholarly world
for a full-scale battle. And Kidd did not disappoint. Prior to the appearance of this landmark article in the Joyce Wars, several scholarly assessments of the Gabler edition had taken place, particularly a 1985
conference in Monaco which published the proceeds as *Assessing the 1984
"Ulysses"* (Sandulescu and Hart 1986). In addition, Kidd had published an
article in *The Irish Literary Supplement* (4 [1985]: 41–42) criticizing
Gabler's treatment of Gaelic and other foreign languages; this article
prompted a biting reply from Danis Rose in the next issue (30–31). G.
Thomas Tanselle had published a critique of Gabler's editorial methods,
"Historicism and Critical Editing" (*Studies in Bibliography* 39 [1986]:
1–46), and Anthony Hammond published an untitled review in *The Library* (Sixth Series 8: 382–390) which criticized Gabler's methods as well.
But for the general public, the next real shot in the Joyce Wars occurred
three years after the initial volley, and two years after the trade edition of
Gabler's version had forced other editions off the market. Kidd's article is
witty and succinct, admirably explaining arcane bibliographic details for a
non-bibliographic audience. It makes its case against the Gabler edition,
but without addressing textual theory—Kidd critiques the reading edition
more than the synoptic text, but makes clear that the several historical and
textual inaccuracies in the trade edition stem from flaws in the synoptic
edition. A look at Kidd's rhetorical stance in the *NYRB* article shows why,
in the name of non-Joyceans and non-scholars at least, Robin Bates
"award[ed] the era to John Kidd" ("Reflections" 136).

   Kidd opens the article with an anecdote about one Harry Thrift, a real
person who lived in Dublin and who came in second in a bicycle race in
1904. This race was a part of the "Wandering Rocks" episode of *Ulysses*
(*U*86 209.1258). But in the Gabler trade edition Thrift's name was
changed to Shrift. Kidd asks, "Did it occur to anyone to check whether
Thrift was a real person before changing him to Shrift? Apparently not"
(32). He goes on to call the trade edition's appearance a "transparent
scheme to replace *Ulysses* outright with another version" in hopes of a new
copyright, which "could only be accomplished by creating an entirely new

work, which in an unintended sense has been done" (32). Kidd takes the edition to task for calling the 1922 edition defective due to the French printers' mistakes; he writes, "Yet for six of these [Joycean coinages supposedly corrected for the first time], the majority, the 1922 and 1984 spellings are identical. Is no one awake at the wheel?" (32). Kidd asks such rhetorical questions throughout the article, creating a sense of outrage at the apparent crimes committed against Joyce's text. He uses words like "radically new *Ulysses*" and "disastrous," describes "bizarre assumptions" of the editors, calls the edition "worthless," and says that pages are "mangled." (32–36). He summarizes the *Corrected Text* in his final paragraph as "deceptive and inaccurate" (39). He refers to the widely repeated quote from Ellmann (originating in the *New York Times* article in 1984— see previous chapter) and wittily undermines this influential nod from Ellmann:

> . . . what did Ellmann think of the edition as a whole? Full page ads in the literary weeklies quoted him in banner blurbs:
>
> AN ABSOLUTELY STUNNING SCHOLARLY ACHIEVEMENT
> —Richard Ellmann
>
> This is far and away the most widely-known puff for the edition and is still in use in both America and England. Yet Ellmann never spoke such words. In a letter to me dated "22.iv.985" (sic) Ellmann wrote:
> Incidentally, the quotations from me in the press were inaccurate. "Stunning" was not one of my words, though of course I was approbatory. After this clarification, those promotions can blaze:
> I AM APPROBATORY
> —Richard Ellmann (38–39)

Kidd exhibits no restraint in his article, and given the response he had so far encountered from the scholarly world, it is easy to say that animus disguised as humor was the only intended effect. But it should also be noted that Kidd's use of humor and rhetorical flourishes was also an attempt to garner sympathy for his cause from the readers of the *NYRB*, and as such the sarcasm serves two audiences at once. Kidd's article shows a writer fully cognizant of the power of humor to win over an audience which might otherwise have dismissed his criticisms as uninteresting academic squabbling.

Rhetoric or no, many of Kidd's criticisms are worth considering. He lists several inaccuracies which derive from the use of facsimiles, by far the most serious charge against the Gabler edition to date. Kidd writes, ". . . facsimiles cannot be used to spot erasures, or decipher blurred and faint writing" (33), and he castigates Gabler's team to task for failing to consult the originals. He does allude to Gabler's methodology, but in predictably negative summary terms: "The palpable genius of Joyce's typescript revision is absent from the 1984 synopsis. The breakdown is traceable to the odd theory of the *Synoptic Edition* that all the fragments in Joyce's hand from early drafts through last proof insertions can be assembled like mosaic chips" (36). In criticizing this theory, he charges that the synopsis eliminates any typist's errors, even when they led to further revisions by Joyce. It is consequently impossible to see how such errors led to the changes Joyce made to his text during revision, and therefore the synoptic apparatus is incomplete. Kidd lists thirteen categories of change from "what Joyce actually wrote" introduced into the reading text; most of these revolve around spelling, names, and punctuation. The most serious category is listed eighth: "rejection of specific typographical features ordered by Joyce (and intentional suppression of Joyce's instructions to the printer, making a patchwork of *Joyce Archive* transcriptions)" (37). Further, Kidd outlines several instances of documents he turned up himself during research into the matter: Joyce's correspondence with Ezra Pound, letters to a typist of "Circe," the identity of one of the typists in Zurich, a set of Shakespeare and Company proofs with Sylvia Beach's changes, and a postcard to typist Claud Sykes giving instructions for alterations in the text which Gabler denied ever seeing ("Does the postcard exist at all? If so, where? And what are its instructions?") in his response to Kidd's paper, "Errors of Execution," among others. Kidd ends this extensive listing, which serves in part to quiet those who would impugn his own scholarly acumen, by lobbing a grenade: "Scavengers, good luck! Remember, facsimiles don't lie. But liars facsimile" (38).

By far, the most damaging charge against the Gabler edition was over the use of facsimiles. Yet the Rosenbach facsimiles, published in 1975, are in fact as remarkably clear as Kenner made them out to be in the *Harper's* article. They show erasures, faint markings, fingerprints, even the blue lines of the paper Joyce used (one notebook consists of graph paper, while the other manuscript pages are plain, loose-leaf pages). To the general reader, however, the word "facsimile" carries connotations of inferiority, particularly since "facsimile" can conjure up images of the common office technologies of "fax" machines and photocopiers, both unsatisfactory methods of reproducing text for editorial purposes. The Rosenbach facsimiles are closer to photographic reprints than photocopies. A check of the "Nestor" episode manuscript revealed sixty-three erasures, easily visible when holding the individual pages up to lamplight. All sixty-three of these erasures are detectable in the facsimile. For example, on MS page 7, line 49, the name "Cochrane" is written over an erasure, with markings of the original word still faintly visible around the edges of the erasure, and these markings are clearly reproduced in the facsimile. However, in the "Penelope" episode, MS page 3, there is a purple-hued ink smudge and on MS page 18, there are two fingerprint smudges; in the facsimile all three of these markings are visible, but only faintly so. In these particular instances, the facsimile is clearly inferior to the original, but none of these smudges affect the legibility of the writing. The facsimiles, contrary to what Kidd implies, were an excellent choice to begin transcription of the Rosenbach manuscript. Gabler consistently maintained that he or his team checked the originals when questions arose about individual emendations or when confirmation was required for particular findings. Such a policy seems adequate, given the detail in the facsimile. However, the common reader, not having access to the manuscript and highly unlikely to have a copy of the three-volume facsimile, is left with an impression from Kidd's description that this procedure was a sloppy way to go about editing *Ulysses*. Kidd's rhetorical flourish, "liars facsimile," serves to yoke dishonesty and inferiority in a damaging attack on Gabler's professionalism and a blatant attack on his integrity.

Kidd then moves from carefully documenting his criticisms to lapsing into an account of his grievances against the Joyce establishment. He states that it was "unfortunate" that the *NYRB* review fell to Richard Ellmann, "the godfather to the text," and he finds Kenner's review in the *TLS* suspicious, since Kenner had already undertaken what he called a "relentless American campaign" in favor of the edition. He also criticizes the *James Joyce Quarterly*:

> Without appearing to build a conspiracy theory, I must add that the *James Joyce Quarterly* assigned its only review of the new *Ulysses* to Michael Groden, who had long been a collaborator in the edition and was named on the title page of both the 1979 edition prototype and the finished 1984 text.
>
> And so it fell out that the players reviewed the play and found it pleasing. (39)

Of course, the coy beginning of this passage which pretends to eschew a conspiracy only serves to foreground such an idea, and the use of the word "collaborator" in such a context makes it sound very dark indeed. Perhaps Kidd can be forgiven for feeling as though he was surrounded by the enemy, but it is clear that by placing the suggestion of conspiracy in an article read by those outside the lines of battle, he is making a pitch for his own case. By 1988, then, Kidd had fully assumed the mantle of David battling Goliath which the *Post* article placed on him three years earlier. The final section is polemically charged, calling the 1986 edition "a radical version forged of shoddy scholarship and puffed out with grandiose claims" which "pushed Joyce's authorized version off the shelves"; Kidd states that the "publishers are victims as much as Joyce's readers and certainly are not to blame for this fiasco" (39). He calls the trade edition "corrupted" and says that "the stock should either be destroyed or given a new title page without the word 'corrected'," and that the 1961 edition should replace it. At this point Kidd's final paragraph states:

> With the deceptive and inaccurate *Corrected Text* out of the way, Joyce's publishers and estate will need to consider editing *Ulysses* afresh. If a foundation agrees to help, the scholarship can get under way. Until then, the Modern Library edition, the book roughly as Joyce last saw it, is the

best we have, and Random House can start shipping copies tomorrow if it wishes. (39)

It is clear that Kidd is making a pitch for "a foundation" to support a fresh edition of *Ulysses* edited by himself; again, his phrasing is coy ("if a foundation agrees to help": help whom?), using the third person in a disingenuous attempt to disguise such an obviously self-promoting gambit. This final section of the *NYRB* article, combined with Kidd's sarcasm throughout the piece, prompted a blitzkrieg of letters to the editor which continued for almost a full year.

Interestingly, the *New York Times* carried an article on June 15, 1988 on Kidd's charges and the ensuing controversy, mentioning the *NYRB* article (McDowell "Corrected *Ulysses* Sparks Scholarly Attack" C30). The *Times* piece describes Random House's decision to form a committee headed by Tanselle that would consider the charges and make a recommendation on whether or not to withdraw the Gabler edition. In this article, Jason Epstein, editorial director of Random House, stated that "Tom Tanselle and a group of experts" would advise the publisher, but that he was "inclined to think that the edition . . . is seriously flawed." McDowell summarizes the points in "Scandal of *Ulysses*," but quotes Gabler as stating that "[w]hat much of the dispute boils down to . . . are differences of opinion." McDowell also quotes Kenner, as he did for the 1984 article on the edition, who agreed with Gabler's description and characterized the dispute as "what are known in baseball as 'judgment calls'." Kenner is again described as "an authority on Joyce" from Johns Hopkins University, certainly another indication to a reader outside the fray that the Gabler edition still had support from the Joyce establishment. But Christine Froula, who had in a 1985 issue of *The Yale Review* praised the Gabler edition,[12] reversed her earlier assessment: "It turns out, as Kidd shows, that the groundwork was inadequately laid and the scholarship haphazard and unprofessional. . . . Now I don't think it can be patched up, the editing will have to be redone from the ground up." Other established scholars are quoted in support of Kidd, including Harry Levin, author of one of the most influential works on Joyce (see Chapter One). Curiously, he is only listed as a professor emeritus at Harvard; McDowell does not note Levin's venerated position in the Joycean academic world or as another "authority on Joyce" to balance Kenner's view. Certainly, Levin would be qualified for such a description. Denis Donoghue is also quoted in support of Kidd, and has the last word in the article:

> Professor Donoghue said the publishers should halt the distribution of the Gabler edition. But when told of Random House's plan to abide by the judgment of a committee headed by Professor Tanselle, he said, "That is an eminently reputable thing to do." (C30)

By ending with this quote, the article creates the impression that a disinterested scholarly investigation was being held on the issues involved; in reality the committee was racked with its own internal disputes, and was disbanded before ever reaching a conclusion.[13] The *Times* piece ran almost two weeks before Kidd's article appeared in the *NYRB*, and served in effect as advance advertising for it.[14] Further advertising the dispute, a small paragraph in *Time* magazine ran in the June 27, 1988 issue. The paragraph summarizes the controversy thus: "John Kidd, a scholar at the University of Virginia, charged that the edition had multiplied the errors that have plagued the masterpiece since its publication in 1922. Among the gaffes are misspellings that break up chains of allusions, and the reinsertion of a passage on love cut out by Joyce. Random House is considering a recall. As for Kidd, he is coming out with his own *Ulysses* in November" (47). It was this piece that broadcast Kidd's intention of editing *Ulysses* himself, and gave a specific time frame for that edition. It is not clear from the *Time* piece where this information comes from, and it seems inaccurate to say the least; unless Kidd had been editing *Ulysses* for years already, there is no way he could have published his own edition in five months' time. But indeed, Kidd had been involved as an advisor to the Robert Motherwell-illustrated Arion Press edition of *Ulysses*, which did come out later that year, a special collector's edition of 150 copies at $7500 apiece. The *Time* article, however, implies that Kidd is the editor of a rival *Ulysses*, rather than being involved in someone else's project. The article is also inaccurate in attributing the claims against the infamous "love passage" to Kidd; his *NYRB* article does mention this passage, but only in describing Ellmann's reversal on the issue as support for Kidd's contention that the edition is flawed, not as a defect pointed out by Kidd himself. Inaccuracies aside, the effect of the last sentence in the *Time* paragraph is to underscore the commercial implications of the debate, and leaves the impression that Kidd's criticisms stem from his own interests rather than any scholarly investigation. Further, since it appeared in a general interest news magazine in a section devoted to celebrity gossip, and placed as it was between a paragraph on a race horse that bites and a piece on the break-up of recording artist Bruce Springsteen's marriage, the seriousness of the debate seems questionable. The vast audience outside the confines of the debate are given the impression that the conflict is simply a dispute between personalities. Even so, given this advance advertising there is no doubt that, for the principals at least, the *NYRB* piece would make a huge impact on the debate. And so it did.

Meanwhile, Roger Shattuck and Douglas Alden's "Searching for the True Text" appeared in the *Times Literary Supplement* (10–16 June 1988: 640–641). While their article is primarily a critique of another controversial editing project on Proust, they mention early in the piece that copyright considerations are tainting classic literature with "spurious" new editions; below are the excerpts relevant to the Gabler-Kidd controversy and which sparked most of the letters to the *TLS* following the article's appearance:

For certain commercially valuable works an association of publishers, holders of expiring copyrights, and scholars can produce a "definitive critical edition" that establishes a new copyright. Instead of releasing the great works of the twentieth century into the public domain of more varied and less expensive copies, the new editions seek to recapture the books for commercial exploitation. In the past few years precociously classic works by Joyce and Proust have fallen into the public domain and offer us two test cases in this confusing state of affairs.

. . .We now know, thanks to John Kidd (see the *TLS* of May 10, 1985; a comprehensive essay will appear soon in the *New York Review of Books*), that the allegedly corrected text is a travesty of editorial procedure and creates more errors and confusions than it corrects.

. . . In Britain and the United States commercialism triumphed and almost cowed Joyce scholarship into silence. (640–641)

The May 10, 1985 article they refer to is by the *TLS* editor, Jeremy Treglown, who called for a halt to any trade edition after hearing Kidd's initial paper, "Errors of Execution," at the Society for Textual Scholarship conference in April 1985 ("Editors Vary" 520). Shattuck and Alden's article prompted almost as many letters to the *TLS* as did Kidd's "Scandal" to the *NYRB*. The following chapter analyzes the letters in both publications as examples of Foucault's description of polemics as "a parasitic figure on discussion and an obstacle to the search for the truth" ("Polemics, Politics, and Problematizations: An Interview" 382). The "true" text of *Ulysses*, ostensibly the reason for all the quarreling, became secondary once the battles began in earnest, primarily because it seemed that the combatants were trying to score points rather than rationally discuss their differences. The more minute the points of contention became, the less relevance the arguments seemed to have for the reader of *Ulysses*. The common reader, to use Amis' words, remained unconsulted on the matter, and eventually the whole schism became fodder for parody in popular publications. And Joyce's book became even more firmly entrenched as a "special case" within the ideology of literature, as it began to appear that every name, every comma, was imbued with significance—and an unholy lot of scrabblers was claiming to know the "truth" of *Ulysses*.

NOTES

[1] "The Critical Reception of the 'Gabler *Ulysses*': or, Gabler's *Ulysses* Kidd-napped" *Studies in the Novel* 21 (1989): 175.

[2] Robin Bates offers a similar perspective on Kenner's enthusiasm for computers: "Kenner is a computer-buff. He likes computers and sees them as the way ahead. He recognized Gabler as a pioneer—correctly; computerizing *Ulysses* began a half-dozen years before most of us had workstations on our desktops. As a pioneer, Gabler needed encouragement and protection, irrespective, almost, of the eventual outcome. Kenner became the technology's champion" ("Reflections on the Kidd Era," *Studies in the Novel* 22 [Summer 1990]: 134). Bates's article leans heavily in

favor of Kidd, with little real understanding of Gabler's methods; however, his analysis of Kenner's role here is perceptive.

[3]Gabler's articles were: "And Now: *Ulysses* as James Joyce Wrote It: Working on a Critical Edition," *German Research: Reports of the DFG* (1979): 25–26; "Computer-Aided Critical Edition of *Ulysses*," *ALLC Bulletin* 8 (1981): 232–248; "The Synchrony and Diachrony of Texts: Practice and Theory of the Critical Edition of James Joyce's *Ulysses*," Text 1 (1981): 305–326. This latter article was not actually published until 1984. Gabler's lone article, prior to the publication of his edition, appearing in a volume aimed at literary critics rather than textual scholars appeared in a publication of the James Joyce Society of Sweden and Finland: "James Joyce as Author and Scribe: A Problem in Editing 'Eumaeus'," *Nordic Rejoycings 1982—In Commemoration of the Centenary of the Birth of James Joyce*: 98–105. Another article was privately published and made available by Gabler at the 1979 James Joyce Symposium held in Zurich: "*Ulysses* II.5: Prototype of a Critical Edition in Progress" and created little stir, according to Bruce Arnold (110). The Zurich James Joyce Foundation also has copies of this article available in its collection.

[4]Gabler's stated vision of his edition's place as a complement to other editions of *Ulysses* also seems a bit disingenuous. The reality is that the prohibitive size and cost of the synoptic edition virtually guarantees that it would not be used in the classroom, or that the non-professional Joycean would purchase it. An interesting discussion of this issue can be found in Patrick McGee's "Is There a Class for this Text? The New *Ulysses*, Jerome McGann, and the Issue of Textual Authority" *Works and Days: Essays in the Socio-Historical Dimensions of Literature and the Arts* (Fall 1987: 27–44).

[5]The only other letter received in response to Kenner's review was from Ruth Bauerle, a noted Joycean from Ohio Wesleyan University. She corrects the Latin in Kenner's citation of the infamous restored "love" passage: "Kenner cites, as an important restoration to the text, the passage (p 419 of the new edition) identifying the 'word known to all men' but only inferred by Joyce's readers for six decades. Thinking of this word 'love,' Stephen Dedalus muses '*Amor vero aliquid alicui bonum vult unde et ea quae concupiscimus . . .*' This Latin passage has emerged from Kenner's typewriter or from the *TLS* typographer as '*Amplius veri alius* (sic) *alicui bonum vult unde et ea quae concupiscimus.*' Even Joyce could err: *Amor vero aliquid* is, apparently, *not* known to all" (10 Aug. 1984). This letter evinced no published response from Kenner.

[6]Ellmann's presentation published in *Assessing the 1984* Ulysses, eds. C. George Sandulescu and Clive Hart (London and New York: Colin Smythe and Barnes & Noble, 1986).

[7]This phrase was included in the Garland prospectus for the edition, which presumably provided much of the information for the *Times* piece (I am indebted to Hans Gabler for pointing this out to me in a phone conversation on March 23, 2002).

[8]In a letter cited by John Kidd in "The Scandal of *Ulysses*" (*New York Review of Books*, 30 June 1988:39), Ellmann stated, "Incidentally, the quotations from me in the press were inaccurate. 'Stunning' was not one of my words, though of course I was approbatory." For Kidd's use of Ellmann's letter, see p. 144.

[9]This characterization of Kidd continued with an article in *The Observer*, titled "James Joyce and the Nutty Professor" (Warren St. John, 23 Dec. 1997: *The Ob-*

*server* archive online, observer@aol.com, 24 July 1998; also available at the Joyce Wars website, http://home.att.net/≈fnord32/jjnp.html, 19 Mar. 1998). St. John compares Kidd to a "grandiose Hollywood director who has run over budget and out of time," referring to Kidd's long-awaited edition of *Ulysses*. Further, Kidd is described as "an amiable but driven eccentric" who rescues injured mice, pigeons, and worms on the campus of Boston University, and who, "on one occasion, . . . showed up at his office with a sick duck." He calls some of his graduate students "Joyce nuts," an ironic designation given the earlier description of Kidd in the 1985 *Post* article. More recently, an article in the Boston Globe detailed Kidd's health problems after leaving Boston University amid allegations of misconduct, and portrayed Kidd as out of touch with reality: "Kidd became 'estranged from the community of academics' and obsessive about Joyce, even affecting the novelist's appearance"; "Kidd promises a comeback. He contends that the publishing companies have conspired against him to block the release of his manuscript"; and the article ends with a quote from Kidd that on bad days he is "just like a brain in a jar . . . [He] can't do anything" (Abel). Kidd does say that he is "not a basket case . . . [He's] planning to get well and to retire in [his] 70s," but this quote seems buried among other, less flattering descriptions. The article paints him as a rebel and a fire-brand, paying the price for "rocking the boat." For the general public, Kidd is still the "nutty professor," but rather than the slightly bemused tone of the *Observer* article five years earlier, this article evokes pity.

[10]Curiously, the designation of Joyce being a "writer's writer" is echoed over ten years later in a *New Yorker* article on the exhibition of some first editions of *Ulysses* given to Joyce's supporters and admirers. See chapter 2.

[11]An early review by a novelist which takes a similar approach is Arnold Bennett's "James Joyce's *Ulysses*", first printed in the *Outlook*, April 29, 1922: 337–339 and reprinted in *The Author's Craft and Other Critical Writings of Arnold Bennett*, edited by Samuel Hynes. Lincoln: University of Nebraska Press, 1968.

[12]"The Adventures of *Ulysses*," *The Yale Review* 74 (1985): 454–466.

[13]See Bates, "Reflections on the Kidd Era" *Studies in the Novel* 22 (Summer 1990): 136–138 for a quoted lengthy conversation with Jason Epstein, who left the committee in a dispute unrelated to the Gabler edition. Epstein refused to divulge the nature of the disagreement but Bates reveals that it had to do with Epstein and Tanselle's membership on the board of the Library of America, where Epstein and Tanselle had had numerous disagreements. Epstein was removed as treasurer, then voted off the board within a two-month period; Tanselle voted for Epstein's removal. Tanselle learned of Epstein's dissociation from the Gabler committee through Bates's article in the *Smithsonian* (detailed later in this study), and said that he had "set up the committee as a favor to Epstein." The future of the committee was then cast into doubt, since it was solely to advise Random House that it was set up in the first place; the committee disbanded in 1990 without Gabler ever reporting to it in response to Kidd's criticisms.

[14]The June 22, 1988 edition of the *Chronicle of Higher Education* also ran an article ("Much-Heralded New Edition of Joyce's *Ulysses* Is Badly Flawed, Virginia Scholar Contends" A6+) about Kidd's charges and forthcoming article in the *NYRB*, but the article only mentions that this piece is a shortened version of Kidd's paper for the *Papers of the Bibliographical Society of America*. The *Chronicle*, aimed at the academic community, served to advertise Kidd's piece in this forum as

well, and contributed to the interest in the *NYRB* article. The *Chronicle*, however, went to Michael Groden for quotes in support of Gabler, and to Tanselle for information about the committee; there are no quotes from Kidd or any indication that the *Chronicle* attempted to contact him. The article specifically mentions that Gabler, "who was attending a Joyce conference in Venice, could not be reached for comment" (A13). On the whole, the *Chronicle* article appears to be less allied with Kidd than the *New York Times* piece.

CHAPTER FIVE

# SELECTED PAPERS OF THE JOYCE WARS,
## in which
# A MIDDEN HEAP BECOMES A PILE OF LETTERS

*Few combatants of the wars anticipated the fame (and infamy) which came to redound and rebound upon them.*

—*John Kidd*

*Strange things happen in the groves of academe . . .*

—*William Robertson,*
Miami Herald *Book Editor*

The first letter of reply to Kidd's article in the *NYRB* was from Gabler in the August 18, 1988 issue, a lengthy piece which explains in somewhat vague terms the theoretical aims of Gabler's edition, and responds to several of Kidd's specific charges of error in his article. The letter states that Kidd's allegations of not checking originals against facsimiles "scandalously rebounds upon [Kidd] himself" (63). Gabler rebuts a specific charge of error (a spelling variant of "tway" and "twey"), citing evidence to support his own reading, and then turns the allegations of inconsistency back upon Kidd: "Clamouring for bibliographic analysis, Dr. Kidd yet wilfully closes his eyes to the editorial consequences of its results." He does give credit to Kidd for catching some errors, but primarily he condemns Kidd:

> The scanty array of examples provides not even the flimsiest of foundations for a critique, let alone a condemnation of the critical and synoptic edition, or, particularly, the current trade editions—not to speak of the slurs on the competence and scholarly integrity of the editor and editorial team—such as they are flourished in Dr. Kidd's rhetoric of allegations, insinuations and sweepingly generalising assertions. (63)

Gabler states that he was not responsible for the subtitle "The Corrected Text" on the trade edition; it was "a phrase coined . . . by agreement between the James Joyce Estate and the publishers." Clearly he is distancing himself from the commercially exploitative implications of the subtitle.

Gabler then devotes the rest of his letter to explaining in vague terms the fact that Kidd's objections stem from misunderstanding Gabler's editorial theory: "the critical edition is a text edition, not a manuscript edition . . . it telescopes textual developments into a synopsis, using diacritics and symbols to refer its textual and editorial results to the manuscripts and other documents where the writing acts implicitly or explicitly took place. . . . [The] reading text is the editorial suggestion—as any and every edited text is an editorial suggestion—of a valid text for *Ulysses*." Gabler closes with a scathing assessment of Kidd's suggestion to do away with the Gabler edition and go back to the 1961 edition: "To profess, in the end, to be unable to deal with the critical scholarship internationally invested in the editing of James Joyce's novel of the century in any other way than by scrapping its evidence and returning to the highly inauthentic printing of 1961 is to admit utter helplessness before the challenge of *Ulysses*."

Gabler seems frustrated in this letter; he patiently attempts to explain his theoretical approach and answer Kidd's specific charges, although he more or less dismisses their importance. He does try to be even-handed in acknowledging that Kidd has uncovered some new material, but overall he feels that Kidd missed the fundamentals of the theory behind the edition. It is certainly less fiery than his reply at the Society for Textual Scholarship conference three years prior, but the letter still ends on a challenging note. With a knowledge of Gabler's intended aims, the letter makes a great deal of sense in its rebuttals; but for a general public with little understanding of the textual theory involved, it seems inappropriately dismissive of Kidd's charges. The other letters in this "round" show that Kidd had made more than a few respected converts: the novelist John Updike, and the scholar Robert M. Adams, whose 1962 *Surface and Symbol: The Consistency of James Joyce's "Ulysses"* is a highly respected work in Joyce circles. There were also three other respondents, only one of whom identified herself as an academic. Updike's letter raises the issue of the dialogue dashes for the first time, stating that Gabler's edition places them flush left, rather than indented as Joyce passed in proof (63). Adams's letter states that he "is persuaded by Mr. John Kidd's evidence that the Gabler edition is fatally flawed." He suggests that a "proper edition of the book will be cumbersome, pedantic, and encyclopedic—beyond the powers of any but a team of trained and disciplined researchers. It will take a long time, and by itself may not be worth the effort; but it will provide an indispensable basis for a reading edition of the book in which the common reader can feel at least a minimal confidence" (63–64). Although Adams's description could also be said of Gabler's edition, he shows a literary critic's traditional understanding of the stability of a text derived from critical editing. Updike's letter, not unexpectedly, sticks up for authorial intention; he writes that the Gabler edition is "a mistaken scholarly fidelity to holograph mannerisms that were never meant by the author to be translated into type" (63). Updike bases his inference on the fact that Joyce passively authorized the

French printer's indention of the dashes in proofs for the 1922 edition. Whether or not Gabler can justify placing the dashes flush left through his editorial intentions to render the pre-production *Ulysses* in an "ideal" state is an arguable point since, as Kidd points out in his reply printed after these letters, the manuscript shows the text flush left and the dashes further left, *into* the margin. Neither Gabler's flush left dashes nor the indented dashes follow the manuscript practice. But Updike's contention that Joyce did not seem to mind the indented dashes in proof throughout the typesetting of *Ulysses* would seem to be a valid one for recommending the indentations be put back in, particularly since all three of Joyce's other major works— *Dubliners*, *Portrait*, and *Finnegans Wake*—show the dashes indented.

Robert Craft wrote to question Kidd's own command of English. Craft says that Kidd does not inspire much confidence in his assertions, since Kidd wrote ungrammatically, "neither . . . are mentioned" at one point in his article. Craft further quotes Kidd: "'The "Eumaeus" episode is cliché, euphemism, redundancy, and mashed metaphor ambered in a gooey senti- mentality.' To amber in goo?" (64). Beverly Fields, the only one to identify herself as an academic, wrote in support of Kidd, stating in her first sen- tence that though "the study of James Joyce is not my specialty, the fire- bomb that John Kidd flung at the 'corrected' text of *Ulysses* sparked my intention to complain someplace about a small misdemeanor in the Gabler edition" (64). This "misdemeanor" is the substitution of "chord" for "cord" in the 'Sirens' episode (*U* 86 227.791). She ends her letter: "John Kidd is to be commended generally, and specifically for forbearing to ana- grammatize Gabler's name as Garble."

John Kidd's reply to this set of letters is a witty and sardonic response couched inside of a fictional story:

> In the year 2088, the general editor of *Selected Papers of the Joyce Wars* has her hands full. She finds the documents (paper, electronic, and plasmic) surviving from 1988 incomplete, contradictory, error-prone, stylistically archaic and a touch comic. Letters in one issue of *The New York Review* keep Professor Futura and her textological lexica busy for weeks. (64)

Kidd, in the persona of a reporter describing Professor Futura's thoughts, says that John Updike's "protest against the 1984 quotation dashes . . . strikes Professor Futura as long overdue" (64). He continues, "Professor Futura regrets having to correct Updike's statement" that Joyce's manu- scripts show the dash without indentation, but manages to make a quick stab at Gabler in his correction: "Updike is misled by Gabler's cunning phrase 'without indentation.' Gabler refuses to say that no manuscript of *Ulysses* has his own system of flush-left dashes. Rather, all the manuscripts have the dashes well into the margin" (64). He agrees with Adams that "an editor seeks 'balanced probabilities,'" implying that Gabler did not. Fur- ther, in a parenthesis Kidd states that the "'absolute confidence' sought by Robert Craft is unattainable." It would seem that Kidd mistook Adams's call for an edition the common reader could feel "at least minimal confidence" in with Craft's judgment on the editors of *James Joyce's Letters to Sylvia Beach,* a work that exposed errors in the Gilbert and Ellmann edition of Joyce's letters. Craft points out that those editors "do not inspire absolute confidence" because they misspell "financial strai*gh*ts," among other oversights (italics in original). Kidd seems to believe that Craft calls for an edition one can feel absolute confidence in; what Craft's letter makes clear is that he simply desires for editors to proofread their own material. Craft's own criticisms of Kidd's grammar and syntax go unanswered. Kidd does defend Ellmann's work on the Joyce letters, saying that at times he followed "the sloppy transcriptions typed by Sylvia Beach. [Professor Futura] notes that . . . [t]extology was less sophisticated in the Pre-Post-Modernist age. The Joyce Wars of Eightyeight changed all that" (65). This was the first time that the name Joyce Wars saw print.

Kidd devotes the rest of his narrative to further criticizing Gabler. He begins by mocking Gabler's style: "The letter of H.W. Gabler is in a prose unfamiliar to Professor Futura. Her plasma syntactic collator cannot identify the dialect. She inserts a sample Gablergraph for a plasma search under 'academic prose' and retrieves only 'Thomas Carlyle *SEE* Professor Diogenes Teufelsdröckh.'"[1] Kidd moves on from this wry comparison of Gabler to Carlyle's often dense and syntactically challenged alter ego to repeat his charges that the Gabler team relied overly on facsimiles and never checked them against the originals. After quoting Gabler's claims that originals were checked, Kidd again pokes fun at Gabler's speech patterns:

> Convinced by Kidd's examples from documents in Philadelphia, Buffalo, and at Harvard that the Gabler team could not possibly have checked all editorial work against originals, Professor Futura wonders why Gabler insists in his letter to *The New York Review* that:
> > They did. Dr. Kidd knows and has known this since the early 1980s when we first met. For him to assert otherwise scandalously rebounds upon himself.
> [Irony abounds. What redounds to Dr. Kidd rebounds. On several grounds, it sounds; he's out of bounds.] (65)

After this humorous and Joycean play with words, Kidd addresses the theoretical issues Gabler raised in his response—but he does so in a deft sleight of hand which allows him to sidestep the theory:

> Some of the most forceful arguments in Gabler's letter [Professor Futura] finds plausible, yet [she] searches in vain for the Kidd passages Gabler purports to refute. Powerful blows strike against the air . . . [She] is unable to locate any book, article, paper, interview, lecture, draft, panel discussion, radio broadcast, jotting, or doodle in which Kidd used the terms *manuscript edition, diplomatic fidelity, topographic fidelity,* or *layout of manuscripts.* The "basic misconceptions in Dr. Kidd's assumptions" that haunt Gabler are lost to history. (65)

Kidd focuses in on specific phrases rather than theoretical conceptions here, and neatly avoids any discussion of his own theoretical basis for editing. Such a move in essence naturalizes his own author-centered, traditional approach to editing: it is unnecessary to expound upon his own basis because it is obviously the right way, and Gabler's methodology is cast as heretical and strange. Such a rhetorical move falls neatly into Foucault's formulation of polemics: "The polemicist . . . proceeds encased in privileges that he possesses and will never agree to question. . . . his final objective will be, not to come as close as possible to a difficult truth, but to bring about the triumph of the just cause he has been manifestly upholding from the beginning. The polemicist relies on a legitimacy that his adversary is by definition denied" ("Polemics, Politics, and Problematizations" 382). Kidd had, from the start of his campaign against the Gabler edition, positioned himself in the service of the true text of *Ulysses* and against what he saw as the dishonesty of calling the Gabler edition a "corrected" text.[2] Kidd ends his narrative of Professor Futura's *Selected Papers of the Joyce Wars* with more "Kidding" prose: "Few combatants of the wars anticipated the fame (and infamy) which came to redound and rebound upon them" (65). Kidd slyly leaves unclear who became famous and who infamous; either epithet could apply to him, based on this particular performance.

Meanwhile, in the *TLS* Gabler also responded to Shattuck and Alden's article, saying that they derived their information from "a journalistic piece of writing in the *New York Review of Books*" (1–7 July 1988: 733). Gabler states that the

> economic and legal side-issues of the trade publication of *Ulysses* do not here concern me, although I assure you they are ludicrously misrepresented by your reviewers' remarks. What troubles me is the facile dismissal of the foundations of the *Ulysses* edition . . . The critical and synoptic edition may claim the scholarly attention that your reviewers give the Proust editions they discuss. The separate trade publication of the reading text fulfills a demand for expensive scholarly editions to be made available in affordable forms. (733)

Here Gabler again distances himself from the commercial interests surrounding his edition, but seems to pass over the fact that, if his edition was intended to be primarily the synoptic text, then publishing the reading text without the apparatus is, frankly, dishonest. This decision, based as it was on the Joyce Estate's ignorance of the real textual theory Gabler used, was not entirely Gabler's doing. He is walking a fine line in this letter: he cannot publicly castigate the Joyce Estate for its decision to go ahead with the trade edition (and market it as the definitively "corrected" text), but he cannot simply let the accusations go, either, since they impugn his own scholarship. The Joyce Estate in effect left Gabler between Scylla and Charybdis. Gabler explains his editorial practice in greater detail in this letter than he did in his letter to *The New York Review of Books*. In fact,

Kidd's article so focuses the debate on specific errors that he virtually single-handedly dictated its direction. As such, Gabler had little choice but to respond to a few of the specifics, but his refusal to go further is apparently based on his firm belief that John Kidd misunderstands his project. In fact, Kidd understands it perfectly well, but he espouses a completely different concept of editing than Gabler, choosing instead to follow the traditional, author-centered school. Kidd's focus in "Scandal" had to center on specifics simply because Kidd showed a full understanding that a general readership (the audience for the *NYRB*) would either get lost in or bored by bibliographic arguments grounded in theory rather than specific instances of variation. He was not aiming his article primarily at the academic textual establishment, but at a broader audience of readers and scholars unfamiliar for the most part with textual editing theory. In this respect, Gabler lost before he even got started, since he could not debate the issue in terms of theory but had to refute Kidd's specific allegations or look like a fool.

Gabler's letter is followed in the next issue (8–14 July 1988: 755) by one from Peter du Sautoy, defending the Joyce Estate from Shattuck and Alden's charges of commercial exploitation. Du Sautoy states that the "Trustees did not authorize the publication of the 'Corrected Text' because they wanted to secure continuing royalties but simply because they were aware of the corruption of the existing text and they wanted to get it right if they possibly could."[3] He goes on to say that "[t]exts that are comprehensively edited acquire a copyright status of their own and the Trustees accepted this fact." Du Sautoy shifts responsibility to the publishers: "The trade publishers, Bodley Head and Random House, were parties to the contract for the Gabler text, as they had to be since they hold exclusive licenses to publish *Ulysses* during the copyright period. But there was no suggestion that they would have to take the Gabler text if they didn't want to." The publishers, of course, relied on the credentials of the academic advisers to guarantee that the edition was worth taking; with the approval of Richard Ellmann and the Joyce Estate, what reason could they have had for rejecting Gabler's edition? There is no indication in du Sautoy's account of the edition's history that the publishers were even notified of any disagreements arising among the advisers. He further states that he was "aware that our advisers occasionally had reservations but at no time did they say 'This edition must not be published,' and I think it is fair to claim that the edition now available is in general the best there is" (755). Given the doubts which surfaced during the project (see Chapter Three), this claim seems disingenuous; by the time the Estate was aware of the objections of the advisers (here he refers to Gaskell and Hart), and that some scholars had real misgivings about the edition, including the chief adviser Richard Ellmann, the Estate felt that it was too late to scrap the whole project. But du Sautoy, in his letter, understandably puts the best face on the situation possible; Charles Rossman's article "The New *Ulysses*: The Hidden Controversy" had yet to be published in the *NYRB*, so the public had no way of knowing at this point that du Sautoy's version of events in this letter was slightly off the mark.

In the July 22–28, 1988 issue of *TLS*, Kidd apprises British readers of his side of the story. He mentions the "Scandal of *Ulysses*" and Gabler's response to it, and defends Shattuck and Alden against Gabler's charge that Kidd is the "sole source for their condemnation of his work. However, scholars the rank and experience of Professors Shattuck and Alden rightly make up their own minds on the evidence before them." But Shattuck and Alden cite Kidd's *NYRB* article, so Gabler's conclusion is not unreasonable. Kidd answers Gabler's volley that he (Kidd) has not published his views and findings in scholarly forums by listing, for the bulk of the letter, all of his scholarly output concerning the edition, and enlists the *TLS*'s own editor, Jeremy Treglown, in support of his cause: "You yourself, Sir . . . concluded that the Joyce Estate should delay publication of the Gabler text."[4] He then mentions his forthcoming piece for the *Papers of the Bibliographic Society of America*, and that "Gabler will be asked to reply, and other experts will be approached for comments." He continues:

> In the meantime, the articles cited above can be found in libraries. If any are unavailable in Britain (such as "Errors of Execution"), requests for photocopies can be made to me. Offprints of the *NYRB* "Scandal of *Ulysses*" will be sent by me gratis.
>     Letters of support or criticism may be sent to the chair of the Random House investigative committee, G. Thomas Tanselle, Vice-President, John Simon Guggenheim Foundation, [address follows]. (818)

Gabler would reply to this letter by saying that "Dr Kidd's letter highlights the problematics of a mail-order business in academia . . . [which] constitute[s] an unprecedented form of scholarly exchange" (*TLS* 12–18 Aug. 1988: 883). Kidd responds to Gabler's attack in the next issue:

> Now Hans Walter Gabler . . . portrays your Proust reviewers Roger Shattuck and Douglas Alden, who in passing criticized the new *Ulysses* as a "textual travesty" . . . as dupes of international mail fraud. May I interject some geography into the Scandal of *Ulysses*? No "mail-order business" sent my published articles, reviews and interviews, as well as a single unpublished paper, to your Proust reviewers. Professor Shattuck walked down the hall from the French Department, past the watercooler to my office ten yards from the candy machines. (*TLS* 19–25 Aug. 1988: 907)

Again, it seems that Kidd deliberately misreads Gabler's words, though perhaps not their spirit. Gabler did not refer to Shattuck and Alden's acquiring of Kidd's paper, but rather Kidd's publicizing of his willingness to mail copies of articles in his own support. And it seems curious that in his previous letter, Kidd implies that Shattuck and Alden did not read his article; here he states that he is "down the hall" from Shattuck, which would seem to indicate a passing familiarity with each other. By this point in their

exchange, however, neither Kidd nor Gabler were interested in the meat of
the debate; they were out for each other's blood, and contradictions
abound in their letters. Kidd abandons the measured tone he took in his
prior letter to the *TLS* and levels the same sarcastic wit he showed in his
*NYRB* article:

> Your readers doubtless scarfed up my article in the June 30 *New York Re-*
> *view of Books* and tittered over the exchange of long letters with Gabler
> in the August 18 *NYRB* (another, longer exchange is now being set in
> type). In Gabler's latest complaint to the *TLS*, my writings are "mailing
> materials." Does he mean the paper, cardboard and tape to wrap a parcel?
> ("Junk mail" may be the *Poststoff* Gabler is grappling for.) (907)

Kidd audaciously presumes to teach Gabler how to translate German, and
such sarcasm characterizes his tone throughout. He continues:

> Gabler imagines that Professors Shattuck and Alden did not see me set
> right before they dismissed his edition. But Shattuck read Gabler's *Kidd-*
> *Schlag*—it is so thunderous, so thrilling, so theatrical, that I have sent
> eighty copies of it to Joyceans in a dozen nations. (I learned what he calls
> this "unprecedented form of scholarly exchange" from Gabler himself,
> who circulated amused Joyceans with his Response. . . .). (907)

Kidd quotes Gabler's response, but only those parts "which refer to
[Kidd's] detested person." He ends the letter with another offer: "Anyone
seeking *portofrei* copies of Gabler's and Rose's roaring rebuttals, or the
*Poststoff* which roused their wrath, may request them from me." At this
point, all pretense at civility is gone.

In the 2–8 Sept. 1988 issue, Charles Rossman responds to Peter du
Sautoy's letter (963). He describes the letters he recently turned up in the
Ellmann papers at the University of Tulsa which would lead to his article,
"The New *Ulysses*: The Hidden Controversy" in the *NYRB* (8 Dec. 1988:
32–39; see Chapter Three). Rossman refutes du Sautoy and Gabler's assertions that commercial interests had nothing to do with the new edition. He
quotes a letter from du Sautoy to Gaskell in which du Sautoy states that he
has become aware of the divisions between Gabler and the committee of
advisers, and that the first concern of the estate is that the changes made to
the edition justify new copyright. Rossman cites another letter from du
Sautoy which stated that two years would elapse between publication of
the critical edition and a trade edition, in order for scholars to assess it.
Rossman writes, "one might conclude from du Sautoy's letter to Richard
Ellmann of August 13, 1985, that the Estate regarded Gabler's critical edition as under siege, and that they were eager to get out a trade edition before too much damage had been inflicted" (963). Rossman quotes the same
letter to refute du Sautoy's explanation to the *TLS* that the Joyce estate
agreed that two years would elapse before a trade edition would appear:
"the Estate had to make a decision as to whether a trade edition 'was desir-
able' within those two years . . . . Du Sautoy frets about the 'flurry caused

by Kidd' and by the Monaco symposium. . . . This haste hardly comports with du Sautoy's recent assertion in the *TLS* that the Estate's principal concern was an edition carefully assessed by scholars" (963). The second grenade had been thrown at the Gabler edition, and this one seemed even more damaging than Kidd's. For a scholarly edition to be 'tainted' by monetary concerns insults the kind of image that the academy holds about itself—and the image it wishes to broadcast to the public. Following this letter in the next issue of *TLS*, du Sautoy responds that "[a] careful reading of Charles Rossman's letter . . . does not suggest to me any basic incompatibility with what I said in my letter. . . . The really important point at issue is the text itself and I can only infer that Professor Rossman does not feel up to tackling that. Instead, he has chosen to concentrate on a side-issue on which there is really very little to say" (9–15 Sept. 1988: 989). Du Sautoy chooses to ignore the implications of this "side-issue" and does not respond to Rossman's allegation that the Estate decided to publish the trade edition before "too much damage" had occurred to Gabler's edition.

Below du Sautoy's letter Stephen James Joyce, grandson of James Joyce, speaks up on the issue. His letter is worth quoting at length:

> Much ado about nothing? A tempest in a teapot? The blind leading the deaf and dumb (no offense intended to each of these categories of afflicted people)? Scholars trying to build reputations? The Kidd-Gabler controversy is assuming ludicrous proportions and the assurance, even arrogance, of the arguments of the protagonists, including Messrs Alden, Shattuck and Rossman, is quite staggering.
>
> I do not wish to immerse myself in any way in this unseemly, undignified "scholarly brawl" or to discuss the merits and demerits of either side. I would add that I was not in any way involved in the preparation and publication of the "Corrected Text" of *Ulysses*. When I was given the first symbolic copy in Frankfurt on June 16, 1984, I stated: "Whether it will prove to be the definitive version of *Ulysses* is another matter, and only time will tell."
>
> It is my view that this dispute is *essentially* of interest to a hundred-odd Joyce scholars and possibly also several times that number of students. The reading public can and should continue to read and enjoy either the 1961 text or the 1986 "Corrected Text," whatever the edition, until the scholars and the Estate agree on a text, whenever that may be. (989; italics in original)

The letter ends: "Sensationalism will not solve the problem, nor will the glare of spotlights." Stephen Joyce places the debate firmly within the Ivory Tower, and implies that such debate is unrelated to the real business of reading his grandfather's work.

Stephen James Joyce has never been friendly to scholars; according to a story titled "The Wars of the Joyces" that ran in *The Washington Post* on July 10, 1988, the Joyce family blocked publication of the epilogue of Brenda Maddox's biography of Nora Barnacle Joyce, which dealt with "the life of James and Nora Joyce's schizophrenic daughter Lucia in the years after both her parents had died" (Mundy F8), and Maddox was not permitted to quote at length from the infamous "dirty letters" exchanged between Joyce and his wife while he was in Ireland briefly in 1909.[5] The *Post* article also reveals that Stephen Joyce, "in response to Maddox's book, . . . has burned a collection of letters written by . . . Lucia to prevent their falling into the hands of future biographers" (Mundy F1+). He states that he "'believe[s] that the Joyce family privacy has been invaded and abused, if you wish, more than that of any literary figure in this century'" (Mundy F8). Stephen Joyce here taps into the mythic Joyce, greatest writer of the twentieth century; the words "invaded and abused" are somewhat melodramatic and indicate Stephen Joyce's long opposition to scholars, based on his idea of Joyce as an international monument.

The *Post* article continues, describing the Kidd-Gabler dispute and referring to Kidd's *NYRB* article, the answering letters, and the *New York Times* article of June 15, 1988 (see above). Mundy quotes A. Walton Litz in support of Gabler, and lists his credentials as a "professor of English at Princeton University and author of 'The Art of James Joyce'"; what she doesn't point out is that Litz assisted Gabler on the 1984 edition. Mundy writes: "Others remain loyal to the Gabler edition. . . . Contending that 'only about 20 people in the world understand this issue,' Litz said that 'if John Kidd wants to discredit the edition, he must do it in great detail in a scholarly forum, and not through the news media'" (F8). Again, the result of such a statement is that these editorial issues are removed from the world of general readers, and almost made to seem irrelevant as a result. The use of the "news media" (which, ironically, is precisely where Litz's words are being read) is denigrated as an unworthy outlet for the concerns of scholars and critics.

Later in the article, Mundy writes that scholars agree "that any attempt to create a truly 'authoritative' edition of *Ulysses* is impossible, given the novel's chaotic printing history" (F8). What goes unremarked here is that it's not just the printing history which prevents an "authoritative" edition but the fact that textual scholars for the most part do not subscribe to the notion of a definitive text. This theoretical understanding is based in their experience of the material existence of documents, but that is not the idea presented to the public. The myth of a stable text which can be realized through careful editing is here taken as the unspoken truth which Joyce's text, due to its unique nature, can never achieve. This idea was widespread among literary scholars as well, until the revolution in textual editing and the resultant controversies forced us to confront our blasé acceptance of the texts we analyze. There is nothing unique about Joyce's text; all texts are unstable. Even literary theories which championed an unstable meaning for text (for example, Derridean deconstruction) did little to examine the actual texts themselves as unstable objects in their material manifestations. The public operated (and continues to operate) under the impression that the texts they read are what the author intended to put before them; textual editors know that texts are the result of less sturdy constructs. The fact that such instability does not seem to prohibit the public from enjoying literary works seems to escape scholars in the Joyce debate, and their disputations over what appear to the public as "nits" seem childish; the Kidd-Gabler debate did nothing to dispel this impression, and much to solidify it.

The *Post* article ends with an account of the Motherwell-illustrated *Ulysses*, for which Kidd "served as [an] adviser," and closes with this paragraph:

> Asked if he would consider editing a completely new *Ulysses*, Kidd responded much like a potential vice-presidential nominee. "I would have to be commissioned," he said, but grudgingly conceded that if commissioned he would accept the job. (F8)

Just like the last section of his *NYRB* article, this paragraph leaves the impression that Kidd's position is little different from Gabler or the Joyce Estate's; his criticisms are undermined (just as he charges the scholarship on the Gabler edition is undermined) by personal ambition and economic motivations in the form of grants. The perception of the debate formed through this article supports Stephen Joyce's assertions in the first paragraph of his letter to the *TLS*.

### INSULT AND INJURY

In September 1988, the exchange moved back to the *NYRB*, with a long letter from John O'Hanlon (an editorial assistant to Gabler during the editing project), and two short letters from Gabler and Thomas Staley, then editor of the *James Joyce Quarterly*; these were followed by a lengthy reply from Kidd (29 Sept. 1988: 80–83). O'Hanlon's letter begins by addressing the issue of facsimiles, and states that the transcriptions made from the facsimile "were later checked against the originals personally by Professor Gabler"(80). O'Hanlon allows that Kidd has uncovered some errors, but states that "Kidd outrageously, preposterously, and, frankly, quite slanderously suggests" that the Joyce Estate "conspired" to ensure that the editing process "yield the kind of results that it did in order to support a new copyright" (80). He addresses the Conolly/Connolly name change which Kidd also included in his *NYRB* article, and blasts Kidd with a damaging rebuttal:

> The third and last of Kidd's name changes, Conolly/Connolly, is instructive in illustrating his (lack of) scholarly integrity and the ethics of his presentation. When I read his analysis, I found it mighty odd that he should have noted seven places (most of them very obscure) in *Thom's* Dublin Directory. Referring to my own copy, I discovered precisely why this was so. In the most obvious place where I, or Kidd, or Joyce, would look up Mr. Norman—the alphabetical list of the "Nobility, Gentry, Merchants, and Traders" at the back of the book (the section that includes John Joyce

and that, indeed, Kidd looked up for "Buller")—his name is printed as "Connolly Norman"; i.e., the identical form that Joyce wrote down in the Rosenbach Manuscript. Further, the list includes only one cross-reference (to his home address on the North Circular Road convenient to the Richmond) and, notably, here also his name is spelled "Connolly." Why did Kidd not see fit to include this relevant information in his article? I submit, because it is his unscholarly practice to suppress evidence not supportive of his claims. (80)

O'Hanlon then refutes the infamous postcard to Claud Sykes by printing an "open letter dated 21 May, 1985" from Gabler to Kidd which explains why the edition does not list the postcard as a source. Kidd was led to the postcard by looking through Jack Dalton's index card file which Gabler had assembled in Munich. Gabler states: "You did not know and did not understand Dalton's conventions of encoding information and decisions on his cards. Nor did you seek out the Buffalo postcard to make sure you understood the issue" (80). The letter continues:

> The Dalton cards—his memoranda to himself about his research findings, featuring much private code—were seen by you in Munich last January, when I offered you the opportunity to take a look at them. Much of the time I sat in my office next door and would have been available at any time to discuss queries. (While you had merely a couple of hasty afternoons with the cards, my familiarity with them was formed over a long time of using them.) You preferred to appropriate clandestinely a fragmentary piece of information and, irresponsibly mistaking your understanding of it for the truth of the matter, never bothered to seek verification. Thus compounding professional ineptitude with an act of personal double-dealing you rushed before the public to disparage my scholarly integrity. This I deeply resent. I expect you to seek, and I hope you will find ways to redress the insult and injury. (80)

This paragraph explains, in part, the source of Gabler's heated response to Kidd's paper in 1985: he felt betrayed. O'Hanlon loyally continues: "One can but marvel (and even perhaps perversely admire) the nerve of the man posing as a friendly colleague in Gabler's office in Munich only a few weeks before he launched his vitriolic campaign. Present-day patrons of Kidd, take note: watch your files and your backs!" (80).

O'Hanlon then addresses Kidd's charge that Kenner and Ellmann should not have reviewed the edition. He states, correctly, that Kenner's only involvement with the edition was that he observed the project and wrote an article about it for *Harper's*; O'Hanlon asks, "Did this transform him into one of the editors and disqualify him from reviewing the finished work? Obviously not" (80). Here O'Hanlon turns Kidd's own rhetorical method of question and answer against him. However, in the matter of Richard Ellmann's review, O'Hanlon is on shakier ground, and he attempts to sidestep the apparent conflict of interest:

> Strictly speaking, [the function of the Academic Advisory Committee, of which Ellmann was Chair] was to advise the Estate of James Joyce, and not the editorial team. In practice, of course, their advice was passed on to the editor. It is a moot point whether this state of affairs disqualified Ellmann from writing a review. Yet Ellmann is surely an exceptional case; as the most senior of senior Joyceans, everybody wanted to hear what he had to say about the edition; and normal practice was, reasonably, suspended. (80)

O'Hanlon doesn't explain why it is "a moot point" whether or not Ellmann's role should have disqualified him from reviewing the edition; surely, any involvement in the edition should have done so. Kidd's charge is not quite dismissed by saying that Ellmann is a "special case." Ellmann's foreword to the trade edition seems a more appropriate venue for his evaluation of Gabler's work; the formal review could have been assigned to any number of eminent Joyceans who were not involved with the edition.

O'Hanlon maligns Kidd as a "neophyte" while calling Gabler an "experienced professional," and compares Kidd's list-making to Senator Joe McCarthy's lists of communists in the State Department, a rhetorical escalation worthy of Kidd himself. O'Hanlon closes his letter with one final volley:

> On first looking into Kidd's article—and being like any normal person initially impressed—I called upon the shade of James Joyce to give me a sign by way of which I might understand his feelings on the matter. A few hours later, after a good dinner of stuffed roast pork, cabbage and potatoes, I was idly turning the pages of *The New York Review* when I saw it: the picture on page 39 of Joyce sitting in Shakespeare and Company's bookshop with, behind him, a poster announcing "The Scandal of *Ulysses*." That title was originally employed over a scurrilous piece of gutter journalism denouncing the first edition of *Ulysses*. By what unerring insight did Kidd appropriate it for his own similar efforts? As all other editions derive directly from that first edition, the 1984 *Ulysses* can correctly be designated the second independent edition. I suggest that Hans Walter Gabler have a copy of the corresponding page of *The New York Review of Books* blown up into a poster and have himself photographed sitting before it; copies to be sent to all the libraries in the world, including Marsh's and Alexandria. (81)

Turning Kidd's use of narrative and rhetorical questions against him, O'Hanlon delivers a stinging blow to Kidd in this round of the Joyce Wars. And invoking the parallels between Kidd's article and the "scurrilous piece of gutter journalism" also implies that the Gabler edition is the same as the original *Ulysses* in that formulation: assailed by the great unwashed who just don't understand the art behind it. In some ways, this equivalency is accurate; the general public was not privy to the theoretical basis for the Gabler edition. Yet the appropriation of those roles also rhetorically positions the Gabler text as *the* *Ulysses*—the *real* *Ulysses*. O'Hanlon's letter is the longest yet in response to Kidd, and many of O'Hanlon's counter-charges would go unanswered in Kidd's reply (below).

Gabler's own letter is short and more measured than O'Hanlon's; he wrote that he was "[w]rily amused by John Kidd's brand of critifiction" and made only two comments on Kidd's response: one was to address the charge that he had adopted changes in the edition which came from Kidd but went unacknowledged—a continual sore point with Kidd and alluded to repeatedly in his letters and articles—and this comment:

> "Professor Futura's" failure to locate in Dr. Kidd's published or unpub-lished pronouncements such terms as "manuscript [*vs.* text] edition," "diplomatic fidelity" or "layout of manuscripts" is revealing. It means that he refuses to allow theoretical and methodological grounds to the fault-finding he is forcing on the public. Yet on his own reduced and lim-ited scale, a discussion of the problems of editing *Ulysses* must, I am afraid, remain futile. (81)

Again, Gabler points out that Kidd's arguments are not worth respond-ing to unless they are couched within a theoretical construct, underlining his own contention that the editing of *Ulysses* was a theoretical enterprise which can only be assessed on its own terms rather than on the resulting reading text. In his refusal to debate Kidd he consistently upheld the view that there was nothing worth responding to because Kidd's charges did not touch on the *theory* of his edition. But Kidd's lists of "errors" was impres-sive to those outside of the world of textual theory (and quite a few within it), and as such it damaged Gabler's credibility to imply that the theory was unassailable whether or not the results were "correct."

Thomas Staley's letter takes umbrage at Kidd's "conspiracy" barb in his original *NYRB* article. He refutes Kidd's contention that Michael Groden's article in the *James Joyce Quarterly* was a review, and writes that "Gro-den's essay is neither labeled a review, nor does it appear in the review sec-tion of the journal where there are five reviews. *JJQ* has never formally reviewed the Gabler edition, and to suggest a conspiracy between *JJQ* and the editors of the new edition is irresponsible if not libelous" (81). Kidd had a strong comeback against Staley's letter in his reply:

> Mr. Staley declares it a near-libel for me to call the Groden article a re-view. The word is Mr. Staley's own. In the Fall 1984 issue, page 5, he wrote: "*Ulysses: A Critical and Synoptic Edition* has been published, fol-lowed by front-page articles in newspapers around the country and the world. We will review the edition in the next issue." The next issue . . . featured Michael Groden's endorsement. For using the word "review" I am called "irresponsible if not libelous"; I am not "precise"; I lack "credence." (83)

But the bulk of Kidd's reply is devoted to refuting O'Hanlon. Kidd calls O'Hanlon's letter "long" and "defiant," seeming to ignore the fact that his own letters have been equally long. He insults O'Hanlon:

[O'Hanlon] calls himself "a member of the editorial team that oversaw the critical edition of James Joyce's *Ulysses*," yet Mr. O'Hanlon is named nowhere in *Ulysses: The Corrected Text . . .*, the chief target of my article. In the 1984 Garland edition, Mr. O'Hanlon is not listed as a co-editor but as one of six editorial assistants. True, he writes a racy line. A research assistant who flashes Overseer credentials deserves a response as much as anyone else. (81)

The label of "neophyte" which O'Hanlon flung at Kidd seems to have touched a nerve. But it seems beside the point to say that O'Hanlon is not listed in the trade edition and that this edition was the "chief target" of Kidd's article; since the trade edition is derived from the synoptic edition and is a result of its editorial procedures, criticizing one effectively criticizes the other. Kidd continues: "Not wishing to trade remarks of a purely personal character, however, I must pass over some of Mr. O'Hanlon's paragraphs. The editing of *Ulysses* can be debated without a reply to taunts that I am a 'neophyte'." It would seem a little late to claim that he does not want to trade personal insults, and hypocritical to any reader following the debate. Kidd had been trading personal insults from the appearance of his article "Scandal of *Ulysses*."

Kidd continues his charges of inadequate checking of originals, and refutes O'Hanlon's claim that Gabler personally checked the originals: "The issue can be resolved if Gabler will publish a list of dates that he signed the register of the Rosenbach Museum while collating the manuscript from end to end" (81). While collating the manuscript end-to-end is not the claim of the Gabler team, and never was (they checked where there was some question or inconsistency detected in their editing), it is still a damaging charge because Gabler never answered with a list of dates. This request seems reasonable, and his refusal to do so therefore looks suspicious. Kidd, in his "Professor Futura" letter, had written that the "registers of the libraries with major Joyce holdings, which patrons are required to sign daily, also yield no evidence of Gabler or any co-editor spending the long months in the reading rooms necessary to verify facsimile transcription" (*NYRB* 18 Aug. 1988: 65). The implication here is that Kidd checked those registers himself. However, neither the Rosenbach Museum nor the libraries at Harvard and Buffalo allow access to patron registers, so it is unclear how Kidd came by his information.[6] What is clear is that Gabler's reputation, in the eyes of the public, would have been damaged by these accusations, as it began to look as though Gabler had not looked at original manuscript materials at all.

Kidd's next rebuttal point quotes O'Hanlon's explanation of the editorial method, and says that O'Hanlon "adopts a turgid style meant to boggle the reader" and says of his own writing that he (Kidd) "sh[ied] from unnecessary jargon." The use of the word "diplomatic" Kidd defines as "erasures, additions, deletions, even slips, are recorded faithfully without editorial correction in the genetic apparatus" in a parenthesis, and then shows where Gabler and O'Hanlon contradict each other: "Gabler protested in his letter of August 18 that the edition never claimed 'diplomatic or topographic fidelity.' Now Mr. O'Hanlon asserts that diplomatic transcription *was* central to the edition" (81; italics in original). Then Kidd throws out another rhetorical flourish: "Having never seen the original Harvard proof, on which Captain Buller's name is obscured, Mr. O'Hanlon tries to assure us that it is no more legible than the facsimile which he has seen. Trust me, he says, them originals ain't worth the bother" (81). The use of the pronoun "us" immediately brings the reader within Kidd's circle, and the last sentence acts as a metaphorical arm around the reader's shoulder, encouraging the reader to see things Kidd's way.

Kidd's long reply refutes O'Hanlon's letter point-by-point, but of particular interest are his continued metaphorical and rhetorical jabs at the Gabler team. In one instance, he quotes O'Hanlon as saying that if one name had been investigated, then the host of others in the same paragraph should also have been checked. O'Hanlon writes: "Did Kidd do this? I very much doubt it" (80); Kidd responds: "Actually, I have done precisely what Mr. O'Hanlon doubts very much" (81). He then replies to O'Hanlon on the Conolly/Connolly issue by saying that "Now Mr. O'Hanlon insists that I must cite any passage of *Thom's* that supports the 1984 misspelling. That's Gabler's job not mine" (81). This flippant statement brushes aside the issue of Kidd deliberately leaving out evidence which contradicted his own claims, which rightfully should have been included in his article and addressed.

Kidd continues his reply to O'Hanlon for another two columns before getting to Gabler's letter. The last point in this section mentions his involvement with the Arion Press Motherwell-illustrated *Ulysses*, and Kidd writes: "Far from being under my sway, the printer-designer-publisher-cum-entrepreneur Andrew Hoyem has his own ideas about how Joyce should have spelled and punctuated *Ulysses*. Such typographic splendors rarely carry an authentic text anyway, and Motherwell's illustrations command the price. . . . Arion Press had bought a reprint license for *The Corrected Text* but decided not to use the Gabler version. Too many errors" (82). But in his letter to the *NYRB* of August 18, Kidd told a slightly different story. He stated that the Gabler edition had "inspired Hoyem to tinker with the Joycean system" (64), not that Hoyem had rejected the Gabler edition as having "too many errors." This is not fundamentally a contradiction, but it reveals Kidd's willingness to tailor his prose for the occasion; that last "too many errors" is a parting shot, delivered for rhetorical effect.

In replying to Gabler's letter, Kidd paraphrases him by saying that "Gabler dismisses as 'futile' our debate over the text of *Ulysses* because I don't share his love for obscure theorizing" (82). Here he plainly attempts to paint Gabler as the out-of-touch academic by dismissing theory altogether as "obscure." No doubt, those unaccustomed to such theory would applaud Kidd's position, but curiously enough, throughout his reply he refers readers to articles by Fredson Bowers and G. Thomas Tanselle to support his own contentions against the Gabler edition. These articles surely fall under the rubric of "theorizing" and would most likely appear "obscure" to readers unfamiliar with textual scholarship. Kidd's position here reveals that he has been stung too often as being unscholarly, and wishes to point scholars to his own theoretical leanings by citing Bowers and Tanselle, as well as showing the general reader that he is indeed scholarly; in other words, he has abandoned his earlier attempts to reach specifically the general readership of the *NYRB* for an attempt to reach the two audiences, general and scholarly, by combining the conventions of both.

## TransAtlantic Fight

Following this series in the *NYRB*, the letter-writing campaign shifted back to the *TLS*. In the 11–13 Oct. 1988 issue, on pages 1109 and 1132, Michael Groden defends the Gabler edition against Kidd. Groden's letter occasionally rivals Kidd's for acid humor. He begins by ironically stating that Kidd "has enriched our summer with four contributions to his three-year campaign" against the Gabler edition, and that the date Kidd published in his July 22–28 letter to the *TLS* for the appearance of his *PBSA* paper "has passed"; Groden continues: "The time seems appropriate to look at the way he has conducted his campaign, the state of events at this time, and possible future developments. I mention at the outset that my own connection with Gabler's edition is long-standing and public" (1109). Groden prevents Kidd from leveling any accusation of conspiracy by stating his relationship to the Gabler edition so clearly.

Groden accuses Kidd of being "lively and entertaining" in order to "[obscure] the facts and issues, in this case complex scholarly and theoretical issues"; he accuses Kidd of distorting evidence, omitting what "would weaken his case, and redefin[ing] words to suit his purposes" (1109). Groden proceeds to illustrate these charges, allowing a full paragraph for each one. But he is not above a few rhetorical flourishes himself; witness this shot at Kidd in the context of showing where Kidd distorts the number of errors in Gabler's edition: "He asks . . . if anyone was awake at the wheel: it seems preferable to nod briefly in the back seat than knowingly to adjust the odometer before showing your goods to unsuspecting customers" (1109). Groden mentions the alternate spelling of Conolly/Connolly found in *Thom's*, which O'Hanlon points out Kidd omitted from his article: "One of Kidd's most consistent procedures has been to accuse other people of precisely the scholarly transgressions he himself is most guilty of and to call other people exactly those names that best apply to him" (1109). This statement rings with echoes of the schoolyard chant of "I'm rubber and you're glue," and contributes to the air of childishness surrounding the entire debate.

Further on, Groden casts aspersions on Kidd's own scholarly pursuits. He cites Kidd's dissertation on "Rabelais's influence on Joyce, . . . a source that Joyce consistently denied," and then cites Kidd's interest in numerological patterns in *Ulysses*, as reported in the *Post* article which started the Joyce Wars (see Chapter Four). Groden writes:

> Gabler's editorial decisions destroyed the perfect patterns. Now Kidd justifies the need for the name "Captain Buller" in the text of *Ulysses*, apart from what seem like valid textual grounds, on the basis of a far-fetched Byron pattern that he claims runs from "Flowers of idleness" (an allusion to Byron's *Hours of Idleness*) at the beginning of the "Lotus Eaters" episode to the identification of Captain Buller's address in Thom's Directory as Byron Lodge. According to "The Scandal of *Ulysses*", this is Joyce "priming his hidden machinery." A mind that finds hidden patterns throughout the texts not surprisingly finds conspiracies in the real world. . . . It is ironic that, of the Joyce scholars I know, only Gabler thought that there might be some merit to Kidd's numerological ideas. Kidd responded by telling a reporter that Gabler might be encouraging his numerological investigations only to deflect him from looking at the errors in Gabler's text (*Washington Post*, April 2, 1985). Do we want an editor of *Ulysses* who finds hidden and secret patterns, conspiracies, enemies and deceivers everywhere he looks in both art and life? (1139)

In the same letter, Groden writes almost libelously, "If Kidd finds 'so much order, perfect order' hidden in the numerological patterns of the 1922 text, would he as editor be able to resist making those patterns just a little more perfect" (1139)? Groden justifies such a serious accusation of possible future malfeasance by saying that it "is important to scrutinize Kidd's potential ability as an editor because he may get the chance to edit a text to replace Gabler's" (1139). Ironically echoing Kidd's own conspiracy-finding, Groden charges that the Tanselle committee, charged by Random House with deciding the fate of the Gabler edition, is biased towards Kidd because Tanselle was quoted in support of Kidd's efforts and had arranged to have Kidd's *PBSA* article published (*Washington Post*, April 2, 1985). Groden calls Tanselle a "booster of Kidd's campaign against the text" and also points out that Tanselle has written critically against the Gabler edition[7]; he grudgingly allows that "Tanselle may have been encouraging Kidd's efforts, as he has said, to allow the critique to be heard, and his own criticism of Gabler may be a legitimate scholarly and theoretical disagreement" (1139). "But," he correctly states,

> Kidd's supporters and sympathizers would be justifiably concerned about the fairness and impartiality of a committee headed by a scholar associated with the Gabler edition, and I feel that anyone who wants the debate to proceed fairly and impartially should be just as concerned about a committee headed by someone who has criticized the conception and execution of Gabler's edition and boosted Kidd's efforts as much and for as long as Tanselle has. (1139)

If Kidd can make accusations of conspiracy, Groden implies, then so can Gabler's supporters. Groden closes his letter by urging people "concerned about the issue, whether they agree with my position here or not, should communicate their opinion to Tanselle," and he lets fly one last shot at Kidd: "I think that if Kidd is allowed to produce his text at the expense of the Gabler text, Tanselle and Epstein will be perpetrating the real 'scandal of *Ulysses*' " (1139).

Of course, Kidd did not let Groden's remarks go unanswered, and in the next issue of the *TLS* he writes an uncharacteristically short response. He calls Groden a "collaborator of ten years' standing" with the Gabler team and says that in "the space of 2,000 words Michael Groden manages to disagree with me on a single textual crux, the spelling of Conolly Norman's name, which is historically correct in all editions of *Ulysses* except Gabler's. The charge of suppressing evidence about Conolly Norman I answered previously in the *New York Review of Books* published on September 15 and dated September 29, page 81, column 4" (*TLS* 21–27 Oct. 1988: 1175). His response, however, did not really answer this charge; he merely stated that *Thom's* spelled it "correctly seven times and incorrectly twice" (of course implying that the spelling used by the Gabler team is incorrect), and flippantly stated that it was "Gabler's job not [his]" to show where *Thom's* supported the Gabler text (see above, Kidd's reply to O'Hanlon).

Kidd calls Groden's letter a "rambling *excursus ad hominem*" which "leaves him room for only one point on the theory of editing" (charges that could just as easily be laid at his own feet), but does not challenge Groden's assessment of Kidd and Gabler's different approaches. Rather, he argues that the difference in editorial theory comes down to a definition of "error" and that he has "carefully distinguished between factual error, editorial judgment, and the inevitability of differing textual versions." Kidd offers his letter in the September 29 issue of the *New York Review* as an example of his addressing theory; but that letter does not show that "he is entirely in accord with the authorities cited against me by Mr. Groden" (1175). Groden cites Jerome McGann, and in his *NYRB* letter Kidd cites Zeller and Thorpe's definitions of versions. Kidd further states that Groden's letter "merely repeat[s] what has been debated at great length and in fullest detail in America. That is why Mr. Groden was unable to find a publisher for his letter over here" (1175). This last statement seems to have a curious subtext; obviously, Kidd is attempting to impugn the merits of Groden's letter by stating that no one would publish it in the United States; but it also implies that the *TLS* is the place where unneeded scraps of the debate are heard, rather than being a legitimate forum. Perhaps this subtext was unintended by Kidd, because in the final paragraph of his three-paragraph letter he writes:

Personal attacks on me cannot mask the documented inaccuracies and glaring aesthetic flaws of the Gabler *Ulysses*. Readers who missed "The Scandal of *Ulysses*" in the June 30 *New York Review* or the long exchanges with Gabler and Company in the August 18 and September 29 issues may request free offprints from my new address at Boston University. (1175)

On the pretext of offering his "mail-order" distribution of materials, Kidd manages to saucily convey his new status as an "authority on Joyce" through his new address: the James Joyce Research Center at Boston University, of which had recently become the head. It was partly this kind of self-aggrandizement which earned Kidd his abrasive reputation.

Following this reply was a letter from Ian Gunn, who does not identify himself as the co-compiler (with Alistair McCleery) of *The "Ulysses" Pagefinder* (Edinburgh: Split Pea Press, 1988). Gunn supports Groden's letter by saying that John Kidd's dismissal of it is "unconvincing" (*TLS* 4–10 Nov. 1988: 1227). Gunn states that "With the suppression of Groden's informative letter by the *New York Review of Books* the feeling grows that maybe they are in cahoots with Kidd as he appears always to be given acres of space and the last word." Gunn continues, echoing Groden's needling over the delay in Kidd's *PBSA* article, and says that "we need more than wind to sink the Gabler." He also calls Kidd a "bragging schoolboy" who "should lie low until such a time as he is prepared to bare all for admiration or ridicule." From here on out, Kidd's promised article for the *PBSA* is brandished as a weapon because it had not appeared. The next letter in the *TLS* is from Gabler (12–22 Dec. 1988: 1345), in which he, too, referred to Kidd's promised *PBSA* article; he writes that the "*PBSA* editor, however, has so far not been able to tell me more than that he would ask me to respond 'if and when' such an essay was received . . . A letter just received from the chairman of the Random House committee expressly confirms that the Kidd essay is not in hand. Yet only if and when it becomes available, and only then, will it be possible to begin to investigate what substance, if any, there is in it to contend with" (1345).

Curiously, Gabler's letter begins with a move to dissociate the trade edition from the critical edition, echoing moves he also made in previous letters to distance himself from the commercial concerns of the publishers and the Joyce Estate: "The debate of the past months around the *so-called* "Corrected Text" of James Joyce's *Ulysses* and, indirectly, its "parent," the Critical and Synoptic Edition of 1984 . . ." (my emphasis). Gabler continues to differentiate his real project, the synoptic text, from the reading text it produced. Since Charles Rossman's article, "The New *Ulysses*: The Hidden Controversy" had appeared in the *NYRB* at this point, Gabler was again forced to remind the public that the commercial considerations which Rossman uncovers were not part of his project. With Rossman's article, the debate moved once again onto the pages of the *NYRB*, and the letters continued for another six months.

REINFORCEMENTS ARRIVE

When Charles Rossman's article appeared detailing the disagreements and doubts plaguing the advisory committee and the Joyce Estate about Gabler's editorial methods, John Kidd suddenly appeared less iconoclastic in his criticisms against the edition (Rossman's article is fully treated in Chapter Three). But his article did not receive a response in the same issue; instead, the *NYRB* finally published a letter from Michael Groden which exposed the reluctance of the periodical to publish his letter earlier, and which had forced him to send it to the *TLS* instead: "I recently sent *The New York Review* a letter that questioned Kidd's tactics and motives and doubted the objectivity of the committee . . . that Jason Epstein of Random House established to investigate his charges. The *Review* rejected the letter on the grounds that considerable space had already been devoted to responses to Kidd and that he had recently addressed issues I raised. The editors said that they would consider a new letter of no more than five hundred words" (61). Groden, in the next paragraph, states that the explanations offered by the *NYRB* for rejecting his letter were not "justified," because "while the editors were telling me that there was no space . . . they were giving Kidd even more space for his repetitive responses than they gave to all his critics combined." This kind of score-keeping further characterized the dispute as a "schoolboy scuffle" (to borrow a metaphor from Ian Gunn's letter to the *TLS*). Groden's letter here does briefly address Kidd's evasion of O'Hanlon's point about *Thom's* spelling of "Conolly/Connolly," and Groden characterizes this evasion as "sleight of hand." He closes his letter by referring readers to a "condensed version of the letter rejected by the *Review*" which "appeared in the . . . *Times Literary Supplement*. [Groden] urge[s] readers who find the arguments in that letter compelling" to contact Random House and Tanselle.

Giving credence to Groden's scorekeeping, Kidd's reply to Groden's letter covers almost two columns of print. He begins by painting a picture of behind-the-scenes campaigning by those arrayed against him:

> When Hugh Kenner and A. Walton Litz wrote to protest *The New York Review*'s refusal to print a long letter from Michael Groden, they claimed that he had refuted "many of Kidd's allegations." Eventually Mr. Groden, who is named on the title page of the edition he defends, found space in the *Times Literary Supplement*. In the three versions of the letter seen by me, of which 2,500 words are now in print, Mr. Groden mentions only a single textual crux, the name of Dublin physician Conolly Norman, which is historically correct in all editions of *Ulysses* except Hans Gabler's. (61)

For Kidd to point out that Groden is "on the title page of the edition he defends" seems to show his paranoia again; wouldn't readers expect those involved in the edition to defend it? Kidd's attempt to play the battered David to the Joyce Establishment's Goliath begins to wear thin at this point, because he has offered as evidence only the fact that those involved in the edition and those who find it to be satisfactory are defending it. In light of the revelation that the periodical which has given him so much space to carry out his campaign has also suppressed letters from those on the other side of the issue, his mantle of hounded scholar appears to be a false one. If this exchange had appeared in an issue separate from the Rossman article, Kidd might have begun to lose ground. But coming, as it did, in the same issue as the economic charges against the edition that Rossman laid at the feet of the Joyce estate, Kidd's carefully built air of conspiracy seems more plausible. Rossman's article, then, appeared just in time to bolster Kidd's position, and served to reach the *NYRB* audience with the allegations he had made earlier in the *TLS* (2–8 Sept. 1988: 963; see above).

STRANGE THINGS HAPPEN IN THE GROVES OF ACADEME

While several letters appeared in response to Rossman's article, they repeated charges already made in previous sallies in the first Joyce War. Matters were supposed to be settled at the 1989 gathering of the annual Joyce conference held at the University of Miami. The conference itself was covered by the *Miami Herald* on the front page ("Every *Ulysses* Jot and Tittle Fires Scholars' Debate at UM," 6 Feb. 1989: 1A+), in an article written by the *Herald*'s Book Editor, William Robertson. He describes a "substantial academic industry devoted to studying Joyce" which "immediately hailed" Gabler's *Ulysses* on its appearance as "a monumental work of scholarship and at last the definitive *Ulysses*"; the next paragraph, however, shifts attention to the debate by stating: "But strange things happen in the groves of academe, and Gabler's edition is now under assault" (1A). Already, Robertson creates the impression that the academy is a "strange" world unto itself, and he continues this separation by stating that "[t]o those who read *Ulysses* for pleasure, the disagreement may seem trivial. Even the principals concede that the flawed editions of the book have little bearing on its overall meaning and pleasures" (4A). Further showing that academics and general readers are two different species, Robertson states that "in Joycean circles, a misplaced comma in *Ulysses* . . . can provoke hours of debate" (4A). The *Herald* article underlines the textually extraneous issues: "Academic reputations are on the line. And money, perhaps a lot of it, is potentially at stake," quoting the figure that "100,000 copies of *Ulysses* [are] sold annually, mostly to university students who must buy a definitive text for study"; this statement further places Joyce's work in the world of the academy. The article concentrates on the vitriolic nature of the debate, although Robertson indicates that Gabler seemed above the fray: "The University of Munich professor patiently replied to Kidd's questions and never lost his temper during a challenge to his authority so charged at times that a conference participant suggested it would have led to a duel in another age" (4A). Kidd is described as a "young academic in a hurry" at one point, "intent on destroying the credibility of the Gabler text"; one unidentified scholar at the conference joked that "Academic entrepreneurship has been around for a long time, but this . . . is something new . . . What do we have here, a hostile takeover or a leveraged buyout?"[8]

The article emphasizes the commercial aspect of the debate, noting that Kidd has stated he would like to edit his own text of *Ulysses*, and that Gaskell and Hart's "repair kit" correcting the "Gabler 'corrected text'" would, "though it was never said, [fill] another niche in the market." The article repeats Rossman's views that the Estate rushed the project because of copyright considerations, and that Clive Hart replied in his capacity as Trustee for the Joyce estate that the publishers were at fault for speeding up the publication of the trade edition "because they wanted to make money on it." The article concludes that nothing was settled at the conference, but that "few things are in this sort of dispute." In a sidebar, there is a brief biographical sketch of Joyce and a synopsis of *Ulysses* and its importance, obviously for general readers unfamiliar with Joyce's works. The sketch states that even in *Portrait*, "his first novel" (completely ignoring *Dubliners*), "Joyce was already preoccupied with the sordid realities of life." This description invokes the public Joyce's reputation as a "dirty" writer. The description ends by reminding readers of *Ulysses'* central position in literary culture: "Although Joyce wrote another novel, *Finnegans Wake*, it is *Ulysses* that has established him as one of the most important writers of the 20th Century" (4A). This last sentence assures that even if a reader did not know much about Joyce or his works that his importance would be understood.

'TWAS THE NIGHT BEFORE BLOOMSDAY

Prior to the conference, the January 2, 1989 issue of *The Nation* published a parody of the controversy, casting the debate in a new light. Titled "St. Nicholas: A Textual Scandal," the parody opens with a note from the editors:

> Still groggy from five months of letters disputing the merits of the revised text of James Joyce's *Ulysses*, readers of *The New York Review of Books* will face an even nastier confrontation in the periodical's next issue. Judging from the . . . initial exchange, advance copies of which were obtained by *The Nation*, this one could go on till next Christmas. The *casus belli* was the publication of *"A Visit From St. Nicholas": A New Definitive Synoptic Corrected Edition Collated From Original and Collateral Sources* (Kansas Institute of Mining and Science Press, $450), edited by Dr. Hartvig Ludendorff of the Spielvogel Archives. The letter opening the assault on the Ludendorff version came from Dr. Sebastian Ramsforth. We reprint a condensed version of it below. (1)

From this opening, with its parody of Gabler's dense style in the title of the farcical new edition of "'Twas the Night Before Christmas," and its poke at Kidd with the name "Ramsforth," it is clear that the satirists

believe the debate to be petty, and the parody offers a glimpse into the public perspective on the debate only hinted at through newspaper articles like
the *Post*'s and the *Herald*'s (see Remnick 1985; Mundy 1988; Robertson
1989 above). The article begins with a parody of Kidd's "Scandal of
*Ulysses*" in which Ramsforth states that "we now have an alleged 'corrected edition' cobbled together by textual editor Dr. Hartvig Ludendorff
and his band of right jolly elves at the Spielvogel Archives in Bad
Moutheim, West Germany" (1). The authors, Richard Lingeman and
Thomas M. Disch, have captured Kidd's sarcasm well. The fictitious article
continues by stating that "Scholars only recently cracked the code of Dr.
Moore's 'Visit,' unlocking a hidden subtext that reveals the poem to be a
profound evocation of the dark night of the soul . . . the good cleric had
long been plagued by dipsomaniacal demons and . . . the poem about
Santa Claus was an attempt to exorcise them" (1, 21). This "hidden subtext" parodies not only Kidd but also academics in general, who (in the
public's eye) see hidden meanings in the most apparently innocuous of literary passages. This satire continues with a list of fictitious articles that
Ramsforth has published in scholarly journals, and the ubiquitous colon in
academic titles is present in all three: "'St. Nick and Old Nick: Clement
Moore's Satanic Vision,' *Susquehannah Review*, Winter 1985"; "'Clement
Moore: Dionysian Poet,' *Scholarly Offprints*, June 1986" (this title contains a more specific cut at Kidd's offer to send offprints of his articles to
interested readers); and "'St. Nicholas Revisited: Moore's Dark Vision,'
*Air Force Academy Quarterly*, Winter-Spring 1986" (21).

The article also parodies Kidd's conspiracy charges and strongly worded
accusations, as well as his witty use of metaphor:

> [The textual editors'] computerized labors have now given birth to a
> chubby tome, weighing in at 5 pounds, 7 ounces, including acknowledg-
> ments, appendix and footnotes. This "definitive edition," launched by a
> fulsome, self-serving Festschrift in the Fall 1987 issue of *Clement Moore
> Studies*, well recognized as the mouthpiece of the Ludendorff cabal,
> plumbs new depths of scholarly ineptitude. (21)

For those who have been following the debate, such paragraphs are a won-
derful send-up of Kidd's style. Ramsforth castigates "Ludendorff and his
drones" for using a manuscript which was written on a cocktail napkin
(which, in a footnote, is placed at the "Howard Hughes Collection, University of Las Vegas"), and he states that one of the changes made in
Ludendorff's new edition not only doesn't scan but that "Worse, we lose
the religious double-entendre of 'St. Nick' (as in Old Nick—Scratch, the
devil)" (21). This change is "worse," readers understand, because it undermines the whole of Ramsforth's scholarly work on the Moore poem as a
"Satanic Vision." The self-interest in Ramsforth's accusations, in this parody, serve to carry over to an evaluation of Kidd's own accusations against
the Gabler edition of *Ulysses*.

Lingeman and Disch further parody academic attention to minutiae (and Gabler's synoptic edition, which is not a reader-friendly enterprise) by mentioning that the change Ramsforth deplores above is justified in "footnote 2007, page 563"; Ramsforth states that Ludendorff's "arguments are too tedious to adumbrate here, but they come down to the simple proposition *in vino veritas*" (21). Ramsforth offers the "so-called Morning-After Holograph . . . considered, until Ludendorff and his wrecking crew took up their cudgels, the true text" as evidence that such revisions as the Ludendorff team rejected were closer to Moore's intentions, even though they were dictated to his wife "after taking to his bed with a severe case of the megrims" and therefore not in his hand (21). The reference here to Joyce's dictation to Budgen and the controversial spellings of names and places which resulted cannot be missed. Ramsforth continues: "But Moore hung-over was Moore twice armed, as I have argued elsewhere (see Ramsforth, 'The Morning After Christmas: Moore's Revisions of "A Visit from St. Nicholas",' *Elsewhere*, Spring 1983)" (21).

The "article" breaks off here, with an editor's note that "for reasons of space we have omitted the remaining 10,000 words of Dr. Ramsforth's letter"; the note summarizes Ramsforth's charges, which include misplacing a specified number of punctuation marks, plagiarizing from Ramsforth's work, misappropriating $500,000 from the National Endowment for the Humanities (some of which, Ramsforth charges, went to feed Ludendorff's gambling habit), libel meant to destroy Ramsforth's reputation (ironically in light of the charges Ramsforth makes here), and closing with charges of "certain felonies and misdemeanors, 'which have been duly reported to the proper authorities'" (21). The escalation of charges here is plainly humorous, but also echoes the escalation of financial charges in the Joyce Wars stemming from the Rossman article. Ludendorff's reply follows this note, and the major players and issues in the Joyce debate find their parodic equivalent in the scholars that Ludendorff arrays against Ramsforth: "E. VandeConolly" and "Hugh O'Connor" clearly refer to the "Conolly/Connolly" argument and to Hugh Kenner, and Ludendorff repeatedly refers to Moore as the "Good Doctor" and the "Beloved Author," showing the reverence to Joyce evident in both sides of the debate (21). He also states that Ramsforth's description of the cocktail napkin Holograph—which in his footnote he says depicts a "wine glass emitting bubbles and several scantily clad females"—is nothing more than Ramsforth "project[ing] his own fevered imagining on the Rorschach-like wine stain on the recto side" of the napkin (22). Further accusations of not visiting original manuscripts in the "Spielvogel Archives" and a reference to Ramsforth's name not appearing in the registers for this fictional archive refer explicitly to the accusations Kidd makes against Gabler, except the positions are reversed in the parody.

But Gabler does not escape so easily; his alter ego's "restoration" of "original" lines to the Moore poem are pedantic and heavy-footed, and he, too, is the author of humorously named journal articles. For example, he has changed the lines "When what to my wondering eyes should appear,/ But a miniature sleigh and eight tiny reindeer" to "When, all amaz'd, I saw upon the snowy road/ A wint'ry phaeton with four bays to pull its load," changes Ludendorff attributes to correcting the "embarrassing whimsy" of alterations made by Moore's wife to the poem as she took it down; Ludendorff states that "it was she who 'corrected' the Beloved Author's stately alexandrines to anapestic doggerel" and "wrench[ed] . . . Keatsian echoes" out of Moore's original (22). The "scholarship" behind these changes stem from Ludendorff's work which showed that Moore's "equine and coaching imagery" was appropriate to one about Santa Claus, who was "not only the patron saint of children, merchants and pawnbrokers but also of high-waymen (see Ludendorff, 'Stand and Deliver': The Other Side of Santa,' *Clement Moore Studies*, Spring 1986)" (22). The parody ends with Ludendorff's dismissal of Ramsforth's "scribblings" and his apology to "the readers of this journal for the necessity of defending my own work, and Clement Clarke Moore's, against his imputations" (23). The closing of Ludendorff's letter reads: "Finally, . . . in the spirit of the Yuletide season, and in the immortal words of the Beloved Author: A Merry Christmas Day to you, and now good-night!" (23).

Clearly, this parody exemplifies the attitude of those outside the direct line of fire in the first Joyce War. The "article" brilliantly reaches two audiences: the specific digs at Kidd and Gabler are obvious to those who have been following the debate, and the general digs at academic squabbling over minutiae reach those who may not have been following the Joyce War, through the use of a popular Christmas story as a stand-in for *Ulysses*. There is a curious subtext revealed in this substitution. By implication, *Ulysses* is as beloved a story as "'Twas the Night Before Christmas," and as easily understandable. But since that is not, in fact, the case, and no one would make such a preposterous claim, the function of this substitution underscores the shift of the real debate from the actual business of determining the text of *Ulysses* into the world of personality conflict and career aspirations—it's not about the book anymore. While the scholars involved in the debate remain convinced that they are arguing over serious textual matters, the witnesses to the fighting (the general public) can discern that the scholars have abandoned any real concern with the "true" text of *Ulysses*.

## THE LAST ACT

Once the Miami conference was over, the combatants retreated to their camps and regrouped. The letter campaign continued in the *NYRB*, spanning a six-month period, and generally repeating accusations already made and escalating the name-calling and rhetorical flourishes already exhibited in the first Joyce War.[9] The subject was just about exhausted now, neither side really having anything more to say; after June 1989, the letters ceased and the first Joyce War was over. Almost a year later, in March 1990, Robin Bates published "Much Ado about James Joyce and His *Ulysses*," an article covering the whole of the debate for *Smithsonian* magazine. Bates is an Emmy-award winning producer for the Public Broadcasting Corporation's series *Nova*, and as an outsider to the scholarly world he offers the perspective of the common reader. His article uses language that ultimately trivializes the world of scholarship, and curiously, the title of his article, while perhaps meant to point toward the scholarly debate as "much ado about nothing," substitutes Joyce and *Ulysses* for the "nothing" of the Shakespearean allusion. The effect is to cast not only the debate, but the very subject of the debate, as irrelevant. But Bates makes no comment on the title's subliminal dismissal of *Ulysses*, so presumably this effect was unintentional. His trivializing is reserved for the editorial enterprise: he writes that scholars had long known that *Ulysses* had "tiny textual errors" and that once Gabler's edition was heralded as 'fixing' *Ulysses*, "[s]cholars and the few Joyce readers who worry about such things" were delighted with the edition; when he describes the controversy, he calls it "the kind of bizarre fuss that scholarship is prey to"; he describes the "arcane" world of scholarship around *Ulysses*, and says that "Joyceans, in fact, are the prime bloodhounds of modern literature"; and comments that most of "the alterations that have caused all the current fuss would slip by the ordinary reader of *Ulysses* undetected. Few had anything whatever to do with the book's richness or literary authenticity" (129–141). The implication here is that the debate was indeed a tempest in a teapot, unimportant to the real business of reading *Ulysses*.

Bates paints the controversy in terms of its personalities, and his article clearly leans towards Kidd. He describes Kidd as a "man who claims Irish blood and has flaming red hair and a beard to match" (130); Gabler is simply described as a "professor of English at the University of Munich" (129). Apparently, Bates's audience is supposed to privilege Kidd's view because he shares Joyce's nationality. Later, Bates writes of the 1985 conference that brought the world's attention to Kidd: "It was an antagonism made in heaven: Kidd, agile, brash, a natural-born gadfly; Gabler, safe and secure, Germanic, standing on his dignity, the professor versus the privateer" (141). This image is harder to analyze; on the surface it would seem to be less flattering of Kidd than of Gabler. But there is a subtle connection between "privateer" and "buccaneer," and the romantic image of Captain Kidd braving the stormy seas of the Joyce world emphasizes the public perception of Kidd as heroic scalawag: his is the worthy quest. The balance of the article shows that Bates finds Kidd's charges hard to dismiss, and that at one point, Gabler is said by Bates to "[admit] that he didn't actually do a complete collation of each letter and word in the facsimiles he used against the originals, a process usually considered essential by many textual editors" (142). By using the word "admitted" (changed above for grammatical reasons), Bates

frames such a statement as a guilty one—Gabler, he says, has done something wrong. Gabler never claimed to have checked "each letter and word"
against originals, so using "admit" implies that Gabler has covered up
something unseemly. It is apparent that Bates has not seen the facsimile, or
he might be more inclined to give Gabler the benefit of the doubt and avoid
words like "admit." Bates gives Kidd the last word when describing various
points of contention (141–144). For example:

> Kidd (and many other Joyceans, let it be added) objects to the way Gabler
> presents dialogue, retaining the dash, but placing the quote flush left.
>     Why the change? Gabler theorizes that Joyce wished to blur the dis-
> tinction between narration and dialogue; by placing his dashes left (with-
> out indentation), he is thereby making dialogue an inseparable part of the
> narrative text.
>     Retorts Kidd: "Joyce would quibble with his printers over the size of a
> period, but there is not a single scrap of evidence, anywhere, that he ever
> complained about indented dashes to mark dialogue." (143)

While Kidd is correct, the structure of this passage pits Gabler's claim
against Kidd's "retort," and while Gabler is paraphrased, Kidd is quoted.
The effect is to validate Kidd's position at Gabler's expense, and shows
Bates' own bias toward Kidd's position. Further on, describing four word
changes on the first page of *Ulysses* made by Gabler, Bates writes: "They
are errors made by Joyce's typist, says Gabler. There is no evidence for this,
says Kidd: 'They were Joyce's revisions. He passed on five sets of proofs
without complaining. Do you really think he would keep missing them—
on the very first page of his book?'" (144). Again, Gabler is paraphrased
and Kidd is allowed to speak directly. The effect of such an arrangement is
that Kidd's words have more force and overshadow Gabler's. Further,
Bates quotes a letter from Richard Ellmann (also quoted by Charles Rossman in his *NYRB* article; see Chapter Three) that questioned Gabler's
command of English, with no further comment upon the charge. It is left to
hang there, in the audience's mind, as an unanswered criticism of Gabler.
But Gabler's English is flawless and tinged with a British accent;[10] the
xenophobic implication that he doesn't speak the language well enough to
edit *Ulysses* is ludicrous. There is no indication that Bates ever actually
spoke to Gabler for his article, and to include this aspect of the controversy
is irresponsible. The cumulative effect of Bates' presentation indicates that
only Kidd is correct, when the truth of the matter is far more complicated.
    Bates recounts the history of *Ulysses*, focusing on the censorship trials
and a brief overview of the book's content. Showing the public Joyce's connection to pornography and the concurrent reputation for inaccessibility,
Bates mentions its reputation as a "dirty" book, one that is "impenetrable
without help" (131), and refers to the various reviews given it by famous
writers of the modernist era but with an eye toward the negative:

> Ezra Pound and T. S. Eliot recognized the novel's greatness from the start. But Virginia Woolf snippily dismissed it as "underbred." Yeats called it a "mad book" and confessed he had never finished it. George Bernard Shaw thought it a masterpiece, but he didn't want to finish it either. H. G. Wells, down-to-earth as always, complained about how hard Joyce's books were to read. Wells was right. As generations of college lit students would learn, *Ulysses* is hard to tackle without one of several guides that have been written to explain Joyce's hidden plans and games. (136)

What Bates doesn't include in his description of reviews here is that Woolf also found it to be a work of genius using methods similar to her own, in spite of her revulsion for its coarseness, and was later "impressed and illuminated" by Eliot's essay on the book (Bell Volume II 56, 84); while it is true that Yeats never finished reading the book, he also retracted his "mad book" statement and said, "It is a work perhaps of genius. I now perceive its coherence" (Ellmann 530); Shaw never finished the book, either, but he formed his opinion that the book was a masterpiece from reading excerpts in *The Little Review*, and stated of Joyce that his writing was of "classic quality" (Ellmann 576*n*); Wells's criticism was mostly aimed at *Finnegans Wake*, although in the letter to Joyce (reprinted in Ellmann 607–8) he writes "Your last two works [*Ulysses* and *Work in Progress*] have been more amusing and exciting to write than they will ever be to read"—but Wells also found value in Joyce's experimental work and wished him well in pursuing it.

These rebuttals to Bates's list of reactions to *Ulysses* are not to defend Joyce's work as much as to show that Bates, by presenting the negative reactions out of context, reinforces the view of Joyce's work as impossible for ordinary people to read. This view, combined with the presentation of the academic controversy as a "bizarre fuss" with little implications for the "ordinary reader of *Ulysses*" is a contradictory one: who is this ordinary reader if *Ulysses* is so impossible that even two of the acknowledged literary giants of our century couldn't finish it? Bates places Joyce yet again in the world of the ivory tower, and this world is rife with meaningless battles over spelling and punctuation. Bates further removes the controversy from "ordinary Joyce readers" in describing Kidd's charge that Gabler did not collate every printing of *Ulysses* during Joyce's lifetime (a charge without merit given Gabler's project of producing the ideal text built from manuscripts); Bates writes: ". . . does this really matter? Not to ordinary Joyce readers. But to textual scholars, Kidd insists, it could matter a good deal since any edition done in a writer's lifetime may contain authentic changes that he meant to have in the text" (142–43). Textual scholars, it is implied, are in charge of preserving the author's intent at all costs. Bates makes no mention of the reality that such intent can never be definitively ascertained, as such an issue is based on textual theory which presumably does not interest Bates' readers. The idea that there is a way to know the author's intentions, and that this aim is (or should be) the central concern of a textual scholar is the unspoken assumption behind Bates' article, an assumption shared by the vast majority of "ordinary readers"—witness this paragraph, which comes close to the end of the article:

> More textual infighting is sure to come, some of it fascinating, none of it significant to the reading of Joyce for pleasure and instruction. Scholars, after all, do have a duty to struggle toward an accurate text, down to the minutest of details. (144)

There is truth to his statement that scholars do have an obligation to work towards an accurate text; but different approaches to editing can produce different editions, and these editions can all be called accurate if they follow their editorial principles faithfully. The assumption behind Bates' statement is that one accurate text can be reached, that only one ought to be reached. The theoretical understanding of the instability of texts is far removed from the world Bates and his readers inhabit. Kidd's entire campaign in the Joyce Wars was predicated upon a knowledge of this condition and he carefully selected examples which would play to the public's expectation that the author's intention is a stable, unchanging, and identifiable entity. By avoiding a discussion of theory, Kidd ensured that the public, at least, would agree with him that Gabler's edition was flawed because it did not adhere to this understanding of authorial intention. This strategy appears to have worked. The 1961 edition was reissued, and the Gabler trade edition's title was changed from *Ulysses: The Corrected Text* to *Ulysses: The Gabler Edition*.

Perhaps much of the controversy could have been avoided had it been issued under that title in the first place; the publishers apparently operated under the same assumptions as the rest of the public about the stability of edited texts, and this misunderstanding of Gabler's project was fostered by the Joyce Estate long after they knew what Gabler was about. In the end, the picture presented to the public of academics was an unflattering one, and it solidified stereotypes of obsessed men in an ivory tower. Bates writes that "it seems likely that all the fuss created by the fracas at least may encourage Joyce readers to pick up whatever edition of *Ulysses* they have and dive into its intricacies again" (144). What is also likely is that the Kidd-Gabler controversy, played out in the popular press, only served to widen the dichotomy between the worlds of academia and the general reading public. Joyce's reputation, however, emerged unscathed as the writer who achieved immortality by keeping the professors busy.

The entire debate, as it appeared in the public documents, illustrates with uncanny accuracy Foucault's understanding of polemics as heresiology:

> polemics sets itself the task of determining the intangible point of dogma, the fundamental and necessary principle that the adversary has neglected, ignored, or transgressed; and it denounces this negligence as a moral failing; at the root of the error, it finds passion, desire, interest, a whole series

of weaknesses and inadmissible attachments that establish it as culpable. ("Polemics" 382)

The intangible point of dogma, as determined by John Kidd's position, is the will of the author, and it is easy to see which of Kidd's charges fall under Foucault's categories of transgressions here: Gabler, as the adversary, neglected and ignored Joyce's authority in the matter of the dialogue dashes and the full stop at the end of "Ithaca," among others; his "moral failing" lay in calling his edition the "definitive" *Ulysses*; and the attachment to what Kidd called "obscure theorizing" established Gabler as culpable in trespassing against Joyce and the ideology of the authorial will. Such polemics can be effective, as the renaming of the Gabler trade edition and the reissue of the 1961 edition show. But polemics also, as Foucault writes, are "nothing more than theater . . . And yet, in the order of discourse they are ways of acting which are not without consequence. There are the sterilizing effects: Has anyone ever seen a new idea come out of [polemics]?" ("Polemics" 383). The sacred ideology surrounding *Ulysses* was left in place throughout the polemical exchange because of the increasingly hermeneutical quality of the points of contention, and the priesthood of the Joyce Industry kept its position as interpreters of the holy writ of Joyce. In 1997, Danis Rose claimed to free *Ulysses* from the ivory tower with his *Reader's Edition*, and the next chapter explores whether Rose delivered on his promise of creating a "people's *Ulysses*."

NOTES

[1]Complaints about Gabler's prose style were not uncommon throughout the duration of the first Joyce War; Antony Hammond, in his review for *The Library* (Sixth Series 8 [1986]: 382–390), says Gabler's writing is "all too frequently too ponderous and slightly unidiomatic," full of sentences that "[make] one itch for the copy-editor's blue pencil," and "annoying" (385–86).

[2]See Remnick, "The War over *Ulysses*," *The Washington Post* (2 Apr. 1985), in which Kidd states: "When you read a book, you have a right to as good and accurate and edition of the book as possible and an honest statement from the publisher about what you're getting" (B4).

[3]Du Sautoy would repeat this explanation later in his 1989 article for the *James Joyce Quarterly*; see Chapter Three.

[4]"Editors Vary," *Times Literary Supplement* (10 May 1985: 520).

[5]A brief selection of these letters was allowed by the estate to be published in Richard Ellmann's *Selected Letters of James Joyce*. Ellmann justified the inclusion of the letters because he felt they shed light on the sexual content of *Ulysses*.

[6]The libraries at Harvard and Buffalo both corresponded with the author electronically (17 Sept. 1998) on this issue, and the Houghton Library at Harvard specifically stated that their registers are considered University records and as such are sealed for 50 years. The Rosenbach Museum was unwilling to divulge whether or not Kidd had indeed looked at their registers, because the privacy laws of Pennsylvania expressly prohibit such activity.

⁷Groden points to an article cited by Kidd in his July 22–27 letter to the *TLS*; Kidd wrote: "*Studies in Bibliography* (1986), edited by Bowers, had in press an article by Tanselle (President of the Bibliographical Society of America) which calls Gabler's theorizing 'pretentious,' and finds beneath his 'verbiage' that 'Gabler's position has obviously not been carefully thought through'" (818). The Tanselle article appeared as "Historicism and Critical Editing," *Studies in Bibliography* 39 (1986): 1–46, and critiques Gabler's article "The Synchrony and Diachrony of Texts: Practice and Theory of the Critical Edition of James Joyce's *Ulysses*," which appeared in *Text* 1 (1981) [published in 1984]: 305–326. Tanselle has continued to write pieces critical of Gabler's theories, including "Reproductions and Scholarship" *Studies in Bibliography* 42 (1989): 25–54, and "Textual Criticism and Literary Sociology" *Studies in Bibliography* 44 (1991): 83–143; for further examples of Tanselle's views on editing, see also "Critical Editions, Hypertexts, and Genetic Criticism" *Romanic Review* 86 (May 1995): 581–93; "Editing Without a Copy-Text" *Studies in Bibliography* 47 (1994): 1–22; "Books, Canons, and the Nature of Dispute" *Common Knowledge* 1 (Spring 1992): 78–91.

⁸In another bit of humor from the conference, an unidentified scholar made a joke about "textually transmitted diseases" in reference to the editing controversy. Robertson quoted this joke as an example that not everyone at the conference was heavily invested in the controversy or its outcome, and that some attempted to lighten up the charged atmosphere.

⁹Hans Walter Gabler, Alistair McCleery, Charles Rossman and John Kidd (30 Mar. 1989: 43–45); Alistair McCleery, John Kidd (1 June 1989: 40–41).

¹⁰See Remnick's *Washington Post* article. In my own correspondence with Professor Gabler (both electronically and via telephone), he exhibits a perfect command of English.

CHAPTER SIX

# WHOSE BOOK IS IT, ANYWAY?
# or,
# PRUNING THE BLOOM

*Bad editors can make authors look very good. Every author should be blessed by one.*
                                        —William Cain, "Making Texts New"

*Of course, it is a beauty visible only to other textual scholars.*
                                        —Philip Cohen and David H. Jackson,
                                   "Notes on Emerging Paradigms in Editorial Theory"

As Penelope did in Homer's epic, the reading public went ten years before hearing again from (or, more accurately, about) *Ulysses*. In 1997, to much academic hand wringing, *Ulysses: A Reader's Edition* appeared in Britain, edited by Danis Rose. Once again, the Joyce world became a focus of attention for the popular press, and once again controversy over matters Joycean garnered print in the *New York Review of Books* and the *Times Literary Supplement*. The debate was far different from the earlier conflict, though; the tone was more subdued and the duration much shorter. Perhaps Joyceans, still shell-shocked from the first Joyce War, were wary of becoming embroiled in an encore. Perhaps there was little left to say about editorial issues in *Ulysses*. More likely, the changed tenor of the second Joyce War resulted not only from these reasons but also from the fact that the primary force behind the first Joyce War, John Kidd, did not sustain the same zeal against the Rose edition—probably because of his troubles in getting his own edition of *Ulysses* published. The scholarly reactions to Rose's edition were limited to a few reviews, letters to the editor, and quotes in popular press accounts of the new edition.[1] The *James Joyce Literary Supplement* carried some scholarly response to the edition, the summer 1998 issue of the *James Joyce Quarterly* devoted a special section to the Rose *Ulysses*, and the 1998 International James Joyce Symposium held in Rome convened a panel on the Rose edition.[2]

The popular press, however, devoted considerable space to covering the new edition, partly because of its ostensible audience: the common reader. For the better part of 1997, articles on Rose's *Ulysses* appeared in newspapers and magazines across several continents. But these articles in the popular press did not address the editorial issues relevant to Rose's text, nor did they discuss whether or not Rose's edition lived up to its aim of making Joyce's prose easier to read. Instead, they concentrated on issues of personality and the politics of the academy, and they reinforced Joyce's deistic status and the trope of difficulty surrounding the text of *Ulysses*. In short, the controversy, as reported in the popular press, differed only in degree from the first Joyce War: the same combatants were consulted, the same arguments were made, and the same charges of avarice and glory-seeking were leveled at those who would deign to tackle editing the master of modernism. It is not surprising, therefore, that the controversy was not as heated as the first one; nothing really new was being said.

What this propensity toward rehash disguises, however, is that the Rose edition of *Ulysses* raises some deeply thought-provoking issues about readership that Joyceans, at least, seem unwilling to tackle: who reads *Ulysses*? And why? Such questions were left unexplored in the first Joyce War while questions of authorship—i.e., what Joyce actually wrote—held everyone's focus. Yet, the controversy over the Gabler edition was actually about readership—issues of copyright, trade editions, and notions of "definitiveness" speak more of access to Joyce's text than of philosophical and bibliographical theories of manuscripts. Ironically, the controversy over the Rose edition focused on who actually has the authority to write *Ulysses*—i.e., to change Joyce's words and style—instead of the questions of readership that Rose ostensibly wished to raise. And contrary to Rose's claims of "freeing" *Ulysses* from academic ownership, an edition based primarily upon the idea that Joyce's prose is impossible for the non-specialist to read does little to remove or weaken the trope of difficulty surrounding *Ulysses*. While claiming to make Joyce's text into "a *Ulysses* for our time," as the dust jacket proudly decrees, the rationale behind this reader's edition seems to ignore the fact that *Ulysses* is not a document from a culture centuries removed from current readers, but a book less than 90 years old. Modernizing Shakespeare may be logical for twentieth-century readers;[3] but surely a book written in the twentieth century is a book "for our time" already. It is not simply Joyce's use of compound words and punctuation that make *Ulysses* more difficult to read than other kinds of narratives, but that Joyce deliberately (even gleefully) turned narrative practice on its head. Punctuation plays a part in Joyce's stylistic innovations—especially its lack in "Penelope," to use a popular example—but the chapters that seem most troublesome for readers are actually punctuated in a standard way. For example, Rose himself points out that "Oxen of the Sun" is particularly difficult for readers to master, but that chapter contains regular punctuation and spelling within each of its "periods" of English language—and Rose does not explain *why* this particular chapter is difficult. However, in the popular press neither Rose nor the articles written about his edition appear willing to address anything but punctuation and spelling changes. The import of this phenomenon is best addressed by first exploring the editorial theories behind the Rose edition.

## PERFORMATIVE ACTS AND HISTORICAL CURIOSITIES

Rose elucidates his theory by first invoking science; he states that physicists have been "telling us that we are in the era of inbuilt indeterminacy" since around the first publication of *Ulysses*, and that "[w]ith the passing away of the materialistic belief in certainties in favour of statistical probabilities, the contemporary but still widespread fallacy that the extirpation of mere printers' errors, important as it is, is the sole or even the primary function of a textual editor ought also to have passed away" (xi). Rose does not make clear how the shift to belief in "statistical probabilities" reflects a shift in textual thinking about *Ulysses*, but instead relies on induction to legitimize his editing project through recourse to science, a time-honored move in literary circles. Rose then briefly outlines a history of textual editing, as it derived from the study of religious manuscripts, and discusses the need for eliminating errors as important only to establishing accurate manuscripts. He differentiates this procedure from that of producing "works of literary art—books made for readers to be read for pleasure,"[4] which requires literary hermeneutics: "The textual faults underlined by the copy-reader challenge the textual scholar to search for their origin in surviving or in reconstructed lost manuscripts, and the cruxes that defy both these disciplines are as often as not solvable by the critic or the biographer" (xii). What Rose seems to imply here is that traditional editing does not rely on the skills of the critic or the biographer, a premise directly contradicted by Bowers' development of Greg's rationale. It is precisely the reliance on the extra-textual material that helps to establish hierarchy in variant readings for Bowers. But the structure of Rose's explanation implies that he is doing something unique; he ends a paragraph with the statement quoted above, and then begins the next paragraph with "I have sought to bring all these skills to bear in editing *Ulysses*" (xii). The subtle emphasis on "all" here suggests that prior editions have not followed the procedures Rose outlines. Rose thus attempts to differentiate his edition not through its theory or introduction of new material, but by simply saying that other editions, because they do not take into account the "pleasure of the reader," exist in a scholarly world inaccessible to the common reader. His edition, he implies, will be different.

Rose explains his editing procedure by discussing his preparation of an "isotext," which he defines as a "straight manuscript text . . . [that] is an error-free, 'naked' transcription of the author's words as written down by him or by a surrogate . . . It is not a transcription, however edited, of any single text, but a blending . . . of the members of a series or complex of texts" (xii). He states that this "isotext" is similar to the synoptic pages of the Gabler edition (without explicitly mentioning his own work on that edition), but that his manuscript "includes *all* the extant manuscripts . . . in the main line of transmission, excludes the six 'lost final working drafts' Gabler imaginatively reconstructed (or created) which [Rose] argued never existed . . . and replaces the remaining two 'lost final working drafts' with their corresponding protodrafts (which are not lost)" (xii; original italics). In this way, Rose differentiates his own procedure from Gabler's by subtly casting aspersion on Gabler, who "created" lost drafts, which, to a reader unversed in the Gabler method and its ensuing controversy ten years earlier, would appear to be an editorial blasphemy: it would seem that Gabler made up Joyce's texts when he couldn't find them. Rose states that the "isotext is literally *Ulysses* as James Joyce wrote it" (xiii), not only a bold statement that reinforces a traditional notion of authorial sovereignty to give his created "isotext" legitimacy, but also a dig at the Gabler edition which claimed to present *Ulysses* "as Joyce wrote it" ("Afterword").

Converting an isotext into "a text suitable for general reading" by stripping away "all the diacritics and other codes" and then "copyreading the thus-reduced text" for Rose is a "performative act wholly distinct from the original preparation of the isotext itself," which is materially accurate as a document of the manuscript as it developed (xiii). This "performative act" in effect eliminates the author's final intentions as a determining factor in shaping the reading text:

> Two radically different approaches to editing *Ulysses* are in this way combined: that which insists on the primacy of the author's manuscript, and that which takes account of the preparation of the raw manuscript for the public. These two editorial orientations, insofar as *Ulysses* is concerned, inform Hans Walter Gabler's and Jerome McGann's positions, respectively. (xii)

Rose precisely spells out the procedure that lay in the shadows in the preparation of the Gabler trade edition: the editor's decisions (often arguable) to emend the manuscript for ease of reading. For Gabler, this procedure was secondary to his project of creating the "continuous manuscript text" in that the reading text was primarily an aid to reading the synoptic text; misunderstanding—or ignoring—this element of Gabler's project, the publishers and the Joyce estate marketed the 1986 trade edition as a "definitive" text derived from Gabler's manuscript text. This marketing ploy relied wholly on the primacy of authorial final intention as the final arbiter of an edition's "definitiveness." But Gabler's edition, in effect, reversed the traditional editorial procedure that positioned the edited text as a final repository for the author's words. Rose, too, sees his "isotext" as the final repository for Joyce's words but, following McGann, positions the edited text as repository of the author's, editor's, and publishing crew's words—a move that actually pushes Gabler's method one step further. If the edited text is merely one reflection of the possibilities presented in the manuscript text, then the whole idea of definitiveness in that edited text is shown to be a false construct. So Rose takes great pains to explain Mc-Gann's social theory of editing; Rose writes that McGann's theory "is based on a simple insight known to authors and publishers since the days of the Gutenberg press but not taken sufficiently seriously by textual editors before him: *no published book qua book is entirely the work of the author*" (xiii-xiv; original italics). Here Rose disparages the scholarly establishment: this "simple insight" has been known for hundreds of years, but textual scholars apparently don't have enough common sense to take it seriously. It is in this section that Rose begins to separate his edition from the world of scholars which he claims has held *Ulysses* captive and to justify his own emendations to Joyce's text.

But Rose pushes McGann's theory further than does McGann himself. Rose correctly states that McGann is aware that first editions (the text Mc-Gann would prefer to be used as copy-text—see Chapter Three) are flawed, so he wants to incorporate some version of final authorial intention in making editing choices. Rose then explains the term "final authorial intention," but he misreads Greg's rationale when he writes,

> [this concept] arose . . . when textual scholarship sought to provide a set of rules whereby any text could be transformed into a definitive edition . . . It did not matter who did the editing, the result should in principle always be the same. The underlying model was evidently the paradigmatic requirement in the sciences that an experiment should be repeatable and should always give the same results . . . (xiv)

As Bowers has shown,[5] Greg's rationale was much more flexible than Rose suggests here, and it is contradictory for Rose to disparage here the scientific model he invoked in the first paragraph of his own Introduction.

Rose finally justifies his own project by debunking the "second requirement of traditional textual scholarship . . . that the work is entirely the work of the author alone" (xiv-xv). He writes that the idea that the editor has "replaced the contribution of the production crew (defined as textual corruption) with the author's own words" is a "sham" (xv), and relies on McGann and unnamed "others" to support this bold statement. But even bolder, he pushes McGann's theory further by claiming

> that the editor should replace the original production crew when copy-reading, and the edition's publisher's typographers and designers should replace their original counterparts. Only in this way can one produce an edition that is of its own time and that can, intellectually and aesthetically, stand on its own two feet. (xv)

It is this last statement which recasts the McGann-Gabler theories into something open to debate. To elucidate, we must look at the two rules Rose followed in his procedure: following the isotext for all substantives and following "sound practice" for all accidentals (xvi). Sound practice is a slippery idea that "changes over time and also varies depending on the author and the kind of book that one is editing" (xvi). He justifies this laxity by appealing to an odd notion of (forgive the pun) the shelf-life of books:

> It is my belief that an edition based on these principles generates a text that not only more closely preserves and represents the author's words (in that it deviates least from the isotext) but, somewhat paradoxically, also better recaptures the 'flavour' of the first edition. Readers' expectations change with the passage of time. When *Ulysses* was first published, it was received by the public as being thoroughly modern, absolutely the *dernier cri*. Simply to reproduce the 1922 text seventy-five years on, whether as a straight facsimile edition or as a 'corrected' 1922, is to produce nothing more worthwhile than a historical curiosity on the one hand or a 'genuine replica' on the other. I think that Joyce and *Ulysses* deserve better. (xvi)

This notion of the 1922 *Ulysses* as an "historical curiosity" relies on the odd premise that, because readers' expectations change, a book from the past loses its ability to seem "thoroughly modern." But this description is meaningless upon examination. Authors write during specific historical moments, and it seems absurd to think that readers in later periods expect works to "keep up with the times." No one dismisses Jane Austen's books as "historical curiosities" simply because they are written in a two hundred-year-old vernacular; there is no reason why *Ulysses*, less than half that age, should need to be modernized.[6] Rose appears to believe that books are like clothing, needing to be freshened up every few years to stay "absolutely the *dernier cri*." The intriguing combination of Gabler's and McGann's theories falls flat in light of Rose's aims of reaching readers inhibited by *Ulysses'* reputation for difficulty; in the end, he uses it to justify what amounts to editing by personal taste rather than undertaking an exploration of just what makes *Ulysses* difficult to read in the first place. Such an exploration would reveal, however, that those difficulties are not smoothed away simply by adding commas or inserting hyphens.

Rose includes a few examples of his emendations in his "Introduction," and in each case the changes rely upon Rose's sensibilities. In one example, where the original text in "Lestrygonians" reads "Lady this. Powdered bosom pearls," Rose substitutes "Lady this. Powdered bosom, pearls," and states that the original is "manifestly wrong. What is a 'bosom pearl' and why should bosom pearls be powdered?" (xviii). While his emendation does make grammatical sense, there is no extant manuscript with the comma. He hypothesizes that "Joyce mistakenly dropped a comma . . . in copying out the protodraft" (xviii). Earlier, he states his authority as editor in creating an edition of *Ulysses* for general reading allows him to make just such emendations, but here he relies on a postulated authorial basis—

Joyce meant to put the comma in but made a mistake—to justify his own emendation.

This example is instructive in that it shows Rose hesitating in applying his own boldly stated theory. The construction "powdered bosom pearls" could be read poetically as a description of a woman's powdered breasts. It is Rose's own reading that the comma ought to be inserted, but just because it makes grammatical sense does not mean that it is manifestly correct; such a decision is an editorial judgment. Under Rose's theory, which freely allows him to correct what he sees as errors in grammar and syntax, such a judgment is eminently defensible. But Rose shuffles his feet, so to speak, and justifies his decision on the quite conservative grounds of authorial intention. In effect, Rose tries to have it both ways and thus places his own project within the very bounds of Bowersian editing that he claims to set aside. Each of the examples given in his "Introduction" fall into the same trap, with all of the various kinds of textual faults attributed to Joyce's miscopying or misplacing lines and words. While Rose's changes often do, in fact, make sentences grammatically sensible, he relies on an interpretation of these faulty areas as misrepresentations of Joyce's intent (Joyce *meant* to insert a comma here, he *meant* to put this part of the sentence there), but without any concrete evidence given to support such an interpretation. And, as in the "powdered bosom pearls" example above, some of his emendations rely on his own feeling that things are "manifestly wrong." While this particular judgment call is arguable, under Rose's theory it is admissible in order to make some kind of sense of the text. So why rely on a questionable postulation of authorial intention?

Such sidestepping leaves the editorial changes in doubt, even when they improve the text. In an example from "Eumaeus," Rose compares a passage from the 1922 original to the Gabler edition and his own to show how his changes smooth out unintelligible prose. The relevant part of the passages are as follows:

1922:

> The queer suddenly things he popped out with attracted the elder man who was several years the other's senior or like his father. But something substantial he certainly ought to eat, were it only an eggflip made on unadulterated maternal nutriment or, failing that, the homely Humpty Dumpty boiled.

Gabler:

> The queer suddenly things he popped out with attracted the elder man who was several years the other's senior or like his father but something substantial he certainly ought to eat even were it only an eggflip made on unadulterated maternal nutriment or, failing that, the homely Humpty Dumpty boiled.

Rose:

> The queer things he suddenly popped out with, rather like his father, at-
> tracted the elder man. But something substantial he certainly ought to eat,
> even were it only an eggflip made on unadulterated maternal nutriment,
> or failing that, the homely Humpty Dumpty boiled. (all qtd. in Rose, xxii)

The 1922 version is nonsensical, and the Gabler version merely eliminates some punctuation without changing the word order. The passage is
still nonsensical. Rose's version does make grammatical sense, and does
ease the reading of that particular passage. In this case, the authority Rose
takes upon himself indeed improves the reader's understanding of Joyce's
prose. Yet, instead of simply resting on his laurels, he places this example
under the heading "Textual faults arising through Joyce's omissions in cre-
atively copying out a protodraft" (xxi). He does not explain what "cre-
atively copying out" means; presumably he means that Joyce composed
additional text while copying an earlier draft, a habit that carried well into
the proof stages of *Ulysses*. But Rose relies on the existence of a "protodraft" to justify his changes, not because the new text exists in this protodraft but because Joyce made mistakes. This is not, of course, inconceivable
and in fact is quite probable. Rose, although invoking McGann's poststructuralist theory, in essence reverts to an earlier method of textual editing by
divining authorial intention: here is what Joyce meant to do. In so doing, he
reifies the notion of the author/god, whose word is accessible only to those
with the special decoder ring. What continues to make Rose's position intriguing is that it suggests that what Joyce meant to do was to take readers'
needs into account, that Joyce intended his text to be more accessible. Perhaps, but Rose's retreat into "authorial intention, interrupted," defies his
own carefully explained position that those intentions aren't sacred. And
sometimes, his dependence on such postulated authorial intentions reveals
his own scholarly disdain for the common reader.

### BAD EDITORS AND THE TEXTS THEY LOVE

William Cain, in the essay "Making Texts New," uses the example of Edward Connery Lathem's edition of Robert Frost's poetry to show the editor's "*impulse to reject*. He or she cannot bear the text as it stands; the
human labor that the author did ought to have been done better. And so
the editor intervenes—often in the guise of an honorable, theoretically
based desire for 'regularization'—and willfully skews the text" (201; original italics). Cain describes the editorial project as "a sheer contest of wills
between author and editor" in which the editor is "always tempted . . . to
smooth out what [he deems] to be the author's mistakes" (201). He bases
this conjecture on Lathem's alteration to Frost's "Stopping by Woods on a
Snowy Evening," which changed "The woods are lovely, dark and deep"
to "The woods are lovely, dark, and deep." That simple addition of a

comma turns the modifying "dark and deep" into an artless list of attributes. Lathem, Cain writes, "provides the evidence of his wrongful deed," by listing the variants in the back of his edition. Cain asserts that Lathem has done Frost a favor: "changing the punctuation *away* from what Frost wrote enables readers to understand more readily and richly why Frost wanted it his own way . . . Before he changed the text, readers might not have noticed the purposeful punctuation of the line that Frost wrote, but now, thanks to Lathem, they do" (202; original italics). For this reason, Cain estimates, every author should be "blessed" with a bad editor.

Substitute "Danis Rose" for "Edward Connery Lathem," and "Joyce" for "Frost," and Cain in some ways could be writing about *Ulysses: A Reader's Edition.* Particularly, Rose's decision to offer dual versions of "Penelope" allows readers to compare his version with the original, and theoretically lets readers understand more clearly Joyce's purposes in not punctuating Molly's monologue. Rose's explanation for inserting the apostrophes into the episode signifies his own inability to bear the text as it stands:

> Due to its late completion, the draft that otherwise would have been the basis for a fair copy was the source of the typescript, which in turn (and without a second intervening typescript) was almost immediately sent to the printer. This left no opportunity for Joyce to reverse his decisions on the format. Of these the most controversial—*and the most irritating to the reader*—was the removal of all the apostrophes. . . . The problem is that apostrophes are integral parts of their words, which in many cases ('wed', 'well', 'Ill', 'Id', etc.) cannot be understood without them. In practice, readers of *Ulysses* are compelled mentally to resupply the apostrophes, so that nothing really has been gained by their removal and a great deal—the undisturbed flow of the text—has been lost. (xxv; my emphasis)

In making the claim that contractions cannot be understood without their apostrophes, Rose disregards context; it is highly doubtful that any reader past elementary-school age could mistake "Ill get up early in the morning" as "Sick get up early in the morning." The lack of apostrophes irritates Rose, and he emends according to a rationale based on conjecture and supposition of authorial intention. The Rosenbach manuscript of "Penelope" shows the punctuation intact; the decision to eliminate apostrophes came after the composition of that document, and Rose posits that removing them "was possibly first suggested to Joyce by his friend Robert McAlmon, who typed 'Penelope'" (xxv). Rose proposes that, because Joyce was operating under his self-imposed deadline of publication on his birthday, "Penelope" was sent off to the printer before Joyce could change his mind about the apostrophes. But Rose also says that the process of removing the apostrophes was "continued onto the proofs," surely an indication that this decision was more deliberate than he supposes. Had Joyce changed his mind about the apostrophes, as Rose suggests, he could have indicated to the printer at the proof stage to reinsert them into Molly's monologue. There is evidence that Joyce never wanted those apostrophes to stay in. Joyce was adamant that the French printer setting the French translation of *Ulysses* remove the accent marks on the words of Molly's monologue, and wrote to Adrienne Monnier, "Following my most secret conception, I've taken all the thorns (the grave and the acute) off her" (Ellmann 562). Joyce referred to these accent marks as Molly's "hairpins," something removed before going to bed (*ibid.*). If Joyce felt this way about the accent marks in the French translation, it is likely that he wanted the apostrophes removed in the English printing for much the same reasons. Rose's supposition that Joyce had changed his mind about the apostrophes—or, even more tenuous, would have changed his mind given time—is a highly arguable justification for including them, and another appeal to an authorial intention that he elsewhere devalues.

### ARE YOU TALKING TO ME?

> James Joyce's *Ulysses* is quintessentially a work of literary art. Accordingly, the overriding criterion applied in creating this edition has been to maximize the pleasure of the reader. To this, the scholarship informing the edition—the initial preparation of the isotext and the worksheet-tagged text, the detection and elimination of textual faults and errors, small and large, the copyreading and other acts—must perforce remain secondary and subservient. . . . The Reader's Edition is presented to the reader as an integrated edition of a work of literary art and it is on these terms, primarily aesthetic, that it steps forth to be judged. (Rose v-vi)

So reads the preface to Danis Rose's edition of *Ulysses*. Yet immediately upon turning to the Introduction, the reader is confronted in Part I with the very elements he calls "secondary and subservient": an account of conflicts in editorial theory, Rose's rationale of copy-editing, and the four-part, rather detailed explanation of his categories of textual faults and emendation procedures. It is debatable whether or not a reader unschooled in the editorial conflicts would find much of Rose's rationale worth reading. Compared to Judge Woolsey's stirring words in the 1961 edition, or even Ellmann's eloquent preface to the 1986 Gabler trade version, Rose's "Introduction" falls flat.

Part II, "The History of the Composition of *Ulysses*," narrates the story of *Ulysses* as it took shape, and Rose does address the practicalities of reading the novel in this section, giving an episode-by-episode summation of style and content. For example, he writes that " 'Oxen of the Sun', . . . in which Mrs Mina Purefoy gives birth in the maternity hospital, is perhaps the most complex episode in *Ulysses* and the hardest to get to grips with. The first-time reader should perhaps skip it rather than become bogged down, stop reading and thereby miss out on the more accessible pleasures of the final four episodes" (xliii). This advice is clearly aimed at a non-specialist reader, but he then wanders into territory more suited to textual scholarship. In the middle section of part II, Rose offers a genetic text complete with diacritical markings for selected passages from "Nausicaa," "Eumaeus," "Ithaca," and "Penelope." One or even two examples would be enough to illustrate his point about Joyce's accretive style of writing; four seem like overkill if Rose intends to keep a non-scholar's interest. Part III, which narrates the creation, sale, and history of the Rosenbach manuscript as well as its role in the debate over the Gabler edition, seems to be of unmistakable importance to his own edition, and presumably would help a reader understand why Rose undertook such a project in the first place. It becomes curious, then, that in an edition specifically marketed for such a reader, Rose's introduction begins with what appears to be a calculated defense of his editing methods, rather than the guide to reading and the very intriguing background material on *Ulysses*. If an edition is purportedly for an audience of non-academics coming to *Ulysses* for the first time, then it seems odd that the compelling narrative of the novel's creation, the explication of narrative style, and Rose's rationale behind creating such a reader's edition is not the first (or only) material in the introduction. Placing his editorial rationale first is a move that might be of more interest to textual scholars and those who followed the Gabler-Kidd dispute ten years earlier. Certainly, a general reader buying Rose's *Reader's Edition* based on the marketing hype would want to know what Rose has done to make her reading easier, but it is not clear that such a reader wants to know how Rose's methods measure up against McGann or Greg, two textual scholars who, whatever their individual merits, are not usually found on the best-seller shelves at Barnes & Noble. Part I of Rose's introduction is not aimed at the audience the edition itself supposedly accommodates, but at the Joyce scholars who would dissect his work.

Furthermore, the inclusion of an alternate version of "Penelope" speaks to concerns other than maximizing the pleasure of the reader. Would anyone patient and persevering enough to get to the end of Joyce's novel (and, whatever its delights, *Ulysses* can require a good deal of both) really want to read the chapter twice? Or carry out the kind of textual comparison between chapters that publishing two versions would suggest they do? Such activity may be interesting to a small number of non-academic readers, but the broad appeal Rose claims for his edition would seem to preclude catering to such a small group. It seems inconsistent, to say the least, that he would give both versions of this episode and not any of the others, if presumably he changed them to gain the undisturbed flow of the text as well. Publishing both versions of "Penelope" is a gambit to sidestep the issues raised by his decision to override Joyce's revisions; it is a concession to the inevitable uproar over removing one of the defining elements of Molly's soliloquy—and thereby removing the defining element of the novel as a whole, at least within the discourse of the public Joyce. The effect of Rose's move to print both versions is that the "Penelope" episode is again reified as the most important chapter of *Ulysses* by drawing attention to it as stylistically different than the rest of the book and deserving of special handling.

THE IVORY TOWER SPEAKS

Such a strategem not only reinforces the significance of the episode to *Ulysses*—and its connection to the public Joyce—but also serves to help Rose protect himself from any accusations of claiming to be the definitive text. In fact, Rose's introduction makes a good case for textual indeterminacy and, by extension, his own exercise of what Robert Spoo calls a "broad warrant for editorial search and seizure" (331). Rose's methods follow Gabler's closely (not surprising since Rose was an assistant on the Gabler *Ulysses* project). Key differences arise, though, in how Rose views the importance and ultimate authority of the Rosenbach manuscript (he puts the entire manuscript into the direct line of textual descent, while Gabler only places a portion of it in that line), and in Rose's decision to edit his copy-text into one which more closely follows late twentieth century practices in spelling, punctuation, and italics. Further, Rose's edition suggests the next logical step after the fallout of the Gabler Wars—namely, that there is no one true text; all we can ever have are multiple versions of the same text. If this is the case, then modernizing Joyce's spellings and normalizing his prose is no great sin.

But Gabler himself has serious reservations about the *Reader's Edition*. In the Summer 1998 issue of the *James Joyce Quarterly*, Gabler reviews Rose's *Ulysses* and finds its editorial principles and emendations wanting. He says of the Rose edition that it "employs conjecture beyond a measure commonly allowed in editorial practice," and that it demonstrates "pure copy-editing freewheeling" (567–570); further, he decries the edition's "apparent lack of a methodological foundation" (572). Throughout the review, Gabler compares Rose's edition to his own, and displays a lingering defensiveness when it comes to the 1984 *Ulysses* (which he abbreviates as "CSE" throughout his review; he also abbreviates Rose's edition as "RE"). His rationale for the comparison both justifies it and valorizes his own edition: "Since it is the one scholarly edition that we have, it provides the document reference that RE lacks" (567). But Rose's project was never packaged as a scholarly edition, and here Gabler fails to regard it on its own terms. Instead, this statement may be a veiled jab at Kidd here, in that his long-awaited scholarly edition has still not been published. Gabler also refers to the controversy over the love passage included in his edition, and says that Rose's decision to leave out the paragraph where Stephen names the word known to all men makes the *Reader's Edition* a "wish-fulfilling text, for does not the editorial solution wondrously conform to all Joyce criticism that, since 1984, has balked" at this passage (562)? He states that "what can—or might—be said in . . . favor" of Rose's version is an attempt to "harmonize" the "Scylla and Charybdis" episode with the "Circe" episode (in which Stephen asks his mother to tell him the word), but then says that this harmonizing "puts the cart before the horse. It starts from an interpretation—the balking critics' interpretation" and then "establishes the text" (563). Repeatedly, he states that his own edition offers different options for interpretation by allowing the editorial decisions behind inclusion to be apparent in the synoptic text. The lack of a textual apparatus, in Gabler's view, makes Rose's decisions suspect; by implication, of course, his own edition is valorized because it includes such an apparatus.

At one point, Gabler finds that in some instances, "practical editorial solutions converge" in his edition and Rose's, although reached by different understandings of textual documents' position in the stemma. Gabler writes, "In fact, the hypothesis of a pure linear progression of the *Ulysses* text, were it provable as the transmission model true to reality, may even—be it remarked in passing—be seen to vindicate CSE's editorial procedure in an unforeseen way" (565). The next sentence begins, "At any rate," a sign that Gabler is aware that he has wandered into defending his own work against past accusations of inferiority. When discussing the indentation of dialogue dashes, so contentious in the first Joyce War, he writes parenthetically of Rose and his production crew that "[t]heir incomprehension of the significance of Joyce's nonindentation of dialogue is not unprecedented; it runs through much critical discussion of CSE" (571). He does make an interesting concession later, however:

> In Shakespeare textual scholarship today, "unedit Shakespeare" is a prominent war cry. "Unemend *Ulysses* now!" would be my summing-up call for this review. This goes emphatically and radically for the RE. But the CSE reading text would not be wholly exempt. Some of its (relatively sparse) verbal emendations of its copy-text may justifiably be returned to document readings. (572–73)

Gabler grudgingly allows that the disagreements he has with Rose's edition may be similar to those grievances raised against his own, but carefully distinguishes the "reading text" from his synoptic text, as he did throughout the first Joyce War.

Following Gabler's review is Fritz Senn's. He writes that Rose's edition is "a very handsomely produced book," but questions what the reader will get out of this *Reader's Edition*:

> those entirely nonacademic targeted readers who so much prefer the easy highway, who want signposts in the labyrinth, are unlikely to engage in textual comparison and may never know what they are saved from or what they are missing. Moreover, I am not sure whether a liberal dispensation of hyphens, apostrophes, clearly marked quotations, uppercase letters . . . or rectified spellings will substantially help those readers to sail ecstatically through "Proteus" or the more turgid eddies of "Oxen of the Sun." (574)

Senn also writes of Rose's decision to include the apostrophes in "Penelope" that a reader "who gets unscathed as far as the eighteenth episode will no longer balk at" the lack of punctuation, and he finds that Rose's policy on breaking up compound words is applied inconsistently (575). Twice, he raises objections to Rose's interventions by saying that "Joyce may have known what he was doing," and he sees "no reason why an edition should do the work that Joyce may well have assigned to us readers" (577–79). Senn clearly believes that Rose underestimates the capacities of the common reader to decipher Joyce's unconventional style. Senn writes, "Rose wants to save the reader from being forced 'to make textual decisions throughout' and opts for instant illumination. A matter of taste, perhaps" (582–83). Senn is remarkably fair-minded about Rose's edition, and willing to give it the benefit of the doubt. But doubt he does.

Senn's review positions the *Reader's Edition* as a "well-meant missionary effort [that] has gone unfortunately astray," and ends by saying that "Textually, we are still waiting for our redeemer" (583). This choice of words places *Ulysses* firmly inside the discourse of the sacred text. Rose's "missionary" foray into the dark (unknown?) heart of the general public, in order to bring the light of Joyce's words to the heathens, led to many critics' cries of "The horror! The horror!" His methods, they shouted, are unsound. Further, we still await the redeemer who will give us the true text of *Ulysses*—yet Senn states that such a "definitive, authoritative, best, reliable *Ulysses*" will never come. He precedes this last statement with a mention that "the long-delayed Kidd/Norton edition looms on the horizon," and unconsciously raises the spectre of a rough beast slouching toward Dublin to be born.

HERE WE GO AGAIN

In America, the appearance of a new *Ulysses* was, as in the earlier Joyce War, first noted in the *New York Times* (23 June 1997: *New York Times* archive online 20 Apr. 1998). Adhering to the public Joyce's attribute of obscurity, the article by Sarah Lyall begins with a reference to the work's difficulty: "Even James Joyce didn't always know the precise words he intended to use in *Ulysses*, his masterpiece and a book that was as challenging in the writing as it is in the reading," a curious statement in that, presumably, Joyce's intentions were clear to himself if not to his editors. Further, this statement clearly places Lyall—and by extension, her audience—as adherents to the traditional view of authorial intention. In Lyall's formulation, it is Joyce's muddled intentions which make editing *Ulysses* so difficult, not conflicting editorial theories about pre- or post-publication copytexts.[7] Lyall also quotes Joyce's overworked line about printer's errors that prefaced so many articles in the first Joyce War. She further differentiates the academic world from the common reader's by describing "Joyce scholars and fanatics" who have been "consumed . . . for the last seven and a half decades" with trying to create a "definitive" version of the text. That most editorial scholars have effectively abandoned the idea of a definitive text is not mentioned. Lyall paraphrases Rose as saying that his new edition is "intended to do nothing less than change the way people approach Joyce's formidable novel." It is not clear whether "formidable"—an expression that foregrounds the trope of difficulty—is her word or Rose's. Further emphasis on this trope occurs when she writes, "In a work characterized by idiosyncratic punctuation (or none at all), creative spelling and sentences that often do not conform to normal standards of sentence structure, Mr. Rose says, such changes are necessary for an ordinary reader to understand the text." Lyall never clarifies what *abnormal* standards of sentence structure might be, but neither does she challenge Rose's claim that the "ordinary reader" requires all of the characteristics of Joyce's prose she lists to be changed in order to understand the text. Lyall simply accepts that *Ulysses* is removed from the grasp of the common reader by its difficulty, thereby reinforcing that assumption for her audience.

Yet another dig at the "scholars and fanatics" occurs when Lyall quotes Jon Riley of Picador (the London publisher of Rose's edition):

> "Mr. Rose is highly respected in the Joyce world, but it's the most fractious and controversy-laden group of practically any area of literary study," Mr. Riley said. (Indeed, it is a world whose inhabitants are consumed with things like the issue of whether Joyce ever used a semicolon after 1919.)

The implication that such a debate is petty serves to underscore the dichotomy between the academic and non-academic worlds. Lyall implies that scholarly Joyceans are unconcerned with the kind of reading activity that the common reader values, which presumably does not encompass wondering about Joyce's use of the semi-colon.

Lyall further puts scholarly editors at cross-purposes with the common reader, by focusing on the editorial controversy over Rose's edition rather than whether or not Rose's changes do, in fact, make the book easier to read. Lyall quotes Lawrence Rainey's review in *The London Review of Books:*[8]

> Danis Rose decrees, by fiat, the reign of an editorial theory which violates every principle and procedure of critical editing, replacing it with nothing more than "making sense" as construed, tautologically, by Danis Rose . . . His edition, if it can be called that, is a chastening example of how an excess of piety can imperceptibly turn into self-aggrandizing fantasy.

Such vitriol is worthy of John Kidd's at the height of the first Joyce War. Kidd's own response in the article calls Rose's procedures "mutilation" and "way out of the bounds of serious editing," but Lyall undermines Kidd's position by immediately identifying him as a scholar who "has made something of a career out of attacking new versions of *Ulysses*" and pointing out that

Kidd "is at work on his own version"—all of which may be true, but the implication here is that market concerns are actually at the heart of scholars' discontent with Rose's edition rather than any real disagreement over the best way to edit Joyce's text. Lyall thereby reinforces the impression that scholars are too embroiled in careerism and pedantry to pay any attention to the needs of the common reader.

Rose defends his work, saying that "Joyce wanted precision, not obfuscation," and that "Joyce wanted a person, on the closest possible reading of *Ulysses*, not to be tripped up. He wanted them to be able to take a microscope to his text and see definition" (Lyall). Rose again appeals to authorial intention while claiming in the edition's "Introduction" that such a notion is outdated (xiv-xi). In the popular press, however, he does not refer to his ideas on final authorial intention as being a "sham" and so reveals that, whatever his own editorial thinking on the nature of textual authority, he comprehends that the public still understands texts as stable entities that express the author's wishes. Further contradictory ideas abound in his rhetoric; for example, taking a microscope to the text does not sound like the kind of simplified reading that Rose repeatedly says is his goal. Throughout his explanations in various articles runs the same inconsistency between what he says he is aiming for and what he sees as the process of reading *Ulysses* as Joyce intended it to be read. Moreover, Rose's (and the publisher's) claims both to have altered the text for easier reading and to have restored it—with the implication of returning to a previous state, unsullied by academic or theoretical interference—are contradictory as well. One cannot radically alter Joyce's original punctuation and chapter structure and still claim to achieve the "scrupulous restoration of a masterpiece," as Antony Farrell of Lilliput Press (Dublin publishers of the edition) claims in a letter to the *Irish Times* (2 July 1997). Farrell defends the *Reader's Edition* by inviting a reader "wishing to judge the quality of [Rose's] achievement . . . to read the new edition and to compare it with any of the other versions readily available." But Rose, in an interview published in the *Irish Times'* special 1997 Bloomsday edition, states flatly that "Readers do not collate" (Battersby). True enough, so his decision to print the two versions of "Penelope" becomes even murkier. Rose does not give a solid reason for including both; in the preface he states that "[i]n practice, readers of *Ulysses* are compelled mentally to resupply the apostrophes, so that nothing really has been gained by their removal and a great deal—the undisturbed flow of the text—has been lost. *For this reason* the Reader's Edition includes two versions of 'Penelope'" (xxv; my emphasis). Rose's justification for including both versions of "Penelope" seems to rely on reading practices, but those practices actually do nothing to explain his rationale for including both. If, like Cain's example of Frost, Joyce's artistic accomplishment is emphasized through comparison of both versions, then Rose should explain this reason to readers in the Introduction. If his aim is, as he states, to gain "the undisturbed flow of the text," there seems little point in printing the second version; such a move would appear to undermine his whole argument for emending "Penelope" in the first place: it's as though he were telling the reader "Here's mine, and now here's the way it's *supposed* to be." Again, the effect is to emphasize that there is some ur-*Ulysses* that the common reader cannot understand rather than establishing textual multiplicity, which seems to be part of Rose's editorial and theoretical aim.

## THE "RAPE OF *ULYSSES*"

The Joyce estate was not silent in the second Joyce War; Stephen Joyce, as he did in the first Joyce War, wrote to the *Times Literary Supplement* to express his displeasure. In the first Joyce War, he called the scholarly quarreling a "tempest in a teapot," and urged people just to read *Ulysses* and ignore the controversy which he said was "essentially of interest to a hundred-odd Joyce scholars" (9–15 Sept. 1988: 989). This time, however, Joyce was incensed at Rose's "outrageous misrepresentation of *Ulysses*" (27 June 1997: 17); presumably his ire this time was because Rose's edition was specifically marketed for an audience of non-scholars, and indicates that, for Stephen Joyce, at least, scholarly concerns are irrelevant to the reading of *Ulysses*. In his letter, Stephen Joyce calls the addition of punctuation to "Penelope" a "major example of the many distortions"; he describes the episode as a "revolutionary continuous stream of consciousness first used by Edouard Dujardin" that has been "destroyed by the addition of well over 750 apostrophes, dozens of hyphens/*tirets* and italicized words and phrases." Again, *Ulysses* is defined for the public through Molly's soliloquy; none of the other episodes is discussed in the letter. Stephen Joyce's inflammatory rhetoric reaches its zenith when he calls for his grandfather's name to be "stricken from the dust jacket" and title page of the edition, and when he states that "What the estate and literary world are faced with today is not another 'Scandal of *Ulysses*'; but is this not 'The Rape of *Ulysses*'?!" (17). His emphatic punctuation makes it abundantly clear that he is outraged at what he perceives to be a violation of his grandfather's masterpiece.

Rose's reply (*TLS* 11 July 1997: 17) dismisses Stephen Joyce as part of the academy Rose claims to be against in his edition. Saying that Stephen Joyce and "a coterie of academics" seek to restrict the text to what they "understand James Joyce's *Ulysses* to be," Rose defends his editorial decisions with an appeal to the dichotomy between the academic and the common reader. After a brief explanation of the idea of textual indeterminacy, he justifies the restoration of apostrophes in "Penelope" by parenthetically stating that Vladimir Nabokov recommended doing so, an attempt at legitimizing his editorial decisions through invoking the reputation of another respected writer. It is a curious strategy, however, as Rose gives no explanation for Nabokov's judgment. Conceivably, a more effective retort to

Stephen Joyce's letter would have been to rely on James Joyce's own pro-
nouncements on the issue, but since Rose's rationale for including the apostrophes, in fact, does not rely on any documented reference from Joyce, he
cannot do so. His reason, as presented in his letter, seems capricious and
serves to reinforce the accusations made against the *Reader's Edition*.

Rose responds to the charge of having raped *Ulysses* by calling such an
accusation "the most intemperate, personally offensive and disproportion-
ately vituperative reactions that have been heard in literary circles for a
decade," an obvious reference to the first Joyce War. The polemical nature
of such an accusation thus moves the debate away from the actual editorial
enterprise and again into the realm of personality. The real issue behind
Rose's edition, which is that it exposes the notion of textual instability, is
left behind in the name of saving *Ulysses* from its attackers. Furthermore,
using the term "rape" feminizes the work—and thus *Ulysses* needs to be
protected, presumably by the very scholars and interested parties who as-
sail Rose's project. This curious metaphor points to a subtext of ownership
felt by the Joyce establishment towards *Ulysses*, expressed in the need to
protect it from being ravished by blackguard editors.[9]

Rose ends his reply with a curious contradiction. He suggests that readers can always turn to the other editions of *Ulysses* that retain the "errors
and incoherencies, and the typographical peculiarities" of Joyce's text.
Then, he writes,

> For those whose lives are shorter and want simply to enjoy *Ulysses*, to
> read the novel as Joyce meant it to be read, as a single coherent whole,
> there is the *Reader's Edition*. It is Stephen Joyce and his allies frozen in
> academia, not I, who are seeking domination over the text. And, his dis-
> claimer aside, Mr Joyce is seeking here, as often before, to suppress schol-
> arship. (17)

Rose here repeats his claim that *Ulysses* can be read more quickly in his
edition because of his "smoothing" of the text. He aligns Stephen Joyce
with academics (and by implication, himself with the common reader), but
then says that Stephen Joyce seeks to suppress scholarship, a strangely contradictory position. Stephen Joyce has in the past blocked scholars from
gaining information, most notably his claim to have burned Lucia Joyce's
letters to prevent biographers from seeing them, as well as his successful efforts to suppress the final chapter on Lucia in Brenda Maddox's biography
of Nora Joyce. But Rose's move here to censure Stephen Joyce's suppression of scholarship also suggests that Rose's own scholarship, as represented by the *Reader's Edition*, is what Joyce is seeking to suppress—an
implication that places Rose within the ivory tower, as well.

This exchange between Rose and Stephen Joyce receives bemused comment in Eric Korn's review in the September 5, 1997 *Times Literary Supplement* (3–4). Korn is listed as an antiquarian bookseller in London by the
*TLS*, and his review places him as a seasoned reader of Joyce but outside of

academia. Korn describes Rose's alteration to "Penelope" as "wantonly toss[ing] handfuls of assorted periods into the final episode of *Ulysses*, like road-grit on the Cresta Run, like intrusive bits of eggshell in that sweetly indecent, frothy confection of everreturn: the Molly Bloomerang" (3). Korn humorously paraphrases Stephen Joyce's polemic: Joyce's grandson has "sworn by the nine gods of Ithaca, where Ulysses enjoys his sempiternal estate, to erase James Joyce's name from the dust-jacket and title-page of this volume, using language meeter for discussing the abuse of an underage nun. The satanic abuse of a handicapped under-aged nun of good family. He speaks indeed of the rape of *Ulysses*" (3). The exaggeration makes its point: Stephen Joyce has gone too far. But Rose doesn't get off easily, either. Korn says that Rose has "lightly dusted" Molly's soliloquy with punctuation so that the reader can "no longer read *I'll* and *we'd* and *she'll* as referring to malaise and marriage and malacology (Did we ever?)" (3). Rose's apostrophes, he intimates, are unnecessary and condescending. Korn has a little more fun with the inflammatory rape metaphor: "[Rose] offers—as rapists will—the defences of justification, provocation and tacit permission. She did it before, in manuscript; she was gagging for it, your worship, going about in that dishevelled prose, with not a comma on; even James Joyce said she'd be all the better for a spot of correction" (3).

The rape metaphor is worth exploring, if only because it conflates the editing of a book for the reader's pleasure with an image of violation, implying that the author's words are somehow pure, virginal, and chaste before the editor has his way with them—and that the author, represented by those words, is unwilling to submit to the wishes of the reader. Such an image removes the writing from the reader, eliding all intimations of openness to interpretation—Joyce's words are stable (read: pure), but need the constant vigilance of the scholarly establishment to keep them that way. The anxiety evidenced here over the actual instability of Joyce's text shows how deeply the first Joyce War affected many Joyceans, and how metaphorically losing bibliographical innocence leads to anxiety over controlling Joyce's loose and always slippery text. Korn's lampoon of the rape metaphor further relies on the old cultural assumption that a rape victim "asked for it" by reason of having demonstrably loose morals—a reference, no doubt, to the book's reputation for obscenity, and in particular, Molly's obscenity. But suddenly, in Korn's essay Molly's monologue is a "handicapped under-age nun of good family"—a complete repression of the pornography connection that unconsciously returns via the comical extrapolation of the rape metaphor. *Ulysses* has become the womanly text, with all of the attendant anxiety evinced in a patriarchal society over her chastity.

Korn shows skepticism not only for Rose's premise of maximizing the "pleasure of the reader" but also for the premise of textual indeterminacy which gives Rose license to do so:

> [Rose] sets this deplorably hedonic credo in a Heisenbergian context . . .
> the notion is that the Uncertainty Principle has abolished classical mechan-
> ics, and thereby abolishes authorial authority. This interpretation danger-
> ously fudges the boundary between the microcosm and the macrocosm.
> You would not buy a ticket for an airline that told you that there is no such
> thing as a correct destination. ("Thank you for flying Air Schrödinger. We
> will shortly be landing at either Narita or Dulles International.") (3)

Korn displays the common reader's skepticism of current literary and bibliographical theory, and distrust of the idea of textual instability. Korn further removes himself (and, by extension, his audience) from the world of
academics; after two columns of examining various textual changes Rose
made and finding them either unnecessary or unsupportable, he ridicules
such quibbling: "This is all stamp-collecting, except to the professionals, so
many horse-manure collectors" (4). Clearly, Korn finds the Rose edition a
curiosity full of unneeded changes that do nothing to alter the way anyone
actually reads *Ulysses*. Korn is presumably part of the audience Rose attempts to reach, albeit not a first-time reader of Joyce (evidenced by Korn's
clever last column, written in the catechismal style of "Ithaca"), but he
finds the edition's changes lacking any real impact on the text. It is for this
reason more than any other that Stephen Joyce's virulent accusation of the
"rape" of *Ulysses* deserves such ridicule in Korn's column; but it also raises
questions of just what kind of reader Rose is constructing and for whom
the edition was undertaken in the first place.

    Approaching the text specifically as the reader Rose claims to serve,
David Wheatley reviews Rose's edition in *Books Ireland* ("Shamiana,"
May 1998: 130–131). Wheatley questions Rose's motives in calling his version of *Ulysses* a *Reader's Edition*: "What was the target audience of all
those previous editions—illiterates? . . . [Rose] believes [he] has finally
smuggled the novel out of 'the ivory tower of the academics' for popular
consumption. This is a cheap shot: the phrase 'people's *Ulysses*' is about as
meaningful as the phrase 'people's Princess'" (130). Wheatley writes,
"[L]et's get real: does this edition work or not? As a reader himself, rather
than a rascally academic, this reviewer is presumably among those whom
Rose hopes to woo. But to the question is this my *Ulysses*, the answer is a
resounding no" (130). Wheatley's claims that he is not a "rascally academic," however, are suspect; he has been published in scholarly journals[10]
and completed a doctoral dissertation on Beckett's poetry at Trinity College, Dublin. But his review here explicitly places his opinion within the
world of the common reader, and he writes with an eye toward the audience that Rose is courting. Wheatley explores several of Rose's emendations of textual faults, as Rose defines them; his objections are based on
Rose's "grant[ing] himself a license to revise and rewrite Joyce that is little
short of breathtaking" (*ibid.*). One of his examples is worth quoting in full,
if only because it discusses Rose's emendations in terms of how readers will
view them:

Does anyone apart from Rose really believe that replacing 'snotgreen' with 'snot-green' is an improvement? Readers who, like this reviewer, first picked up *Ulysses* in their callow teens may remember the shock of that 'snotgreen.' It was strange, it was shocking; here was a word you couldn't put in your school essay. But offputting? On the contrary. It was confirmation in a single adjective that Joyce wasn't like other writers. He was an adventure; he had his own language. Why does Danis Rose want him to punctuate like everyone else? (*ibid.*)

Wheatley's placement of Joyce as a writer with "his own language" works within the trope of inaccessibility, albeit as an initiatory rite of passage rather than a barrier to understanding. The shock of finding words inadmissible to a school essay plays with the value of *Ulysses* as an obscene work, by making it a mark of rebellion against the conformity of the educational system. But curiously, Wheatley does not question Rose's construction of the reader any further; he positions Rose as offering another definitive text of *Ulysses*, a completely wrong one: he says of the edition that it "is a welcome attempt to remedy what is a scandalous state of affairs" (131), presumably meaning the strife-ridden publishing history of the book, and a subtle reminder of the "scandal" of the first Joyce War. He finds the results "profoundly unsatisfactory": "In his introduction Rose compares the task of establishing a manuscript 'stemma' to drawing up a road map. But Rose has done more than draw up a map: where he didn't like the landscape, he has altered it to what he thinks it *ought* to look like. Just imagine the consequences if all mapmakers followed his example" (*ibid.*; original italics). The idea of textual instability, and the license that Rose believes that notion gives him to offer a variant edition of *Ulysses*, never enters Wheatley's review, and his evaluation operates under the mistaken assumption that Rose is attempting to offer a definitive text.

## WAR OF THE ROSE

The marketing and press coverage of the *Reader's Edition* served to extend the confusion exhibited by Wheatley and the other writers in the popular press that the notion of definitive texts still existed in academic circles. And the polemics surrounding Rose's move to reveal the dichotomy between the academic and the public Joyce inevitably—and, no doubt, purposely—ignited controversy and boosted interest in the edition. In the first Joyce Wars, the reader was an invisible presence, sometimes given a perfunctory nod as the one for whom all of this squabbling was taking place, but for the most part relegated to keeping the home fires burning while the boys went off to fight for truth, justice, and the Joycean "twey." The controversy over the Rose edition, however, purposely places the common reader squarely in the battlefield as a combatant for ownership of Joyce, and the academic objections have primarily been found in scholarly journals.

But of course, John Kidd had his say. In the *New York Review of Books*, Kidd once more fired his first shot with his review, "Making the Wrong Joyce" (September 25, 1997: 54–56). This article appeared with the same artwork that accompanied Kidd's article "The Scandal of *Ulysses*" in 1988, no doubt a deliberate move by the editors of the *New York Review of Books* to recall the earlier controversy. The review of Rose's edition seems mild compared to the heat of "Scandal," but Kidd manages (in fewer words) to convey his scorn for the *Reader's Edition*. Within the space of two paragraphs, he denigrates Rose for being an entrepreneur rather than an academic, and rehashes his feud with Gabler—a move he repeats six times in seven columns of text. But Kidd's biggest problem with Rose seems to be that Rose has deliberately and polemically drawn attention to an academic ownership of *Ulysses*, and found the academics wanting. Kidd not-so-subtly places Rose squarely back inside the ivory tower. After delineating all the ways in which Gabler, Rose, and Groden were linked through collaborating on projects and reviewing or introducing each other's work, Kidd writes, "David Lodge's novel skewering academic in-breeding bears a telling title: the Joyce industry is truly a Small World, with Messrs. Rose & Gabler snugly lodged within it" (56). Kidd's flash here of Joycean punning ("lodged") hearkens back to his earlier forays in the *New York Review of Books* during the first Joyce Wars.

But the overall tone of Kidd's 1997 article remains subdued compared to his earlier stinging rhetoric. No one is asleep at the wheel this time around. Kidd does question several of Rose's "corrections" to Joyce's math and science in the "Ithaca" episode, including Rose's change of Joyce's "Sundam Trench" to "Marianne Trench," which is nowhere near the Sunda Trench Bloom was thinking of: "Mr. Rose's trench is seven thousand miles to the northeast, indeed in another hemisphere" (55). Discussing Rose's changes—or lack of them—to incorrect place names allows Kidd another opportunity to swing at Gabler and Rose at once:

> Identifying erroneous place names has been a stated goal of all Joyce editors in recent years, but none seems patient enough to fact-check *Ulysses* line by line. Changing "Landsdowne" to "Lansdowne" is easy for Rose and Gabler. But to notice what is askew about the village called "Arbraccan" in Gabler (14.221) and Rose (371.08) requires the academic toil that Professor Gabler neglects and Mr. Rose maligns. (55)

"Arbraccan" is actually spelled "Ardbraccan"—a mistake that Rose, being a native Irishman, perhaps ought to have caught. This example is reminiscent of the kind of mistakes that Kidd found in the Gabler edition, and the implication here is, of course, that only Kidd is "patient enough" to check *Ulysses* "line by line." Further, Kidd concisely condemns Gabler's scholarship by pointedly naming him a professor who neglects academic toil, and simultaneously attacks Rose for maligning such toil while relying upon it (a point he repeats in a letter answering Rose's response to his article).

The final section of Kidd's article is, like "Scandal," devoted to insinuations of conspiracy at the *James Joyce Quarterly*, repeating accusations that he implied ten years earlier. But he frames this conspiracy in fascinating terms: "odd practices at the *James Joyce Quarterly* exacerbate the threat to *Ulysses*" (56). The unmistakable connotation that *Ulysses* is a monument vulnerable to the machinations of unethical scholars again raises the specter of Stephen Joyce's rape metaphor, and also points to the sacred nature of the text. The purity of Joyce's masterpiece is threatened in Kidd's view, however, not by blackguard editors but by the Joyce Industry, as represented by Gabler, Rose, Groden and the editors of the *Quarterly*. Kidd subtly implies that he is not part of that Industry—a curious position, considering that at the time he headed the James Joyce Research Center at Boston University. Kidd is as much a part of that Industry as any of the other names he mentions.

Conspiracy theories aside, Kidd's article does not reach the feverish pitch of "Scandal" simply because there is no extended, point-by-point argument against Rose's emendations. The particular criticisms Kidd makes are rather arranged as part of a broader argument that Rose's version is merely another Gabler edition, with some additional typographical and punctuation changes. Kidd ends with another subtle plug for his own version: "In the text he wrote for the Picador marketeers, Mr. Rose claimed that 'The *Reader's Edition* liberates the text from the prison of its early publishing history.' On the first page of *Ulysses*, Buck Mulligan has the answer to his historic breakout of error: 'Back to barracks!'" (56). (It is perhaps ironic that both Kidd and Gabler are in agreement about the need to "unemend" *Ulysses*). The implication of Kidd's statement is, of course, that *Ulysses* still awaits a proper editing, and it was well known by that time in the Joyce world that Kidd has his own edition awaiting publication. Making sure that those outside the Joyce world know it, too, Rose points it out in the first words of his reply to Kidd's article by identifying Kidd as the "editor of a forthcoming rival edition" (*New York Review of Books* 15 Jan. 1998: 60). This reply is followed by a response from Kidd, and the two of them engage in semantic and pedantic debate similar to the first Joyce War. But what is more interesting is Rose's continued disparaging of the academy. In two paragraphs which bear viewing in full, Rose reveals what he suggests is the dirty secret of the Joyce Establishment:

> Choices must invariably be made in any serious edition. But there is a strong element of intolerance in the Joyce world. Any intimation that the master may have been less than perfect, may not have been fully in control of his texts, may not have been a very good book designer, or that some of the typographical effects in the first edition have become dated and need revision is instantly repudiated. Even when Joyce's fallibility is acknowledged, that very fallibility is itself immediately declared to be an essential ingredient in the work. This makes editing Joyce especially hazardous.

> Before I began work I spoke to a great many people about *Ulysses*. Al-
> most without exception they had given up *reading* the book after a few
> episodes. This is the unpalatable truth at the heart of Joyce studies. The
> greatest novel of the twentieth century has become a textbook to be im-
> posed on unwilling students and/or a pretext for their teachers to wax
> lyrical on psychology, sociology, gender studies—on anything at all. (60;
> original italics)

Rose points to the sacralizing impulse behind the academic Joyce with
his account of "Joycean infallibility." He also positions the public Joyce as
antagonistic to the aims of an academy that uses Joyce as a "pretext" to
impose on "unwilling students" its theoretical fad-of-the-month (as he
paints it). His exposure of the "unpalatable truth at the heart of Joyce
studies"—that people outside the academy don't read the book, or at least
don't finish it—underscores the divergence between the public and academic Joyces. The trope of the book's difficulty has allowed the academic
world to lay a large claim of ownership on Joyce's text, simply because the
reading public appears to have given up on it. Rose positions himself as the
liberator of the text by removing what he calls "obstacles," but these obstacles as he has defined them—punctuation, spelling, compound words—
are chimeras. In the "Eumaeus" example from his "Introduction," he has
shown how his emendations do smooth out unintelligible passages, and
this is certainly helpful to the reader. But most of his changes are cosmetic
and arguably unnecessary, and he does not in truth free the text from its
difficulty for readers nor does he succeed in freeing *Ulysses* from the ivory
tower. He has, in fact, reinforced a conception that *Ulysses* is inaccessible
in its "original" form and that the common reader *needs* the intervention
of a specially trained scholar to make sense of Joyce's text.

The trope of difficulty surrounding *Ulysses*—as well as the perceived
alienation between the academic and the common reader—is clearly exhibited in an article that appeared in *Newsweek* (23 June 1997: 8). Entitled
"The Bloomsday Massacre," the article is placed in the center of the page
under a large photograph of Joyce, and the caption reads, "Turning over in
his grave? James Joyce in an undated photo." The full text of the article
follows:

> In *Ulysses*, James Joyce wrote "A man of genius makes no mistakes. His
> errors are volitional and are the portals of discovery." One editor seems to
> have taken these words as a personal challenge. Danis Rose's new *Ulysses*:
> *A Reader's Edition* (Macmillan UK) comes complete with 8,000 to 10,000
> changes—based not on some long-lost manuscript but on Rose's personal
> copy-editing. Words like "nightblue" and "dressinggown" are broken up,
> idiosyncratic spellings such as "woful" corrected. Most noticeably, Molly
> Bloom's unpunctuated chapter is now replete with apostrophes, hyphens,
> and italics. "A person can read this in two weeks instead of a year," says
> Rose. "Let's say that I have removed from various rooms in Joyce's man-
> sion cobwebs from the past." Boston University's John Kidd, one of

Rose's biggest critics, is aghast. "What's next, the Reader's Digest Condensed *Finnegans Wake*?" (8)

Beginning with the word "Massacre" in the title, the article makes plain its position on Rose's project. The very first sentence perpetuates the mistaken notion (but one often held) that Joyce's works are completely autobiographical, by presenting Stephen's words in the library chapter as Joyce's words about his own work. While it is open to debate whether Stephen's words echo Joyce's own feelings here, the article simply presents the quote as Joyce's pronouncement, one which Rose took "as a personal challenge." Implicit in the article is an appeal to the inviolability of the text and to authorial intention. The public Joyce is also reinforced here by the reference to Molly's soliloquy. The sentence begins "Most noticeably," emphasizing it over the rest of the book, and Joyce's reputation as obscene is subtly invoked by this emphasis. Rose's statement about removing "cobwebs from the past" also reinforces the trope of inaccessibility, and positions his edition as accessible to the common reader. Kidd's horrified reply also reinforces a notion of the academic as scornful of the general public and its abilities to comprehend "real" literature. There is, in fact, a condensed version of *Finnegans Wake* edited by Anthony Burgess, a respected Joycean and author in his own right. But the reference to *Reader's Digest* emphasizes the scholarly belittlement of that periodical, seen as notoriously middlebrow and beneath academic attention. The implication, of course, is that a *Reader's Digest* version of Joyce's last novel would be the final sign of the apocalypse in literary academic circles.

Popular press articles like the *Newsweek* account imply that Joyce has been completely rewritten by Rose. But, as with most things hyped by the press, it is *caveat emptor* with Rose's edition as well. The changes made to Joyce's text are radical to the scholarly eye, particularly in light of his theoretical base. But, alas, for the reader led to expect that somehow Joyce's text would be rendered into a more standardized format and therefore easier to read, the editorial changes appear superficial, indeed. Whether these alterations make any real change to the actual process of reading the novel is doubtful. The *Reader's Edition*, then, poses as a non-academic interpreter of Joyce's text. In so doing, it reifies academic ownership of *Ulysses*. But even if the reader accepts such a designation at face value, the implication remains that another, not-edited-for-readers edition—the "true" edition—exists, one that is inaccessible to the common reader. As a result, the *Reader's Edition* does nothing to free *Ulysses* from the ivory tower, *pace* Rose.

But is *Ulysses* really trapped in academia? The public Joyce would seem to indicate not. *Ulysses*' status as *differend*, discussed in Chapter Two, shows that it exists on the border between the academic and non-academic world. The recent jump in sales of the book, the result of publicity surrounding the Modern Library's "100 Best Novels" list, attests to its continuing interest for the common reader. Joyce's reputation, begun in infamy outside the academy, has become a self-sustaining entity. His academic reputation grew out of the initial scandal, in part through the trial's transformation of *Ulysses* from obscenity to work of art, and currently serves as a foundation for the public reputation. The curious reality, though, is that neither the public iconography nor the academic seems to acknowledge their mutually dependent existence, and this state is symptomatic of the nature of the *differend*, where speaking one discursive practice silences the other. The two behave at cross-purposes, and the first Joyce War exposed this divergence by painting Joycean scholars in the public mind as being concerned with professional reputations and theoretical concerns rather than real matters of reading. The second Joyce War has reinforced such a picture. While Rose acknowledged the gap in agendas by positing a need for a "reader's edition," the marketing hype and the subsequent arguments simply gloss over the reality that his *Reader's Edition* does not actually appear to be aimed at the common reader. The academics are still quarreling with each other in Joyce's name—but not the reader's. In fact, Rose's particular position appears merely condescending, as though the reader could not access *Ulysses* without scholarly intervention and interpretation. Such an attitude erects further barriers between the common reader and the academic.

## Notes

[1] Further limiting reaction to the Rose edition was (and is) its continued unavailability in the United States.

[2] Fritz Senn shared his impressions of the session on the Rose edition via electronic correspondence. He expressed disappointment that many people had formed judgments against the edition before having read it (29 Aug. 1998). Presumably, these judgments were based on the way the press had presented the edition to the public.

[3] It should be noted, however, that modernizing Shakespeare has become as controversial in editing circles as the Joyce Wars have been. See "The Materiality of the Shakespearean Text" by Margreta de Grazia and Peter Stallybrass (*Shakespeare Quarterly*, 44.3: 255–283) and "Levelling Shakespeare: Local Customs and Local Texts" (*Shakespeare Quarterly*, 42.2: 168–178) for the arguments in favor of multiple texts.

[4] Rose uses the term "pleasure" without examining it, a move that, since Barthes, seems questionable. Presumably, Rose assumes that the common reader does not have the same kind of critical unease with using the "pleasure of the text" as an unproblematic term.

[5] See Chapter Three for a full explanation of Bowers' interpretation of Greg's rationale.

[6] Of course, it cannot be overemphasized that the continuing popularity of Jane Austen's novels are perhaps more than somewhat due to the film industry's recent attention to works like *Emma* and *Sense and Sensibility*. This phenomenon has been given much critical attention; see the collection *Jane Austen in Hollywood*, ed.

Linda Troost (Lexington, KY: UP of Kentucky, 1998), and Claudia L. Johnson's "Austen Cults and Cultures," in *The Cambridge Companion to Jane Austen*, ed. Edward Copeland (Cambridge, England: Cambridge UP, 1997: 211–26).

[7]Joseph Kelly defends Rose's edition on the grounds that it was indeed the exposure of Joyce's muddled intentions which caused most of the scholarly uproar surrounding the edition. While I fundamentally agree with much of Kelly's analysis, I take issue with some of his points (see Conclusion).

[8]First printed June 19, 1997; reprinted in the *James Joyce Quarterly*, Summer 1998: 588–596. The quoted material in the *New York Times* article joins two phrases that are separated in Rainey's review by several paragraphs.

[9]Joseph Kelly makes a parallel argument in "A Defense of Danis Rose," printed in the *James Joyce Quarterly* in the special Summer/Fall 1998 double issue (pp. 813–814), which came to my attention only after this chapter was written.

[10]"Beckett's *mirlitonnades*: A Manuscript Study," *The Journal of Beckett Studies* 4.2 (Spring 1995): 47–76.

# CONCLUSION

*In making the "true" Ulysses inaccessible to the ordinary reader, do we engage in disinterested scholarship or the political act of exclusion?*
—*Patrick McGee*

The Gabler edition, as Patrick McGee points out,[1] "gives physical definition to an ideal text" and places the authority for that text in the synoptic edition rather than the reading edition (29–30). He writes, "In principle, the synoptic edition contains all possible readings; it contains everything that Joyce supposedly wrote with finality" (31). As such, all other editions, including the trade edition derived from the synoptic text, can compete in the marketplace but ultimately derive their authority (and therefore their intrinsic value) from the synoptic text, which then becomes a transcendent text over all public editions (31–32). McGee's analysis hinges on what the implications of this situation would mean for the teaching of *Ulysses*, but does not address the implications for the general reader. The "exclusion" he discusses occurs specifically for students; he ignores the effects of marketing as "definitive" a trade edition that is divorced from, and an imperfect copy of, the synoptic text for *Ulysses*. He does ask whether "the strategies by which we construct a class of readers for Joyce's work also reinforce a social hierarchy that has its cultural as well as its economic determinants," but he pursues his discussion of *Ulysses*'s value in terms of its use inside the academy. For McGee, the Gabler edition posits authority in a text excluded from use in the classroom by virtue of the institutional constraints within the university—the synoptic edition, which holds a Platonic "true" *Ulysses*, is inaccessible due to size, cost, and the need to learn a new language to understand the diacritical symbols, which is not a feasible option in a semester-long course. The existence of *Ulysses* as a public commodity as well as an academic one hardly enters his discussion; as such, his essay naturalizes the ownership of *Ulysses* by the academy.

In an essay entitled, "Danis Rose and the Common Reader," Michael Patrick Gillespie would appear to be addressing the way that the Rose edition constructs its audience, but like McGee ten years earlier he also avoids defining *Ulysses*'s relationship with the common reader. Gillespie writes that "to offer fair assessments of Rose's efforts . . . we must be willing to judge the book on its own terms" (584). If that is the case, then it seems reasonable to expect him to assess how a first-time, non-academic Joycean (the intended market for the edition) would read Rose's text compared to an earlier ("non-reader's"?) edition. In fact, Gillespie's essay blatantly conflates "the reader" with the "seasoned Joycean": he writes, "the initial reaction that most of *us* seem to have had to the pronounced changes introduced into the work by Rose has been to ask how does this affect my reading, or, perhaps more properly, how can I *still maintain my reading* in spite of these changes" (586; emphasis added)? Further, he states that, "Like any reader of *Ulysses*, I have a history with the text" and that some of his uneasiness with Rose's changes may stem from "a paternal regard for the sanctity of meanings I have already worked out" (587). Gillespie's construction of the reader here explicitly does not address Rose's edition "on its own terms"; namely, he writes of Rose's edition as a Joycean scholar and addresses the critical reactions of other Joyceans, whereas Rose claims to be aiming the edition at the new Joyce reader. Gillespie states that without viewing Rose's textual apparatus "[n]one of us will be able to do more than make . . . subjective, idiosyncratic response" to Rose's alterations: "[Rose] has told me that he does not believe it would be financially feasible to bring out a copy of his isotext, and that very well may be the case. I do, however, feel that he must publish an essay of whatever length necessary to make readers more aware of the details of the complex editorial methodology that he brought to bear upon his version of *Ulysses*" (587). Gillespie uses the word "readers" here in an unexamined way; if the audience for Rose's edition is "the common reader," then would that audience be likely to buy a specialized editorial apparatus to go with Rose's edition? Again, only the academic reader is considered within this critique of *Ulysses*.

The institutional forces at work behind the growth of the Joyce industry cannot be overestimated: the requirements of seeking a terminal degree, tenure, and prestige within the field do much to continue the industry's existence. This is not to say that the people working in Joyce studies are cynically engaging in empty theorizing simply in order to publish. But to ignore those institutional forces as elements in the construction of the academic Joyce only strengthens the ideology of the sacred within the field; and the sheer number of theses, dissertations, articles, books, lectures, and conferences devoted to Joyce's work[2] leads to statements like the one found at Jorn Barger's web site: "Joyce is **much** deeper, in **every** work, than anyone can claim to have thoroughly plumbed. And he was **intentionally** laying traps for the unwary reader—every great Joycean has surely been

publicly caught" (12 Sept. 1998; boldface in original). This pronouncement sounds very much like "the secularized and infinitely absent" God-
who-is-not described by Umberto Eco: "He hides himself, is ineffable, . . .
is the sum of what cannot be said of him; in speaking of him we celebrate
our ignorance" (93). Further, the traps intentionally laid for the unwary
reader speak to this absent God's characteristic of being a "Void in whose
regard our aspirations are doomed to defeat" (*ibid.*). Eco was discussing
the nature of the sacred in a secular society; its expression within academic
discourse is replicated in Joyce studies. It is surely no accident that the very
words we use to describe the importance placed upon certain authors are
derived from theology: saying an author or a work is "canonized" immediately positions that author/work as a saint, suprahuman and holder of
miraculous powers.

It is this impulse towards sacralizing authors which Joseph Kelly finds
to be the real reason why there has been so much scholarly gnashing of
teeth over the Rose edition. Kelly defends Rose's project by showing that
Joyce scholars are "programmed" by a paradigm of genius that positions
Joyce as being "in control of every detail in *Ulysses*," and this program-
ming leads to a "syllogistic chain" of reasoning:

- we can find meaning in every bit of minutiae in *Ulysses*;
- where there is meaning, there must be intention;
- therefore, Joyce intended something by all the minutiae in *Ulysses*. (813)

This paradigm, perhaps, can account for Barger's statement about the un-
fathomable depth of Joyce's "**every** work." Kelly, too, finds in the rhetoric
of Stephen Joyce's rape metaphor the subtext that it "betray[s] a fear of un-
supervised reading," and he blames the traditional Greg/Bowers editorial
school and its reliance on the author's intentions for allowing Joyce scholars to perpetuate the notion that unprotected texts will lead to dire consequences. Kelly restricts his critique, for the most part, to scholarly
reactions against Rose's edition and hearkens back to Rose's own statements that "any intimation that the master may have been less than perfect
. . . is instantly repudiated" by the Joyce establishment (see Chapter Six).
Kelly goes on to state that "Rose [is] so threatening [to Joyce scholars because he] suspects Joyce intended a lot less than critics give him credit for"
(818), and leaves the kind of formalist criticism of the last several decades
suspect. The myth of genius, Kelly writes, has restricted Joyce to academia
rather than allowing his work to enter cultural discourse at the larger level
of modern myth:

> This mythic stature, unconsciously and collectively bestowed by a culture,
> is far greater than the puny "genius" we have given Joyce. And it gives a
> writer a more profound influence than academic ballyhooing ever can,
> even if people rarely read his work. . . .
>   There are plenty of allusions in popular culture to James Joyce. Why are
> there no allusions to Stephen and Leopold and Molly? Why hasn't *Ulysses*

inspired a sitcom or at least a miniseries? Why don't college kids call certain rakes "boylans"? We are to blame, who have slain the Roses. (822)

Kelly doesn't champion Rose's edition itself, but rather the impulse behind it to free *Ulysses* from the Ivory Tower. But as I have argued in Chapter Two, *Ulysses* does have a life outside the Tower, and while Stephen and Leopold and Molly are not mythical figures in the way Kelly seems to want, it isn't clear that scholars' "slaying" of "the Roses" is to blame. The common comparison of Joyce to Shakespeare may be useful here. Shakespeare's works were conceived for and dispersed within a public arena; and even though Shakespeare's plays seem inaccessible in written form, when they are performed on stage and film they appeal to the same elements of audience expectation that popular films do: there is action, comedy, drama, even melodrama. Seeing the actions helps interpret the words, which are admittedly difficult to read for today's audiences so far removed from Elizabethan language. The plays find their way into modern films both overtly and covertly, and continue to be performed in free venues like "Shakespeare in the Park"-style productions. Shakespeare was never wholly the property of academia. The same cannot be said for Modernist writers, many of whom deliberately alienated the mass audience through allusion or formalist innovation. But Kelly's point is strong: Joyce the author remains the central figure rather than his works and *Ulysses* the exemplary text of the mythology of Joyce, unlike Kelly's example of *Frankenstein*, which is a story that has taken on a life separate from its author.

This state of affairs seems troubling to a relative few, however. The author, as opposed to the text, holds the privilege for readers outside of poststructuralist academic circles. Either Joyce wrote *Ulysses*, or he didn't. Such a simplistic statement would be given short shrift by textual editors like McGann or Rose. Poststructuralist theorists, too, would find fault with claims that Joyce alone is responsible for the textual life his words enjoy. Conversely, for traditionally oriented scholars and editors such a view appears to be sensible—Joyce is, after all, the author. It is highly probable, however, that the common reader does not consider such issues at all when reading *Ulysses* (or any other book). McGee gives an instructive example:

> I have carefully explained to my students that the text of *King Lear* they study in a sophomore survey or an advanced course is not a text that existed in any of the editions of Shakespeare's time but a modern composite text based on two different versions of the play. This news does not impress them as being terribly relevant to their discussions of Shakespeare. . . . they merely assume that all the editions are fundamentally the same, that the authority of a literary text is ideal and not materially determinate. (36)

McGee's assessment of students' understanding of textual variance illustrates something he does not discuss: the "ideal" authority of literary texts resides in the assumption that they represent fairly accurately *what the author wrote*. The ultimate authority for the common reader, too, resides in those individuals who put pen to paper and create literature, not in the editors or critics who come after them. For the common reader, the text is assumed to be an adequate representation of the author's words. Textual editors know that this formulation is naïve, but it is precisely the continuation of this impression that traditionally oriented editors work towards. For poststructuralist editors like Gabler and McGann, the task becomes more complicated. They must remain true to their understanding of textual instability while still achieving a readable edition. The perils of such an undertaking are well illustrated in the Gabler controversy. Perhaps, in this era of hypertext, such questions will become moot. What remains unclear, however, is how the ideology of authorial intention (textually speaking) will continue to fare when readers can truly write (and rewrite) texts as they read them. In essence, Gabler's synoptic text was a paper version of a hypertext, allowing readers to see all variants in conjunction with one possible reading on the opposite page. The Joyce Wars, in academic circles anyway, presaged a whole new territory for thought on this subject.[3]

For nonacademics, however, the issues are less easily untangled. The first Joyce War seemed to exclude the common reader, who was constructed (when mentioned at all) as the innocent bystander for whom all the fuss was being made. But the issues, as presented in the popular press, were about elements that should be of extreme interest to readers: copyright and accessibility to various (and therefore cheaper) editions. The legal arguments over copyright, particularly in the United States, prevent any new editions of *Ulysses* from being published, and the monopoly enjoyed by Random House and the Joyce Estate keeps the price higher than it might be if several editions were available. The long-awaited Kidd edition is the prime example of this kind of stranglehold: Kidd reported in a private phone call with this author that he has been finished with his edition of *Ulysses* since 1991, but because the Joyce Estate and Random House— who claim that the United States copyright they hold began in 1934—have continually threatened legal action, it remains unpublished.[4]

Copyright status for *Ulysses* is a gray area. Robert Spoo, writing in the *Yale Law Journal*, argues that the 1922 *Ulysses* has always been in the public domain because of the complexity of the copyright laws. To review, an "ad interim" clause in the Copyright Act of 1909 allowed a work published abroad to enjoy copyright for four months after it was deposited with the Copyright Office within sixty days of foreign publication. The work, if published in the United States within that four-month period, could then enjoy copyright protection beginning from the date of foreign publication. There is controversy over what failure to comply with the provisions would mean for the work's copyright: "[some claim] that failure to comply . . . injected the work into the public domain; others, that the copyright in that work was merely unenforceable" (Spoo 648). So the legal threats from Random House and the Joyce estate which had kept W.W. Norton from publishing John Kidd's edition would appear to be empty, since the 1922 (on which Kidd based his edition) would have either already been public domain or would have come out of copyright by 1997. The recent extension of copyright in the United States through the Bono Act, however, reinstates prior copyright even if a work became public domain in the interim. This legislation has now created a further twenty-year hurdle for the Kidd edition, and at present it looks as though Norton will not publish it at all.[5]

The real issues in the controversy over the both the Gabler and Rose editions, contrary to what was emphasized in the popular press, are textual instability and the conflict between two divergent schools of editorial thought. Traditional editorial theory privileges notions of definitiveness and authorial intention, and decrees that the editor be as unobtrusive as possible so as not to get in between what the author wrote and what the reader reads; Rose clearly steps forward, following McGann, to claim without apology the editor's role in shaping what is placed before the reader. In some ways the Gabler edition bridged these two schools of thought, because while privileging the author by focusing on the manuscripts—by giving us "what James Joyce actually wrote"—the *Critical and Synoptic Edition* foregrounds textual instability as an inescapable condition of literature, a highly poststructuralist view which decenters the author by suggesting that all reading acts are essentially editorial in nature. The reading text published separately from the *CSE* sidesteps the theoretical aspects of the Gabler enterprise and re-privileges notions of definitiveness as constitutive of scholarly editing. In essence, the scholarly controversies over the Gabler and Rose editions grew primarily out of shifting theoretical bases for editing.

But these concerns appeared in the popular press as a battle over access to the "true" text, which, in part because of the aura of special status surrounding *Ulysses*, appeared to be solely the domain of academia. Readers were constructed in the Joyce Wars as passive recipients of scholarly efforts to mediate the "real" *Ulysses* as Joyce intended it to be. But the truth is that scholars have a rather vague notion of just who outside of academia reads *Ulysses* and why, and nowhere is this truth more clearly illustrated than in the Rose edition: the general reader of *Ulysses* apparently needs help understanding contractions, but is savvy enough to understand the complex editorial theory in his introduction. Such a contradictory stance towards the audience of Joyce's book prevents Rose from seizing an opportunity raised by his own rhetoric: the real issues of difficulty in *Ulysses* remain untouched because they are left unexamined.

The aura of intellectualism surrounding *Ulysses* is not an empty construct; it can be a difficult text to read. But it's not clear that Joyce deliberately chose his style(s) in an effort to alienate his audience or to keep *Ulysses* accessible only to a coterie of elitists. Readers do not necessarily need to know Homer to understand the book, or to admire its techniques. Neither does *Ulysses* require the reader to know several languages, as reading Pound or Eliot demands. My own experience as an undergraduate reading *Ulysses* for the first time remains for me an example that anyone can appreciate the book's originality, humor, and yes, genius without scholarly guides as a crutch (or a barrier). Certainly, I didn't "get" all the references in the book, nor did I find certain chapters easy reading (I still skim "Oxen of the Sun" because I find it to be . . . well . . . boring, and little more than a technical exercise on Joyce's part). But there remains nothing in the book that *requires* more than close attention on my part, which book lovers tend to bring to their reading anyway. I suspect that *Ulysses*, if it had been left to its own devices, would still have been considered an important text of the twentieth century whether or not a Joyce Industry had appeared. The Woolsey decision alone would have guaranteed the work's place as groundbreaking. The Industry lamented as obstructionist by Rose, Kelly, and the good people who brought us "Ulysses for Dummies" only became so through institutional shifts that had little to do with Joyce and much to do with the codification of literary study as something only academics were qualified to do.

One admirable accomplishment to come out of the Rose controversy was the attempt to reinsert the common reader's needs into the discourse surrounding Joyce's text. How *are* common readers best served in presenting Joyce's *Ulysses*? An annotated edition? We have one. Guides and reference books at their fingertips while reading? We have those, too. An unedited text, the way Joyce saw it into print? We have the 1922 edition for that. A guarantee that the text they are reading is absolutely, positively the exact replica of Joyce's intentions? Can't be done, and these considerations do not appear to enter into the common reader's appreciation for texts (see McGee, above). The answer to the question (with apologies to Freud), "What does the common reader want?" seems to lie elsewhere than in editorial concerns. Kidd's horrified statement in response to the Rose edition in *Newsweek* ("What's next? A Reader's Digest Condensed *Finnegans Wake*?") reveals the kind of appeal to the sacred nature of all of Joyce's words—but perhaps a Reader's Digest version of *Ulysses* might not be a bad idea. Such a move would bring thousands of readers to Joyce's text, and even if they never picked up the "unabridged" version they would have enough of a passing familiarity with Stephen, Leopold and Molly to allow Kelly's cultural mythologizing to occur. To simultaneously bemoan the "fact" that no one reads anymore while turning up our collective noses at methods to disseminate literary works to the masses is hypocritical and self-serving. Shakespeare remained in our collective cultural language through a centuries-old tradition of chopping up the plays into memorizable parts— who among us as schoolchildren did not, at one time or another, have to memorize a portion of *Julius Caesar*, or *Hamlet*, or *Macbeth*?

The common reader is not stupid, counter to her appearance in most of the discourse of the literary establishment. And her number is legion, contrary to the continuous lament that television and the Internet have destroyed the reading base in this country: the 1999 figures from the Association of American Publishers show sales of over six billion dollars for what they categorize as Trade books—there is no differentiation between fictional, nonfictional, popular, or literary texts ("Industry Statistics"). The most recent available statistics on book-purchasing patterns in the United States, gathered by the American Booksellers Association, reveal that in 1998 only 3.9 percent of total book sales were devoted to the "Art/Literature/Poetry" category, which includes an indistinct definition of Literature as "Classics/Contemporary"; the category of Popular Fiction, unsurprisingly, comprised 51.9 percent of total sales, and includes the equally broad definition of Popular Fiction as "Adult, Espionage/Thriller, Fantasy, General, Historical, Male Adventure, Mystery/Detective, Occult, Religious, Romance, Science Fiction, Suspense/Psychology, TV Movies & Western" (Book Web). Yes, we can look at that percentage and smugly point out that there are few "serious" readers anymore; but was there ever a large number of them? What's interesting about these statistics is that the categories maintained by the publishing industry itself show that the Literary is as vaguely defined as the common reader is, and that such a demarcation between "acceptable" and "unacceptable" reading may be ultimately unimportant to those outside academia.

But disdain for mass culture and sweeping condemnations of Americans as unlettered, unsophisticated idiots have a long history, and remain a beloved part of the rhetoric of the culture wars. In *The New Republic*, Ruth Franklin reviews Bernhard Schlink's *The Reader* (an Oprah's Book Club selection, which may have caused some prejudiced response in the first place) by invoking the dichotomy between the book reviewers and the general public:

> That bad books are the books most widely read is an entirely mundane phenomenon of contemporary culture. Every week the major book reviews assess a dozen books in a variety of genres, of varying quality but deemed of sufficient significance or originality or beauty to merit a thousand words or so. With only a few exceptions, these books then vanish forever: good books get reviewed, but bad books get bought. ("Immorality Play")

Franklin's restriction of this "mundane phenomenon" to "contemporary culture" is historically naïve. From the birth of mass literacy in the nineteenth century, the reading habits of the lower and middle classes (who had less access to education) have been disdained by the upper (who had the leisure and means to go to elite universities). Even that widely cited champion of the common reader, Virginia Woolf, penned a half-serious letter excoriating the middlebrow: "If any human being, man, woman, dog, cat or half-crushed worm dares call me 'middlebrow' I will take my pen and stab him dead" (186). Though this letter was dashed off in response to a poor review of Woolf's own work, and in fact has a more complex stance toward the division between high-, middle-, and lowbrow than this quote makes it appear, the Modernist impulse towards elitism remains a central motif of that era. The rhetoric of these diatribes against the middlebrow announces the sense of proprietorship that reviewers and other "authorities" feel for "real" art; witness Franklin's next paragraph:

> Once in a while, though, books of 'literary merit' do take a spin on the best-seller list. These are often just bad books in disguise—*Corelli's Mandolin*, or *A Heartbreaking Work of Staggering Genius*. With regard to style, both of those books are credible imitations of the real thing; but unlike the "designer" handbags hawked on the street, what gives away these knock-offs is not their detailing but the absence at their core. Under the weight of all their trappings—pseudo-historical documents, lengthy digressions on esoterica, winking self-referentiality—they shudder with emptiness.

The interesting metaphor of "knock-offs" clearly reveals that for Franklin there are texts with more acceptable claims to artistic status than these "bad books in disguise"; it becomes plain that these books are using the trappings of modernism, and even postmodernism, like a child trying on its parents' clothes, but without the innocence of intent usually associated with such activity. The "trappings" used by these books have become clichés, because they have become forms without content: "they shudder with emptiness." But, Franklin implies, the mass of readers taken in by these empty works are too stupid to see their essential hollowness and so cannot differentiate between "good" books and "bad" books.

But readers are not as undiscriminating as such rhetoric implies. Across the country, public libraries continue to foster literary study outside of academia through book discussion groups, and such groups may be a good place to begin in identifying the common reader. At the Cambridge Public Library in Cambridge, Massachusetts, the Great Books Discussion group chose *Ulysses* for their reading list for the year 2000–2001. Hugh Crane, the Assistant Head of Reference and leader of the Discussion group, indicated that "the man who nominated *Ulysses* was motivated by its appearance in the #1 spot on the Modern Library's list of Top 100 Novels of the 20th Century," and that "everyone was familiar with the title and knew something of its reputation" (electronic correspondence 24 Apr. 2002). The make-up of the group may be indicative (but not necessarily representative) of the identity of the common reader: "a . . . balance of genders [and] ages . . . Almost all members are college educated and several have advanced degrees. Many studied & have or had careers in fields outside the humanities. They find Great Books a relatively painless way to repair what they feel to be a deficiency in their education. One or two are students

now; perhaps half are retirees. The rest are in various professional, technical, [and] business occupations" (*ibid*). Crane further indicated that, of the
13 members present at the selection meeting, 11 voted for *Ulysses*. His description of the group's reaction to the book after reading it is instructive:
"[m]ost readers found the book very puzzling but also very entertaining.
They felt the book needed more than one reading, and were willing to try
again, but with more guidance. . . . A vocal minority hated the book, finding it pretentious and frivolous" (*ibid*). Such responses indicate not only
that these common readers were able to freely tackle *Ulysses*, but also that
it met the criteria of being "entertaining." The distribution of thoughtfully
positive response and "vocal" negative response echoes the early critical
reactions to *Ulysses*. That these readers were "willing to try again, but
with more guidance" shows that, indeed, scholarship has a place in the
common reader's response to the book—but not necessarily a definitive
one. Like Woolf's idealized reader in "How Should One Read A Book?"
these readers appear to come to the criticism with their own questions and
opinions fully formed; critics, Woolf writes, "are only able to help us if we
come to them laden with questions and suggestions won honestly in the
course of our own reading. They can do nothing for us if we herd ourselves
under their authority and lie down like sheep in the shade of a hedge"
(269). It would seem that at least one group of nonprofessional readers
meets Woolf's criteria; I suspect that there are many more.

Of course, as a representative sample of the common reader's identity,
this particular group is insufficient. Crane indicated that "there are no
African-Americans and only occasionally a Hispanic or Asian-American."
Such anecdotal and singular evidence cannot stand if scholars are to examine the identity and needs of the common reader. And I think we need to in
order to maintain the credibility of scholarship alluded to by Spoo. Theorizing is a necessary part of what we do, but there is a practical side of criticism that too often gets short shrift in the academy. Preaching to the
converted about Joyce's potential as a relevant force in our culture will not
make it so. The question arises here of the value placed upon various forums of critical dispersal by the academy. The kind of publications validated within academia are refereed journals and books published by
university presses, and these publications have the most impact on tenure
and hiring decisions. Scholars are thereby encouraged to write for an academic audience, and the relevance for those outside the academy of much
of the exciting work being done can be lost in a "publish or perish" culture. It is, of course, pointless to advocate a complete divestiture of such
practices. They serve a valuable function within the academy, and are necessary to maintain the kind of quality that all scholars hope to achieve in
their careers. Perhaps, though, the academy might consider reevaluating
publications meant not only for scholars but also for general readers. In
order to address concerns that such forums are "uncritical," this reevalua-
tion must ground itself in a knowledge of real reading practices by real his-

torical entities and an analysis of those elements of the reading experience most prized by the common reader.[6] One place to start is investigating such entities as book discussion groups fostered by public libraries.

*Ulysses*, as Joyce repeatedly tried to tell people, is a funny book: "The pity is the public will demand and find a moral in my book, or worse they may take it in some serious way, and on the honor of a gentleman, there is not one single serious line in it" (Ellmann 523–24). In all of the controversies over editions, throughout much of the critical discourse surrounding the text, this message that *Ulysses* can be fun to read is often lost. The joys of the text draw scholars and common readers alike to an appreciation for *Ulysses*. It is these pleasures that keep them coming back to no. 7 Eccles Street, and this shared experience can serve as a bridge between the common reader and us busy professors.

NOTES

[1]"Is There a Class For This Text? The New *Ulysses*, Jerome McGann, and the Issue of Textual Authority," *Works and Days* 5.2 (1987): 27–44.

[2]In the Winter/Spring 1998 issue of the *James Joyce Quarterly*, the "Current JJ Checklist" compiled by William S. Brockman shows 232 entries, spanning the years 1996–1998. This number does not include the 27 reviews of the Rose edition, also listed in Brockman's compilation, nor does it include the 13 theatrical and musical productions or the 19 listings under the "miscellaneous" category (439–460). This is the 79th such Checklist, and the Joyce industry shows no signs of slowing down.

[3]There are several articles and examples of *Ulysses* in hypertext on the Web: some interesting ones are "A Hypermedia Edition of the 'Sirens' Episode of James Joyce's *Ulysses*" by Laura M. Crook at http://www2.shore.net/~laura/Ulysses/Sirens/home.htm; "James Joyce and Hypertext Theory," by Mark Nunes at http://www.dc.peachnet.edu/~mnunes/joyce.html; "*Ulysses*: A Case Study in the Problems of Hypertextualization of Complex Documents," by David Gold at http://ccwf.utexas.edu/~dgold/joycehyper/title.html; and two sites maintained by Charles Cave, "Visions of Nighttown: A hypertext exploration of the Circe Chapter of Ulysses" http://members.optusnet.com.au/~charles/Circe/ and "Wandering Rocks: A hypertext exploration of Chapter 10 of Ulysses" at http://members.optusnet.com.au/~charles/WR/.

[4]Phone conversation with author, April 21, 1999.

[5]On May 24, 1998, editors at the Norton company revealed via email with this author that they were engaged in negotiations with the Joyce Estate over permission to publish the Kidd edition; however, a recent article in the Boston *Globe* quoted the president of Norton, Drake McFeely, as saying that publication of Kidd's edition was "unlikely" (Abel). McFeely cited the copyright extension as one reason for this development.

[6]Janice Radway, in examining the selection practices of the Book-of-the-Month Club, discusses "a certain hostility toward the academy and the institutionalized teaching of literature, which the editors seem to believe transforms fascinating books into dry exercises in analysis" (269). The value of knowing such an evaluation is that the "Book-of-the-Month Club is well regarded within the publishing in-

dustry as an institution that manages to combine commercial goals with a concern for 'quality'" (259); as Radway writes, the editors are trained by academics and their jobs resemble literary critics', but they are also aware that their readers' taste is not necessarily formed by this same kind of training and they are "always attending to what individuals outside the culture industry actually do with books" (263). As such, their evaluation of the "dryness" of academic discourse is predicated upon their knowledge of what the common reader understands about such discourse.

# Bibliography

Abel, David. "Troubled Chapter: Professor Who Rose Over Joyce Critique Falls From Grace At BU" *Boston Globe* 9 April 2002: B1+.

Adams, Robert M. Letter. *New York Review of Books*. 18 Aug. 1988: 63–64.

Altick, Richard. *The English Common Reader: A Social History of the Mass Reading Public, 1800–1900*. Chicago: University of Chicago Press, 1957.

American Booksellers Association. "BookWeb: Research and Statistics." 14 Apr. 2002. http://www.bookweb.org/research/stats/387.html.

Amis, Martin. "Teacher's Pet," *Atlantic Monthly*. September 1986: 96+.

Arnold, Bruce. *The Scandal of* Ulysses*: The Sensational Life of a Twentieth-Century Masterpiece*. New York: St. Martin's Press, 1991.

*Back to School*. Dir. Alan Metter. Perf. Rodney Dangerfield, Sally Kellerman. MGM/UA, 1986.

Bannister, Frank. " 'Reader's Edition' of *Ulysses*," Letter. *Irish Times*. 8 July 1997: 13.

Barger, Jorn. "IQ Infinity: The Unknown James Joyce" 12 Sept. 1998. http://www.mcs.net/~jorn/html/jj.html

Barthes, Roland. "The Death of the Author," in *Modern Criticism and Theory*. Ed. David Lodge. London and New York: Longman Group, 1988.

Bates, Robin. "Much Ado About James Joyce and His *Ulysses*," *Smithsonian*. Mar. 1990: 129–144.

———. "Reflections on the Kidd Era," *Studies in the Novel* 22 (Summer 1990): 119–141.

Battersby, Eileen. "When is a 'Molly' a 'Welly'?" *The Irish Times, Special Bloomsday Edition*. 14 June 1997. *Irish Times Archive* online. 19 Mar. 1998. http://www.irish-times.com/irish-times/paper/1997/0616/fea1.html.

Bauerle, Ruth. Letter. *Times Literary Supplement*. 10 Aug. 1984: 840.

Beach, Sylvia. *Shakespeare and Company*. 1959. Lincoln: University of Nebraska Press, 1991.

Beckett, Samuel. "Dante . . . Bruno. Vico . . . Joyce," in *Our Exagmination Round His Factification for Incamination of Work in Progress*. London: Faber & Faber, Ltd., 1929: 1–22.

Bell, Quentin. *Virginia Woolf: A Biography*. New York: Harcourt Brace, 1972.

Beja, Morris. "Synjoysium: An Informal History of the International James Joyce Symposium," *James Joyce Quarterly* 22 (Winter 1985): 113–129.

Bennett, Arnold. "James Joyce's *Ulysses*," *Outlook*. 29 April 1922: 337–339. Reprinted in *The Author's Craft and Other Critical Writings of Arnold Bennett*. Ed. Samuel Hynes. Lincoln: University of Nebraska Press, 1968.

"The Bloomsday Massacre," *Newsweek*. 23 June 1997: 8.

Boscagli, Maurizia and Enda Duffy. "Joyce's Face," in *Marketing Modernisms: Self Promotion, Canonization, Rereading*. Edited by Kevin J. H. Dettmar and Stephen Watt. Ann Arbor: University of Michigan Press, 1996: 133–159.

Bowers, Fredson. "Greg's 'Rationale of Copy-Text' Revisited," *Studies in Bibliography* 31 (1978): 90–161.

Brown, Richard. "Marilyn Monroe Reading *Ulysses*: Goddess or Post-Cultural Cyborg?" in *Joyce and Popular Culture*. Ed. R. B. Kershner. Gainesville: University Press of Florida, 1996: 170–179.

Cain, William. "Making Texts New," *Devils and Angels: Textual Editing and Literary Theory*. Ed. Philip Cohen. Charlottesville: University Press of Virginia, 1991: 195–204.

Cave, Charles. "James Joyce" Web page. 18 Mar. 1998. http://www.ozemail.com.au/~caveman/Joyce.

Cheng, Vincent. "The Joycean Unconscious, or Getting Respect in the Real World," in *Joyce and Popular Culture*. Ed. R. B. Kershner. Gainesville: University Press of Florida, 1996: 180–192.

Cohen, Philip, ed. "Introduction," *Devils and Angels: Textual Editing and Literary Theory*. Charlottesville: University Press of Virginia, 1991: ix-xviii.

———. and David H. Jackson. "Notes on Emerging Paradigms in Editorial Theory," in *Devils and Angels: Textual Editing and Literary Theory*. Ed. Philip Cohen. Charlottesville: University Press of Virginia, 1991: 103–123.

"Copyright Basics." United States Government. 28 May 1998. http://lcweb.loc.gov/copyright/circs/circ1.html.

Coren, Alan. "Bloomers," *Punch*. 14 Mar. 1979: 417–418.

Craft, Robert. Letter. *New York Review of Books*. 18 Aug. 1988: 64.

Crane, Hugh. "Ulysses." E-mail to the author. 24 April 2002.

Cullen, Paul. "Director threatens action over new 'Ulysses' film," *The Irish Times*. 19 June 2001. *Irish Times Archive* online. 25 April 2002. http://scripts.ireland.com/search/highlight.plx?TextRes=Ulysses&Path=/newspaper/ireland/2001/0619/hom8.htm.

Dalton, Jack. "The Text of *Ulysses*," *New Light on Joyce from the Dublin Symposium*. Ed. Fritz Senn. Bloomington: Indiana University Press, 1972: 99–119.

Dalziel, Margaret. *Popular Fiction 100 Years Ago: An Unexplored Tract of Literary History*. London: Cohen & West, 1957.

Davidson, Cathy N., ed. *Reading in America: Literature and Social History*. Baltimore: Johns Hopkins University Press, 1989: 259–284.

De Grazia, Margreta and Peter Stallybrass. "The Materiality of the Shakespearean Text," *Shakespeare Quarterly* 44 (Fall 1993): 255–283.

Dettmar, Kevin J. H. *The Illicit Joyce of Postmodernism: Reading Against the Grain*. Madison, WI: The University of Wisconsin Press, 1996.

———. and Stephen Watt, Eds. *Marketing Modernisms: Self Promotion, Canonization, Rereading*. Ann Arbor: University of Michigan Press, 1996.

Du Sautoy, Peter. "Editing *Ulysses*: A Personal Account" *James Joyce Quarterly* 27 (1989): 69–76.

———. Letter. *Times Literary Supplement*. 8–14 July 1988: 756.

———. Letter. *Times Literary Supplement*. 9–15 Sept. 1988: 989.

———. Letter. *New York Review of Books*. 19 Jan. 1989: 58.

Ebershoff, David. E-mail to the author. 24 July 1998.

Eco, Umberto. *Travels in Hyperreality*. San Diego, New York and London: Harcourt Brace & Co., 1986.

Elam, Jack. Letter. *Times Literary Supplement*. 27 July 1984: 732.

Ellmann, Richard. *James Joyce: New and Revised Edition*. 1959. Oxford: Oxford University Press, 1982.

———. "The Big Word in *Ulysses*," *The New York Review of Books*. 25 Oct. 1984: 30–31.

———. "The New *Ulysses*," *The Georgia Review*. Summer 1986: 548–556.

Eliot, T. S. "*Ulysses*, Order, and Myth," *The Dial*. November 1923. Reprinted in *Critical Essays on James Joyce*. Ed. Bernard Benstock. Boston: G. K. Hall & Co., 1985: 25–27.

———. *Introducing James Joyce: A Selection of Joyce's Prose*. London: Faber and Faber, Ltd., 1942.

Ernst, Morris and Alan U. Schwartz. "Four Letter Words and the Unconscious," *The United States of America v. One Book Entitled* Ulysses *by James Joyce*. Eds. Michael Moscato and Leslie Le Blanc. Frederick, MD: University Publications of America, Inc. 1984: 33–43.

Farrell, Antony. Letter. *The Irish Times*. 2 July 1997. *Irish Times Archive Online*. 20 May 1998. http://www.irish-times.com/irish%2Dtimes/paper/1997/0702/lea.htm#l.

Fitch, Noel Riley. *Sylvia Beach and the Lost Generation: A History of Literary Paris in the Twenties and Thirties*. New York and London: W.W. Norton & Company, 1983.

Foucault, Michel. "The Functions of Literature," in *Genealogy and Literature*. Ed. Lee Quinby. Minneapolis: University of Minnesota Press, 1995: 3–8.

———. "Polemics, Politics, and Problematizations: An Interview," in *The Foucault Reader*. Ed. Paul Rabinow. New York: Pantheon Books, 1984: 381–390.

———. "What Is an Author?" in *The Foucault Reader*. Ed. Paul Rabinow. New York: Pantheon Books, 1984: 101–120.

Frank, Jerome P. "Trade Edition of Corrected *Ulysses* is Due from Random House," *Publishers Weekly*. 13 June 1986: 25–26.

Franklin, Ruth. "Immorality Play," *New Republic*. 12 Oct. 2001. *New Republic* online. 26 Apr. 2002. http://www.thenewrepublic.com/101501/franklin101501.html.

Fields, Beverly. Letter. *New York Review of Books*. 18 Aug. 1988: 64.

Friedman, Melvin J. "Ellmann on Joyce," in *Re-Viewing Classics of Joyce Criticism*. Ed. Janet Egleson Dunleavy. Urbana and Chicago: University of Illinois Press, 1991: 131–141.

Gabler, Hans Walter, ed. *Ulysses: A Critical and Synoptic Edition* by James Joyce. New York and London: Garland Publishing, 1984.

———. "Afterword," *Ulysses: The Corrected Text*. New York: Random House, 1986.

———. "A Response to: John Kidd, 'Errors of Execution in the 1984 Ulysses'" given at the Society for Textual Scholars in April 1985;

reprinted with postscript in *Studies in the Novel* 22.2 (Summer 1990): 250–256.

———. "Danis Rose: *Ulysses*. A 'Reader's Edition'," *James Joyce Quarterly* 35 (Spring 1998): 561–573.

———. Letter. *Times Literary Supplement*. 1–7 July 1988: 733.

———. Letter. *Times Literary Supplement*. 12–18 August 1988: 883.

———. Letter. *Times Literary Supplement*. 16–22 December 1988: 1345.

———. Letter. *New York Review of Books*. 18 Aug. 1988: 63.

———. Letter. *New York Review of Books*. 29 Sept. 1988: 81.

———. Letter. *New York Review of Books*. 30 Mar. 1989: 43.

Gates, David and Ray Sawhill. "The Dated and the Dead," *Newsweek*. 3 Aug. 1998: 64–65.

Gillespie, Michael Patrick. "Danis Rose and the Common Reader," *James Joyce Quarterly* 35 (Spring 1998): 584–587.

Goldwasser, Thomas. "Who Was Vladimir Dixon? Was He Vladimir Dixon?" *James Joyce Quarterly* 16 (Summer 1979): 219–223.

Graff, Gerald. "The University and the Prevention of Culture," in *Criticism in the University*. Eds. Gerald Graff and Reginald Gibbons. Evanston: Northwestern University Press, 1985: 62–82.

Gray, Paul. "Odyssey of a Corrected Classic," *Time*. 2 July 1984: 83–85.

Greetham, D. C. "Foreword." *A Critique of Modern Textual Criticism*, by Jerome McGann. 1983. Charlottesville and London: University of Virginia Press, 1996.

Greg, Sir Walter. "The Rationale of Copy-Text," *Studies in Bibliography* 3 (1949): 19-36.

Groden, Michael. Letter. *Times Literary Supplement*. 4-10 Nov. 1988: 1227.

———. Letter. *Times Literary Supplement*. 11–13 Oct. 1988: 1109+.

———. Letter. *New York Review of Books*. 8 Dec. 1988: 61.

———. Letter. *New York Review of Books*. 2 Feb. 1989: 45.

Gunn, Ian. Letter. *Times Literary Supplement*. 4–10 Nov. 1988: 1227.

Hammond, Antony. Review. *The Library: The Transactions of the Bibliographical Society*, 6th Series (8) December 1986: 382–390.

Hart, Clive. "An Inquiry into *Ulysses: The Corrected Text*," *Times Literary Supplement*. 17–22 Nov. 1989: 1279+.

Henke, Suzette A. "Exagmining Beckett & Company," in *Re-Viewing Classics of Joyce Criticism*. Ed. Janet Egleson Dunleavy. Urbana and Chicago: University of Illinois Press, 1991: 60–81.

Hunka, George and Joanne Tzadis. "*Ulysses* for Dummies," *From Hunger*. 1996. 21 Oct. 1998. http://www.bway.hunger.net/ulysses.html.

———. E-mail to the author. 5 Nov. 1998.

"Industry Statistics." Association of American Publishers. 14 Apr. 2002. http://www.publishers.org/stats/prelim.htm.

Johnson, Claudia L. "Austen Cults and Cultures," in *The Cambridge Companion to Jane Austen*. Ed. Edward Copeland. Cambridge, England: Cambridge University Press, 1997: 211–226.

Johnson, Samuel. *The Lives of the English Poets*. Ed. G. B. Hill. 3 vols. Oxford: Oxford UP, 1905.

Jones, William Powell. *James Joyce and the Common Reader*. 1955. Norman: University of Oklahoma Press, 1970.

Joyce, James. *Letters, Volumes I, III*. Ed. Stuart Gilbert. New York: Viking Press, 1957.

———. *Ulysses*. 1934. New York: Random House, 1961.

———. *Ulysses: A Facsimile of the Manuscript, With a Critical Introduction by Harry Levin and a Bibliographical Preface by Clive Driver*. New York: Octagon Books; Philadelphia: in association with The P. H. & A. S. W. Rosenbach Foundation, 1975.

———. *Ulysses: The Critical and Synoptic Edition*. Ed. Hans Walter Gabler. New York and London: Garland Press, 1984.

———. *Ulysses: The Corrected Text*. Ed. Hans Walter Gabler. New York: Random House, 1986.

———. *Ulysses: A Reader's Edition*. Ed. Danis Rose. London: Picador, 1997.

———. *Finnegans Wake*. New York: Penguin, 1939.

Joyce, Stephen. Letter. *Times Literary Supplement*. 9–15 Sept. 1988: 989.

———. Letter. *Times Literary Supplement*. 27 June 1997: 17.

Kaplan, Carey and Ellen Cronan Rose. *The Canon and the Common Reader*. Knoxville: University of Tennessee Press, 1990.

Kenner, Hugh. "Leopold's bloom restored," *Times Literary Supplement*. 13 July 1984: 771–772.

———. "The Computerized *Ulysses*," *Harper's Magazine*. April 1980: 89–95.

———. *Ulysses* (revised edition). Baltimore and London: The Johns Hopkins University Press, 1987.

———. "Reflections on the Gabler Era," *James Joyce Quarterly* 26 (Fall 1988): 11–20.

———. "The Making of the Modernist Canon," *Chicago Review* 34.2 (1984): 49–61.

——. Letter. *Times Literary Supplement.* 17 Aug. 1984: 863.

Kelly, Joseph. *Our Joyce: From Outcast to Icon.* Austin: University of Texas Press, 1998.

——. "A Defense of Danis Rose." *James Joyce Quarterly* 35–36 (Summer-Fall 1998): 811–823.

Kidd, John. "Errors of Execution in the 1984 *Ulysses*" paper given at the Society of Textual Scholars conference April 1985; reprinted with foreword, "The Context of the First Salvo in the Joyce Wars," *Studies in the Novel* 22.2 (Summer 1990): 237–249.

——. "The Scandal of *Ulysses*," *The New York Review of Books.* 30 June 1988: 32-39.

——. "Making the Wrong Joyce," *The New York Review of Books.* 25 Sept. 1997: 54–56.

——. Letter. *Times Literary Supplement.* 22–28 July 1988: 805+.

——. Letter. *Times Literary Supplement.* 19–25 Aug. 1988: 907.

——. Letter. *Times Literary Supplement.* 21–27 Oct. 1988: 1175.

——. Letter. *New York Review of Books.* 18 Aug. 1988: 64–65.

——. Letter. *New York Review of Books.* 29 Sept. 1988: 81–83.

——. Letter. *New York Review of Books.* 8 Dec. 1988: 58–61.

——. Letter. *New York Review of Books.* 2 Feb. 1989: 45.

——. Letter. *New York Review of Books.* 30 Mar. 1989: 45.

——. Letter. *New York Review of Books.* 1 June 1989: 40–41.

——. Letter. *New York Review of Books.* 15 Jan. 1998: 60–61.

——. Telephone conversation with author, 21 Apr. 1999.

Korn, Eric. "Words known to all men," *Times Literary Supplement.* 5 Sept. 1997: 3–4.

Leavis, Q. D. *Fiction and the Reading Public.* London: Chatto & Windus, 1932.

Lehan, Richard. "James Joyce: The Limits of Modernism and the Realms of the Literary Text," *Arizona Quarterly* 50 (Spring 1994): 87–108.

Lernout, Geert. *The French Joyce.* Ann Arbor: University of Michigan Press, 1990.

——. "Anglo-American Textual Criticism and the Case of Hans Walter Gabler's Edition of *Ulysses*," *Genesis* 9 (1996): 45–65.

Levin, Harry. *James Joyce: A Critical Introduction.*1941. New York: New Directions, 1960.

Levitt, Morton P. "Harry Levin's *James Joyce* and the Modernist Age," in *Re-Viewing Classics of Joyce Criticism.* Ed. Janet Egleson Dunleavy. Urbana and Chicago: University of Illinois Press, 1991: 90–105.

Lingeman, Richard and Thomas M. Disch. "St. Nicholas: A Textual Scandal," *The Nation*. 2 Jan. 1989: 1+.

Lyall, Sarah. "A New Edition Purges What May Have Been Joyce's Errors and Enrages Critics," *The New York Times Archive Online*. 23 June 1997. 20 Apr. 1998. http://archives.nytimes.com.

Lyotard, Jean-François. *The Differend: Phases in Dispute*. Trans. by Georges Van Den Abbeele. Minneapolis: University of Minnesota Press, 1988.

Marchant, Peter. "*The Forsyte Saga* Reconsidered: The Case of the Common Reader Versus Literary Criticism," in *Western Humanities Review* 24 (1970): 221–29.

Marcus, Leah S. "Levelling Shakespeare: Local Customs and Local Texts," *Shakespeare Quarterly* 42 (Summer 1991): 168–178.

McGee, Patrick. "Is There A Class For This Text? The New *Ulysses*, Jerome McGann, and the Issue of Textual Authority," *Works and Days* 5.2 (1987): 27–44.

McDowell, Edwin. "New Edition Fixes 5,000 Errors in *Ulysses*," *The New York Times*. June 7, 1984: 1A+.

———. "Corrected *Ulysses* Sparks Scholarly Attack," *The New York Times*. 15 June 1988: 19–20.

McGann, Jerome. *A Critique of Modern Textual Criticism*. 1983. Charlottesville and London: University Press of Virginia, 1996.

———. "*Ulysses* as a Postmodern Text: The Gabler Edition," *Criticism* 27.3 (1985): 283–306.

Mead, Rebecca. "Big Books 101," *The New Yorker*. 26 Oct.-2 Nov. 1998: 54–55.

Modern Library. "100 Best Novels." 24 Oct. 1998. http://www.randomhouse.com/modernlibrary/100best/.

Morrison, Mark. *The Public Face of Modernism: Little Magazines, Audiences, and Reception, 1905–1920*. Madison, Wis. and London: University of Wisconsin Press, 2001.

Moscato, Michael and Leslie Le Blanc, eds. *The United States of America v. One Book Entitled* Ulysses *By James Joyce*. Frederick, MD: University Publications of America, Inc., 1984.

Mundy, Liza. "The Wars of the Joyces," *The Washington Post*. 10 July 1988: F1+.

Nadel, Ira. "Anthologizing Joyce: The Example of T.S. Eliot," *James Joyce Quarterly* 27 (Spring 1990): 509–515.

Norris, Margot. "The Consequence of Deconstruction: A Technical Perspective of Joyce's *Finnegans Wake*," *ELH* 41 (Spring 1974).

Reprinted in *Critical Essays on James Joyce*. Ed. Bernard Benstock. Boston: G. K. Hall & Co., 1985: 206–221.

———. "The Postmodernization of *Finnegans Wake* Reconsidered," in *Rereading the New: A Backward Glance at Modernism*. Ed. by Kevin J. H. Dettmar. Ann Arbor: University of Michigan Press, 1992: 334–362.

"Night Thoughts," *Time*. 8 May 1939: 78–84.

O'Hanlon, John. Letter. *New York Review of Books*. 29 Sept. 1988: 80–81.

Paul, Angus. "Much-Heralded New Edition of Joyce's *Ulysses* Is Badly Flawed, Virginia Scholar Contends," *The Chronicle of Higher Education*. 22 June 1988: A6+.

Pease, Allison. *Modernism, Mass Culture, and the Aesthetics of Obscenity*. Cambridge, U.K. and New York : Cambridge University Press, 2000.

Poldy.com. "About Poldy.com." 3 June 1998. http://www.poldy.com/bloom/about.html.

Pugliatti, Paola. "Who's Afraid of the 1984 Ulysses?" *James Joyce Quarterly* 27 (Fall 1989): 41–54.

———. "The New *Ulysses* Between Philology, Semiotics and Textual Genetics," *Dispositio* 12 (1987): 113–140.

Radway, Janice. "The Book-of-the-Month Club and the General Reader: The Uses of 'Serious' Fiction," in *Reading in America: Literature and Social History*. Ed. Cathy N. Davidson. Baltimore: Johns Hopkins University Press, 1989: 259-284.

———. *Reading the Romance: Women, Patriarchy, and Popular Literature*. 1984. Chapel Hill, London: University of North Carolina Press, 1991.

———. *A Feeling For Books: the Book of the Month Club, Literary Taste, and Middle Class Desire*. Chapel Hill: University of North Carolina Press, 1997.

Raine, Craig. "Pleasures of the Text," *The Sunday Times* (London). 12 Aug. 1984: 39.

Rainey, Lawrence. "How Molly Bloom Got Her Apostrophes," *London Review of Books*. 19 June 1997. Reprinted in *James Joyce Quarterly* 35 (Spring 1998): 588–596.

———. *Institutions of Modernism : Literary Elites and Public Culture*. New Haven, Conn. and London : Yale University Press, 1998.

Read, Forrest. *Pound/Joyce: The Letters of Ezra Pound to James Joyce*. New York: New Directions Publishing Corp., 1967.

Reimer, Andrew. "Joyce Fundamentalists Prefer The Original Bloom To A New Rose," Sydney *Morning Herald.* 6 Sept. 1997: 9.

Remnick, David. "The War over *Ulysses,*" *The Washington Post.* 2 April 1985: B1+.

Robertson, William. "Every *Ulysses* Jot and Tittle Fires Scholars' Debate at UM," *Miami Herald.* 6 Feb. 1989: 1A+.

Rose, Danis, ed. *Ulysses: A Reader's Edition.* London and Dublin: Picador and The Lilliput Press, 1997.

———. Letter. *Times Literary Supplement.* 11 July 1997: 17.

———. Letter. *New York Review of Books.* 15 Jan. 1998: 60.

Rose, Jonathan. "Rereading the English Common Reader: A Preface to a History of Audiences," *Journal of the History of Ideas* 53.1 (Jan.-Mar. 1992): 47–70.

Rossman, Charles. "The New *Ulysses*: The Hidden Controversy," *New York Review of Books.* 8 December 1988: 53–58.

———. "The Critical Reception of the Gabler *Ulysses*: or, Gabler's *Ulysses* Kidd-Napped: Part Two," *Studies in the Novel* 21 (1989): 323–353.

———. Guest Editor. *Studies in the Novel: A Special Issue on Editing Ulysses* 22 (1990).

———. Letter. *Times Literary Supplement.* 2–8 Sept. 1988: 963.

———. Letter. *New York Review of Books.* 19 Jan. 1989: 58–59.

Segall, Jeffrey. *Joyce in America: Cultural Politics and the Trials of* Ulysses. Berkeley and Los Angeles: University of California Press, 1993.

Senn, Fritz. "Prodding Nodding Joyce: The 'Reader's Edition' of *Ulysses,* edited by Danis Rose: Some First Impressions," *James Joyce Quarterly* 35 (Spring 1998): 573–587.

Shattuck, Roger and Douglas Alden. "Searching for the true text," *Times Literary Supplement.* 10–16 June 1988: 640–641.

Shillingsburg, Peter. *Scholarly Editing in the Computer Age: Theory and Practice.* Ann Arbor: University of Michigan Press, 1996.

———. "The Autonomous Author, the Sociology of Texts, and the Polemics of Textual Criticism," in *Devils and Angels: Textual Editing and Literary Theory.* Ed. Philip Cohen and David H. Jackson. Charlottesville: University Press of Virginia, 1991: 22–43.

Sontag, Susan, ed. "Introduction," *A Barthes Reader.* New York: Farrar, Straus & Giroux, 1982.

Spoo, Robert. "Joyce Scholars, Editors, and Imaginary Readers," *College English* 60 (March 1998): 330–335.

———. "Copyright Protectionism and Its Discontents: The Case of James Joyce's *Ulysses* in America," *The Yale Law Journal* 108 (1998): 633–667.

———. "Injuries, Remedies, Moral Rights, and the Public Domain," Introduction. Forthcoming in *James Joyce Quarterly* 37. 3–4 (2002): 1–19.

———. "A Rose Is a Rose Is a Roth: New/Old Theories of Legal Liability in the Joyce World," forthcoming in the *James Joyce Literary Supplement.*

St. John, Warren. "James Joyce and the Nutty Professor," *The Observer.* 29 Dec. 1997:23.

Staley, Thomas. Letter. *New York Review of Books.* 29 Sept. 1988: 81.

Stevens, Kenneth. "*Ulysses* on Trial," *Library Chronicle* 20/21 (1982). In *The United States of America v. One Book Entitled James Joyce's* Ulysses. Eds. Michael Moscato and Leslie Le Blanc. Frederick, MD: University Publications of America, 1984.

Streitfeld, David. "'The Best Novels' May Not Be; Modern Library's Panelists Say They Didn't Rank the Books," *The Washington Post.* 5 Aug. 1998: A1. *Washington Post Archives* online. 24 Oct. 1998. http://www.washingtonpost.com.

Sutherland, John. "Fiction and the Erotic Cover," *Critical Quarterly* 33 (1991): 3–36.

Tanselle, G. Thomas. "Recent Editorial Discussion and the Central Question of Editing," *Studies in Bibliography* 34 (1981): 22–65.

———."Historicism and Critical Editing," *Studies in Bibliography* 39 (1986): 1–46.

———. "Textual Criticism and Literary Sociology," *Studies in Bibliography* 44 (1991): 83–143.

Todd, Richard. *Consuming Fictions: The Booker Prize and Fiction in Britain Today.* London: Bloomsbury, 1996.

Treglown, Jeremy. "Editors Vary," *Times Literary Supplement.* 10 May 1985: 520.

Troost, Linda, ed. *Jane Austen in Hollywood.* Lexington, Kentucky: University Press of Kentucky, 1998.

Updike, John. Letter. *New York Review of Books.* 18 Aug. 1988: 63.

Wells, H. G. "James Joyce," *The New Republic.* 10 Mar. 1917. Reprinted in *Critical Essays on James Joyce.* Ed. Bernard Benstock. Boston: G. K. Hall & Co., 1985: 22–24.

Wexler, Joyce. "Selling Sex as Art," in *Marketing Modernisms: Self Promotion, Canonization, Rereading.* Eds. Kevin Dettmar and Stephen Watt. Ann Arbor: University of Michigan Press, 1996: 91–108.

——. *Who Paid for Modernism?: Art, Money, and the Fiction of Conrad, Joyce, and Lawrence.* Fayetteville: University of Arkansas Press, 1997.

Wheatley, David. "Shamiana," *Books Ireland.* May 1998: 130–131.

——. "Beckett's *mirlitonnades*: A Manuscript Study," *The Journal of Beckett Studies* 4 (Spring 1995): 47–76.

Wilkerson, Isabel. "Textual Scholars Make Points about Points in Books," *The New York Times.* 29 Apr. 1985: B2.

Williams, William Carlos. "A Point for American Criticism," in *Our Exagmination Round His Factification for Incamination of Work in Progress.* London: Faber & Faber, Ltd., 1929.

Wilson, Edmund. *Axel's Castle: A Study in the Imaginative Literature of 1870–1930.* New York: Scribner's, 1931.

——. *The Wound and the Bow: Seven Studies in Literature.* Cambridge, MA: Houghton Mifflin Co., 1941.

Woolf, Virginia. "How Should One Read a Book?" in *The Second Common Reader.* 1932. Ed. Andrew McNeillie. New York: Harcourt Brace Jovanovich, 1986: 258–270.

——. "Middlebrow," in *Death of the Moth and other Essays.* New York: Harcourt Brace, 1942: 176–186.

Woolsey, Judge John M. "United States v. One Book Called *Ulysses,*" in *The United States of America v. One Book Entitled James Joyce's Ulysses.* Eds. Michael Moscato and Leslie Le Blanc. Frederick, MD: University Publications of America, 1984. Also in *Ulysses,* by James Joyce. 1934. New York: Random House, 1961: ix-xiv.

Zeller, Hans. "A New Approach to the Critical Constitution of Literary Texts," *Studies in Bibliography* 28 (1975): 231–264.

Zill, Nicholas and Marianne Winglee. "Literature Reading in the United States: Data from National Surveys and Their Policy Implications," *Book Research Quarterly* (Spring 1989): 24–58.

# Index

Academic Joyce, 6, 11, 12
Adams, Robert M., 114
Altick, Richard, 3
Amis, Martin, 99-101, 108
Anderson, Margaret and Jane Heap,
        14, 32, 53-54
Arnold, Bruce, 57

*Back to School*, 37
Bates, Robin, 108n.2, 139-142
Barthes, Roland, 21
Beach, Sylvia, 12, 32, 53, 54, 77n.3
Beckett, Samuel, 24, 25, 30n.11
Bloom, Molly: monologue as defining
        chapter of *Ulysses*, 31, 34; in
        "Ulysses for Dummies," 45;
        in Rose edition, 153-54, 155-
        56, 160-161
Bowers, Fredson, 61-63, 87, 147, 149
Budgen, Frank, 12, 27

Cain, William, 152-153
censorship trials of *Ulysses*, 14, 15,
        32-33, 50, 53-54. *See also*
        Woolsey, Judge John M.
Cerf, Bennett. See Random House
Cheng, Vincent, 36-38
common reader, xii, 1-4, 180-183;
        Johnson's definition of, xviii;

studies of, 3-4; historical
        view of, xvi, 180-181; dis-
        missed by academia, 4, 180;
        and modernist literature, 5-6;
        as middlebrow, xii, 4, 180-
        181; role in Joyce Wars, 165,
        170, 177, 178; and *Ulysses*,
        179, 181-182; reading tastes
        of, 180; possible make-up of,
        181-182; need to study fur-
        ther, 182-183; *The Canon
        and the Common Reader*,
        xvii-xviii; *Joyce and the
        Common Reader*, xii
copyright law, 56-57, 71, 78nn.5,6,
        177; and 1922 *Ulysses*, xiv,
        56, 57-59, 177; 1976
        changes to, 56-57; Bono Act,
        78n.6, 178; European, 59.
        *See also* Spoo, Robert.
Craft, Robert, 115-116

Dalton, Jack, 56, 59-60
Dettmar, Kevin, 25-26, 30n.11
DuSautoy, Peter, 70-71, 73-74, 118-
        119, 120-121

editorial theory, 81, 87, 178; and
        definitive editions, 8, 165;

For Product Safety Concerns and Information please contact our EU
representative  GPSR@taylorandfrancis.com
Taylor & Francis Verlag GmbH, Kaufingerstraße 24, 80331 München, Germany

www.ingramcontent.com/pod-product-compliance
Ingram Content Group UK Ltd.
Pitfield, Milton Keynes, MK11 3LW, UK
UKHW010813080625
459435UK00006B/64